THE ART OF GRAPHOLOGY

D1259572

THE ART OF GRAPHOLOGY

by
Marie Bernard

edited by
Jeanne M. Reed

THE WHITSTON PUBLISHING COMPANY
Troy, New York
1985

Library of Congress Catalog Card Number 85-051385

ISBN 0-87875-304-4

Printed in the United States of America

In memory of my artistic husband,
Dr. Sinovij Shtokalko

TABLE OF CONTENTS

Preface ix
Acknowledgements x
History of Graphology 1
The Art of Graphological Seeing 7
Symbolism of Handwriting 9
Symbolism of Direction 12
Symbolism of Letters 15

PART ONE: MOVEMENT

Introduction to the three pictures 20
Picture of Movement 21
Picture of Form 23
Picture of Arrangement 25
Relationship of the three pictures 26
Connective Forms 30
Connective Form, The Angle 31
                  The Garland 34
                  The Arcade 38
                  The Double Curve 46
                  The Thread 47
                  The Undefined Form 51
                  Schoolwriting 53
Child-like or Infantile Writing 55
Disciplined Writing 56
Stylized Writing 57
Connectedness 59
Disconnectedness 62
Strong Pressure 67
Weak Pressure 73
Third Dimension in Depth 76
Warmth and Pastosity 84
Sharpness and Coolness 89
Right Trend 92
Left Trend 95
Speed 100
Slowness 108
Pophal's Biotypes 115
Pophal's Tension Degrees 134
Looseness 141
Rigidity 142

Rhythm of Movement...144
Illustrating the Rhythm of Movement...151

PART TWO: FORM PICTURE

Introduction...157
Form Niveau..159
Persona Writing..164
Stylized Writing...166
Regularity...167
Irregularity...172
Enrichment...176
Simplification...179
Fullness...183
Meagerness...186
Initial Accentuation...189
Terminal Accentuation..192
i-Dots...199
t-Strokes..206
Evenness...210
Unevenness...212
Formrhythm...215
Special Forms of Form Rhythm...217
The Stroke...225
Stroke Variations..228
Stroke Direction...232
Signature..236
Extraversion and Introversion..251

PART THREE: PICTURE OF ARRANGEMENT

Introduction...257
Large Size...260
Small Size...264
Width..267
Narrowness...270
Slant..274
Vertical Slant...278
Fluctuating Slant..283
Differences in Lengths...284
Small Differences in Lengths...288
Accentuation of Upper Lengths..292
Accentuation of Lower Lengths..299
Lower Loops as a Key to Sexual Behavior..304
Great Distances Between Words..309
Small Distances Between Words..310
Distance Between Lines...311
Direction of Lines...313
The Margins..318

Table of Contents

Left Margin. 322
Right Margin. 325
The Address 329
The Structure 331

APPENDIX

What we should know before we begin to analyze a   handwriting 339
Nationality 340
Age 343
Profession 345
Gender 347
Left-Handedness 349
Samples of Handwriting Analysis
        Handwriting Analysis of John Hinckley .356
        Handwriting Analysis of David Berkowitz. 361
        Handwriting Analysis of William Shakespeare 366
Document Examination
        Document Examination of Josef Mengele's Resumé 376
        Document Examination of the "Hitler-Diaries" 381
Insincerity in Handwriting. 388
The Four Functions: C. G. Jung's Psychological Types. 395
List of Particular Writing Elements 399
Bibliography 406
Index. 411

PREFACE

Marie Bernard is a handwriting detective, the Sherlock Holmes of graphology. She can perceive almost instantly from a glance at a person's script, not just the character and intellect of the writer but his inner motives. Often she penetrates to the core of his psyche.

Some years ago, when I first encountered Marie, I still supposed, as do many people, that graphology was a sort of tour de force, a pseudo-science in its cradle. But it required only a few hours with this astonishing woman to enlighten me, for in Marie graphology has attained a maturity that makes it almost as exact as any mathematical science.

Last year I was sitting next to Marie Bernard when, on television, she condemned the notorious "Hitler Diaries" as forgeries. She described with devastating accuracy the mentality, age and opinions of the still-uncaptured forger.

Marie's skills in graphology continue to amaze me. I am always awed that she can probe deep into the labyrinth of a mind, even to the very soul, just by a quick reconnaissance of a few curlicues and twirls of a pen.

My friend Huntington Hartford, the noted author on graphology and a great pioneer in the field, once told me that he regarded Marie Bernard as "an intuitive genius."

A letter now lying before me, written by one of America's leading graphologist, describes his first meeting with Marie: "I casually handed her, from the top of my desk, a two-line sentence which was an unsigned note . . to me. She grabbed a red pencil and made all sorts of little marks on the writing at appropriate graphological points. These she assimilated in one of the quickest, most detailed and most accurate graphological analyses I have ever seen.

I told her I thought it was very good and that I was most impressed by her speed. With this encouragement she shuffled through the papers on my desk, grabbing each and every handwriting piece of material she could find. She proceeded to free-associate to each of these in a spectacular graphological performance. . ."

Marie is breathtakingly accurate, concise, very sensitive and not at all superficial. I think that we who plod along with theories and facts have some kind of obligation to recognize natural and uncanny talents on those few occasions when they appear. . . .

I have suggested to Marie that she is a psychic. This she emphatically denies. She insists that her incredible insights are based purely upon scientific observations.

Here in this volume Marie has set forth her method and technique with precision and clarity. Certainly if you can acquire even a glimmer of Marie Bernard's skills from this book, you will qualify as a competent graphologist.

New York, 25th September 1984

Charles Hamilton

ACKNOWLEDGEMENTS

I give my thanks to these generous people who facilitated the appearance of my book on graphology (in alphabetical order):

Ruth Aley who encouraged me to publish the book.

Geneva Bugbee who helped me with her thorough and reliable work to complete the book.

Vincent Caputo whose artistic drawings enriched the chapter on "Lefthandedness."

Bill Davidson who helped me in endless hours to copy my manuscripts.

Yvanne Geltzeiler, Vice President of the National Society of Graphology, who opened her arms for me when I needed love and moral support.

My deepest thanks to my publisher Jean Goode who understands my dedication to the *Art of Graphology.*

And Polly Goode, her lovely intelligent daughter, who set the book.

My thanks to Mr. Charles Hamilton, the greatest autograph dealer in the world, who allowed me to chose samples from his treasures at random.

Bud Handelsman, the known caricaturist of the *New Yorker*, whose charming drawings visualize "The Rhythm of Movement."

Dr. Jean Houston who shares my enthusiasm which she calls "a gift of the Gods," and her husband, Dr. Robert Masters, who sent me the most interesting writing samples of their illustrious friends.

Dr. James Hewitt, the poetical writer, who edited my first chapters and encouraged me to continue in my own natural writing style.

Arnold Hutchins — the *Einstein* of tax and investment consulting — who supervised my personal and financial matters.

My thanks to Mr. A. Malhorta who opened for me the gates to the international world for an inexhaustable supply of fascinating handwritings.

My honest thanks to Frederick Ungar whose wise criticism spurred me to higher efforts.

Marie Bernard

HISTORY OF GRAPHOLOGY

Looking at our small and simply constructed letter forms, it is difficult to imagine that a span of many thousands of years lies between these modern letters and their ancestors. Many may know that today's printed letters differ little from the Latin writing of more than two thousand years ago. But how many are aware of the developmental stages by which the history of the Latin writing can be traced? Or that the Latin alphabet is a progressive change from the Greek alphabet and that Greek is an adoption of a writing which was developed among the Semites of Syria in the middle of the second millennium?

The history of writing goes back even further. The principles of the Semitic writing are those of the Egyptian syllabary. Together with Sumerian, Hittite, Chinese and others, the ancient Egyptian system of writing belongs to the great family of ancient Oriental writing systems.

The history of the oldest of these writings, the Sumerian, which may have been the mother of all the other systems, can be traced back to about 3000 B.C. Its history and prehistory are as long as the recorded history of civilization itself.

Written communication developed around 5000 years ago, from about 3000 B.C. to 2000 A.D., when priests inscribed their religious rites into clay tablets. Around 1500 B.C., the Phoenicians created the first alphabet, which included speech sounds. The new alphabet developed into two different branches: the early Hebrew and the Phoenician alphabet. Early Hebrew is the parent of the classical Hebrew script dating around the 11th century, B.C. From Early Hebrew to Square Hebrew it became a Palestinian Jewish version from which modern Hebrew writing developed over a period of 2000 years. The majority of the famous Dead Sea Scrolls are written in Square Hebrew. These letters are so close to today's Hebrew alphabet that they can be read by Israeli schoolchildren.

Between the second and fourth centuries the Greeks began to add vowels to their writing. They wrote in the boustrophedon way (Greek: turning like oxen in plowing), the Greek way of writing in which the lines run alternately from right to left and left to right. Modern computers use this system to save space and time.

During the fifth century, A.D., cursive writing for daily commercial purposes was

1

introduced by the Romans with shorthand, the so-called Tiro notes. Tiro, a slave of Cicero, invented this stenotype writing. For everyday use for legal, commercial and social purposes the Romans invented a more speedy script, cursive writing (Latin: currere = to run).

From this time stems the first recorded graphological analysis by the Roman biographer Tranquillus who wrote about the Emperor Augustus (63 B.C.-14 A.D.). "The Emperor writes in such narrow lines that he has to press the last words beyond the margin.

TRATTATO
COME
DA VNA LETTERA
MISSIVA

Si conoscano la natura, e qualità dello
Scrittore.

Raccolto da gli scritti del Signor C A M I L L O
B A L D I Cittadino Bolognese,

E dato alle Stampe da Gio. Francesco Grillenzoni.

IN MILANO,

Appresso Gio. Batt. Bidelli. M.DC.XXV.

Con licenza de' Superiori.

He does not separate his words, nor does he carry any excess letter over to the next line. Instead he ties them under the final word with an extra stroke. This speaks for the greed of the Emperor."

Although in Antiquity and in the Middle Ages people were aware of the expression of personality in handwriting, many years elapsed before the first textbook on handwriting was published.

In 1625, Camillo Baldi, a medical professor at the University of Bologna, published a small book entitled: *Trattato come da una lettera missiva si conoscano la natura, e qualità dello scrittore* (a treatise on how to recognize from a letter the nature and the character of the writer).

The next step was taken by Jean Hippolyte Michon, acknowledged as the founder of European graphology. He was a priest, geologist, historian, engraver, archeologist, botanist, architect and novelist. In the last years of his life he gathered thousands of samples of his contempories' handwriting. He presented his graphological findings in his books: *Système de Graphologie and Méthode Pratique de Graphologie.* In 1875 he founded the *Société de Graphologie*, one of the leading institutes for studying graphology at the university level.

Michon's laws of graphology are valid today. All modern graphologists build their research on Michon's ingenious findings. It is he who said: "It is not the hand that writes but the brain. Every movement of the body corresponds with the revelation of the soul. Graphology is the sister of psychology."

Michon called the graphic elements signs. He said: "One sign does not cancel the significance of another sign; the counterweight of the opposing sign must always be con-

French Abbé
Hippolyte Michon
1806-1881

3

sidered. The human being is a complex unit, therefore it is necessary to examine every little element lest we forget the wonderful unity of the entire being. We must do a graphological and psychological analysis in minute detail, to better understand the complexity of the personality. Writing is the art of speaking to the eyes."

Michon's pupil Crépieux Jamin continued the work of his master and moved beyond the school of *signes fixes* to an emphasis of the overall picture. He said: "The study of elements (signes) is to graphology as the study of alphabet to reading prose."

Toward the end of the nineteenth century, German scientists assumed leadership in the development of graphology. Wilhelm Preyer, professor of psychology at the University of Jena, published *Psychology of Handwriting,* which contained the famous phrase, *"Handwriting-Brainwriting,"* on which Professor Rudolf Pophal, at the University of Hamburg, based his main graphological work of the same title, *Handwriting-Brainwriting.*

Preyer conducted experiments with people who had lost their arms and had been taught to write with their mouths or with their toes. The writing characteristics did not change, confirming the hypothesis that handwriting control lies in the brain.

George Meyer, a German psychiatrist, took another step forward in analyzing movement in handwriting. He concluded that character in handwriting is determined by psycho-motor energies. He pointed out that our psyche influences our body movements—special ways of walking, of turning the head, for example. Meyer observed his patients in states of manic elation or depression and described the relationship between their handwriting and momentary states of emotion.

The first German graphological society was founded in 1896 by Ludwig Klages, who soon became the acknowledged leader in the field. Klages established laws and principles of graphology, characterology and expressive behavior (Ausdruckskunde), which he based largely upon his own philosophical theories. It was Klages who introduced the expression *form niveau*, an indicator of the writer's intellectual level and cultural background. The first glance at a person's handwriting can tell us whether he is an individualist—high form niveau—or a stereotyped person without spontaneity and vigor—low form niveau.

For Klages the rhythmical flow in a handwriting was most important. His published works have become the basic textbooks for students in the graphological institutes and universities in Europe.

A very interesting and important dimension was added to the study of graphology when the Swiss poet and writer, Dr. Max Pulver, professor at the University of Zurich, extended Klages' graphological system into the area of psychoanalysis. Pulver applied Jung's depth psychology in his book *Symbolism of Handwriting* and found that Freud's concepts of the personality structure, Id, Ego and Superego, were analogous to the lower, middle and upper zones in handwriting, just as Aristotle had divided the human body into the lower part, the area of instinct and materialism; the middle part, the area of heart and soul; and the upper part, the intellect and spirit.

Ania Teillard introduced Jung's psychological terms into graphology. She brought us the idea of contrasts in the same individual: conscious-unconscious; extraversion-introversion; the *persona* to indicate a mask (as was worn by actors on the stage in ancient Greece).

In this sense, the personality, like the mask, "feigns individuality, and tries to make others and oneself believe that one is an individual. . .fundamentally the *persona* is nothing real: it is a compromise between individual and society as to what a man should appear to be. He takes a name, earns a title, represents an office, is this or that" (Jung).

In graphology, either the signature corresponds to the true, natural representative of oneself, or the whole writing mirrors a façade that the writer wishes to present to the world. At the same time, quite without awareness on his part, it may reveal the hidden aspects of his ego.

Ania Teillard also introduced Jung's psychic function types into graphology: thinking, feeling, sensation and intuition. Ania Teillard discussed the function types as well as the different complexes and their expression in writing. The inferiority complex, anal-sadistic complex, mother-complex, oral-complex, anxiety-complex, flight-complex, guilt-complex, narcissism-complex—all are recognizable in handwriting.

In 1929 Robert Saudek published *Experimental Graphology* in Munich. Basing his work on Crépieux Jamin he continued the introduction of medical and psycho-analytical expressions into graphology. Saudek was the first graphologist to examine handwriting kinematographically, that is to say, he examined the speed in handwriting. He proved, for instance, that a short stroke takes longer to draw than a large, swinging stroke.

Graphology took another giant step forward with the work of Rudolf Pophal, professor of neurology in Hamburg, whose principal work, *Handwriting-Brainwriting,* we mentioned earlier. Pophal introduced an even more important aspect of his view on scientific graphology with his work, *The Stroke Picture.* He used the terms homogeneous, amorphous and granulated to describe the three different strokes in handwriting. Homogeneous refers to a stroke with a healthy appearance—a clear, uniform, internally integrated stroke. Amorphous, meaning without form or inner structure, indicates degrees of psychopathology. Granulated stroke, with its grainy, fuzzy, muddy quality, is usually found in writings of alcoholics and drug addicts.

An examination of the stroke picture, using the above descriptions, can help to detect health problems, degrees of mental disturbances, and can help in the court room, for example, when the stroke picture of the forger differs from that of the true writer of a questioned document. (In Europe a graphologist is required to collaborate with a psychologist in determining the mental health of a defendant in a court case.)

In *Handwriting-Brainwriting* Pophal introduced five degrees of tension in handwriting deriving from the different parts of the brain involved: the pallidum, striatum, brainstem, and cortex. Knowledge of these areas helps us to understand the control of handwriting by the different parts of the brain.

One of the most authoritative works recently added to graphological literature is the *Interpretation of Handwriting* by Professor Robert Heiss. Heiss, who died recently, was Professor at the newly founded Institute for Psychology and Parapsychology at Freiburg University. He combined his profound knowledge of psychology with graphology in a work that has become a standard in Europe.

For the interested student, I would recommend Müller-Enskat's *Graphological Diagnosis*, Pfanne's *Encyclopedia of Graphology*, Wittlich's *Conflicts in Handwriting* and his *Method of Diagram*, a useful technique in analyzing handwriting.

Roda Wieser details her findings during her examination of the handwritings of criminals in her various books about Grundrhythmus (Basic Rhythm). Finally, there is Lutz Wagner's standard work, *Graphological Research,* and Knobloch's *Graphology.*

In this country, *Encyclopedia of the Written Word* and *Key to Personality* by the Hungarian-born Klara G. Roman, has been published, as well as Huntington Hartford's *You Are What You Write,* especially interesting because it includes the *Kanfer Test.* (Kanfer, a Viennese graphologist, studied the signs of cancer in handwriting.) In the *Diagrams of the Unconscious,* Werner Wolff, professor of psychology at Bard College, researched symbols, signatures and doodles. Jane Nugent Green wrote *You and Your Private I,* a graphological analysis focused on the personal pronoun I; and Herry Teltscher wrote *The Key to Successful Living.*

My aim in this chapter has been to present the important events in the scientific development of graphology so that you may have confidence in the information available about determining character from handwriting. It must be noted, however, that graphological information is not derived solely from theoretical knowledge and technical skill. Graphological methodology remains sterile unless infused with the creativity of intuition. The first impression of a handwriting should be formed by intuition—it provides a sense of the whole that the detailed analysis cannot give.

The art of the graphologist consists in his ability to see in the first impression the totality of the writing, which in turn gives special coloration to the detail.

In the next chapter we will examine the role of intuition in graphological analysis. If you devote some time to developing the *Art of Seeing*, the analytical methods we discuss in this book will become more meaningful.

THE ART OF GRAPHOLOGICAL SEEING

We have all been to museums and art galleries where paintings are set off in fairly large, uncluttered rooms with proper lighting. Silence is generally required. This atmosphere is staged so that a viewer may receive an impression from a painting. The purpose is to 'see' more than color and line and detail. Sometimes we stand back and gaze for several minutes, allowing the painting to 'speak' to us through our eyes.

In this book we are going to encourage you to approach handwriting analysis in this manner. The art of graphology consists not only of assembling and evaluating graphic elements, but more essentially of the art of 'seeing', of being capable of receiving an impression from lines of handwriting. Our reaction to the script should be spontaneous and intuitive. We allow ourselves to be struck, for example, by a first impression of a speedy, abrupt, fiery character radiating from the handwriting. Handwriting analysis requires a kind of active passivity, so to speak.

Ludwig Klages, the German philosopher and graphologist, said: "Very rare are those moments where the analyst has to measure the writing elements. Most of the time he simply recognizes the form niveau of the character with one look at the script."

There are other sciences as well where first impressions are weighted in evaluation. Colin Mackay, an expert on Chinese art, can distinguish at a glance a Ming dynasty vase, worth thousands of dollars, from a fake. He knows right away when the paint on a bowl is a shade too dark, when the neck on a vase is a fraction too narrow, when the expression on a painted face is a bit too jovial. Similarly, some medical diagnosticians have said that they know the moment a patient walks into the consulting office the exact nature of the illness.

Who are the people who can rely upon and proceed from their first impressions? They are experts with authoritative backgrounds in their fields. They have this in common: they have become aware of their sensuality and have learned to use their senses—seeing, smelling, hearing, touching and tasting—with great discrimination, whether it be in the fine arts or in matters of taste. Klages said, "When I am going to analyze a handwriting, I silence my will and my intellect and concentrate only on seeing. After several moments of passivity, gathering impressions, I close my eyes and absorb the stream of perception." This artistic experience can be taught, much the same as we learn the techniques of the Yoga exercise.

A German psychiatrist, I.H. Schultz, created the so-called autogenic training, a kind of self-hypnosis which induces a passive state of deep relaxation; will and thought are subdued. Schultz described the renewal and sharpening of the skill by the use of his technique: "A well-known conscientious art critic came to me because he felt insecure in judging the work of young artists. After an autogenic training of four months I recommended that he fall into deep concentration and relaxation when he had to look at a new object of art. With this kind of perception he released a current of emotions toward the object of art, undisturbed by intellectual prejudice. He was forming a *unio mystica*, a mystical union, with this object of art. From then on this art critic won the highest praise from his professional colleagues, and the younger artists especially felt that he now understood their work more deeply."

Modern developments in psychology attest to the fact that this introspective attitude brings increased specific knowledge. Freud wrote in the obituary for his teacher Charcot: "Charcot used to look at things he did not yet know, every day, again and again, to enlarge his impression until he understood. Before his spiritual sight the whole chaos of the symptoms of complete and extreme cases returned. Charcot always emphasized the art of learning to see and not to overlook things, thus recovering new things continually." Freud followed Charcot's advice. "I learned to look at things so often that they began to unfold before my eyes and suddenly I understood. To retain all those numerous dates, the details of my patients' revelations during the months of treatment, I learned to develop an even, floating attention, to gather all information before the intellect began to interfere at too early a stage."

Modern psychiatry recognizes the importance of intuition. The Latin root is *intueri*, to look at, to regard; it refers to the direct knowledge of something without the conscious use of reasoning. It is an immediate apprehension or understanding. Intuition is essential in any diagnostic field. It is the creative faculty which enables art and science to work together. As such, it is critical to the analysis of handwriting, for which we have many reliable methods of measuring, counting and more to evaluate writing elements. But valuable information in handwriting characteristics is not only derived from the use of protractors, rulers and circles. Graphology aspires to a higher level when we use intuition and psychic insight hand in hand with scientific verification. Goethe says in Faust II:

> What you can't touch seems miles away from you.
> What you can't hold you do not understand.
> What you can't see you do not recommend.
> What you can't weigh bears for you no weight.
> What you can't coin you do not appreciate.

Such human qualities as love, trust, devotion, honor, fidelity, integrity, generosity of spirit— cannot be measured. They can only be experienced.

SYMBOLISM IN HANDWRITING

One can see in the evolution of writing how from the beginning man projected the fundamental components of his nature into his writing, unconsciously producing symbols of his most elemental drives and aspirations. One can also see the similarity in his writing formations to his own upright posture. Three zones appeared clearly in his script, perfectly analogous to his stance upon the earth—his feet upon the ground, his foundation; his heart and soul in the middle zone; his spirit in the upper zone. These symbolic projections match Aristotle's division of man into spirit, body and soul. Note the graphic comparison below:

The Swiss graphologist, Max Pulver, introduced the symbolism of the three zones in his work *Symbolism of Handwriting.*

Upper zone, symbol of heaven, spiritual longing, intellect

Past *l g* *Middle zone*, symbol of heart and soul *man* Future

Lower zone, symbol of night, subconscious, earth, riches, fertility, materialism, sexual drives

The line on which we write can also be seen as the horizon, separating the darkness of earth below the imaginary line from the light of heaven above. We pray to the Almighty who is above. Thus, high-striving upper lengths in a script symbolize a yearning for spiritual receptivity and union. Those who write with extremely long upper lengths have a desire to ascend to spiritual and intellectual heights, characterized by the demonstration of the refinement of thought and feeling. Below the imaginary horizontal line is darkness, materialism, earth with its riches and fertility. Here, too, is the world of the subconscious.

Chaim Potok (1929-   ), Jewish writer on Jewish culture.

In his high-longing upper lengths we see high self-confidence combined with a limitless imagination reaching into the upper spheres for answers. We also see great ambition.

A person who writes with long lower lengths is deeply anchored in the physical region with its biological desires. We speak of the good earth on which we build our houses, firmly founded in the soil. Long, lower lengths in handwriting indicate powerful, instinctual drives toward such materialistic things as pleasure, sexuality, money, food, drink and sportive occupation. They also reflect strong, healthy roots clinging to the soil.

John Wayne's powerful anchoring in the earth with his lower loop *y* and the wide-swinging upper loop turning downward to the materialistic regions, with an underscoring in this field.

Those who write with long-striving upper lengths and long-penetrating lower lengths have both dreams and illusions, high ambition and spiritual longing, and a deep anchoring in the instinctual regions and subconscious, as we see in the handwriting of Jean Houston, Ph.D., director of the Foundation for Mind Research, who has written several books on the "potentiation of latent human capacities." In addition to her work in human potentials research, she is co-inventor of a number of machines and electronic devices and environments that serve to alter consciousness.

The desire to expand in both directions—to the heights and to the depths—reflects restlessness and an insatiable longing to explore the world. In these unusually extended upper and lower loops we see high aspiration as well as an interest in the practical.

"Handwriting has a tendency to change from ~hour~ and from task to task

[get] louder, it becomes less

as mind spins along at a different

from my motor capacities .

number 94181, 64 922 743,

Best to you.

Jean Houston

SYMBOLISM OF DIRECTION

Pulver's symbol of the three zones

Symbolism of the Left

Past, mother-principle,
creativity, childhood memories,
introvert, connected with the past

(middle zone) *Life*

(Upper zone)

horizontal writing line

(lower zone)

Symbolism of the Right

father principle,
activity, extravert,
future-oriented

Our European-American writing moves from left to right, going from the *I* to the *You* on the imaginary or prescribed horizontal writing line. We build a bridge from the present to the future, leaving the past behind us. That means, when I write a word I am in the present on the way to the future, and when I have written the word I have left the past behind.

Men have always been preoccupied by a sense of duality in their nature which has found symbolic expression in all cultures. There is good and evil, light and dark, and right and left. Plutarch said: "Right symbolizes the future; the active male principle—willpower, intellect. Left is the symbol of the past: the mother principle - receptivity, childhood, creativity."

Herodotus writes that Lybians shaved the left side of their heads, offering their hair to the goddess of fertility. Plato spoke of sacrificing the right parts of animals to the Olympic Gods.

This duality of right and left is also reflected in law, ritual and religion. We raise the right hand to take an oath. In Christian belief, Jesus sits at the right hand of God the Father. In the Old Testament, King Solomon placed his mother in the seat of honor at his right. On Judgment Day, the righteous man will stand to the right of God's throne.

In Chinese cultural tradition, the mystical Gods, Yang and Yin—light and dark— signify right and left. Yang, on the right, is the male principle. He is heaven, the active, the positive, the straight, the undivided, the favored in the universe. Yin, on the left, is the female principle. She is earth, receptive, submissive, divided and unfavored.

Western man, writing from left to right, is future-oriented, progressive, aggressive, embracing the male principle. He wants to explore the world. He is open-minded, looking for human contact. Life has a constant stimulation for him. He is hungry for sensation. He is eager for social life. He debates thoughts, the opinions of his contemporaries. Any new event awakens his interest.

This is the powerful signature of the famous Texas Senator. They called him *I am Houston* because he scrawled his first name *Sam* so oddly that it looked like "I am." This space-hungry, future-oriented signature reveals extraverted behavior.

If the writing tilts toward the left, the writer tends to the female principle: the past, contemplation, passivity, tradition, introversion.

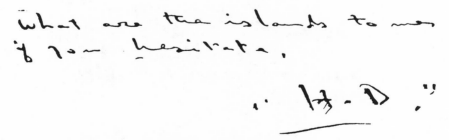

This writing of Hilda Doolittle, the introvert, shows critical distance from people. Yet, behind her reserve, she may hide strong feelings, deep thoughts and fantasies. Whereas Sam Houston writes to the right, expanding into the future, Hilda Doolittle turns in her writing to the left, to the past, to introversion.

Carl Sandburg writes vertically because he has tamed his emotions. He is reason-dominated, writing from left to right with a sober, rational thinking quality.

[handwriting: "you will be lonesome."]

[signature: Carl Sandburg]

In addition to the symbolism of the three zones and the symbolism of direction, we have other symbolisms in handwriting. The straight line, for instance, is a symbol of harshness, stiffness, rigidity and determination. Even more powerful are the zigzag lines, because every change in the writing direction implies a new impulse. These are clear symbols of tenacity, rigidity, stubbornness. Klages compared them with the angular crevasses of snow-covered mountains.

[handwriting and signature: Heinrich Himmler]

Heinrich
Himmler

[handwriting and signature: Reinhard Heydrich]

Reinhard
Heydrich

The cruel, merciless leaders of the Third Reich

SYMBOLISM IN LETTERS

The word symbol comes to us from the Greek *symbolon*. The dove is a symbol of peace. The sign of skull and cross-bones symbolizes death, as does the scythe, skeleton or an extinguished candle.

Handwriting can be richly symbolic in its wide range of formations. Men unconsciously create letter forms which are often symbolic representations of their personalities. The graphologist learns to see these symbols in a script and develops an interpretation of them. Written letter forms are not merely signs of verbal expression but unconscious messages flowing from the brain, drawing a self-portrait of the writer. (The German neurologist Rudolf Pophal stated that certain pre-existing patterns in the brain are transmitted by written letter forms.)

For instance, musical note symbols, formed by musicians, money signs in the signatures of bankers, deadly weapons drawn by murderers, and heart-shaped i-dots by eccentric teenagers are symbols we find in writing.

In the underscoring of the signature of an engineer are the unconsciously-drawn tools of his trade.

Mae West exhibits her large breasts and her preoccupation with the phallus in her well-known signature.

Phallus symbols in handwriting:

We see dollar symbols in writing:

We see numbers (3, 2 and zeroes) in this signature:

We see heart-symbols instead of i-dots in Jayne
Mansfield's eccentric writing:

We see the symbol of a French Horn in the musician's handwriting (the letter *F* in *French* and *Florida* and the *H* in *Horn*):

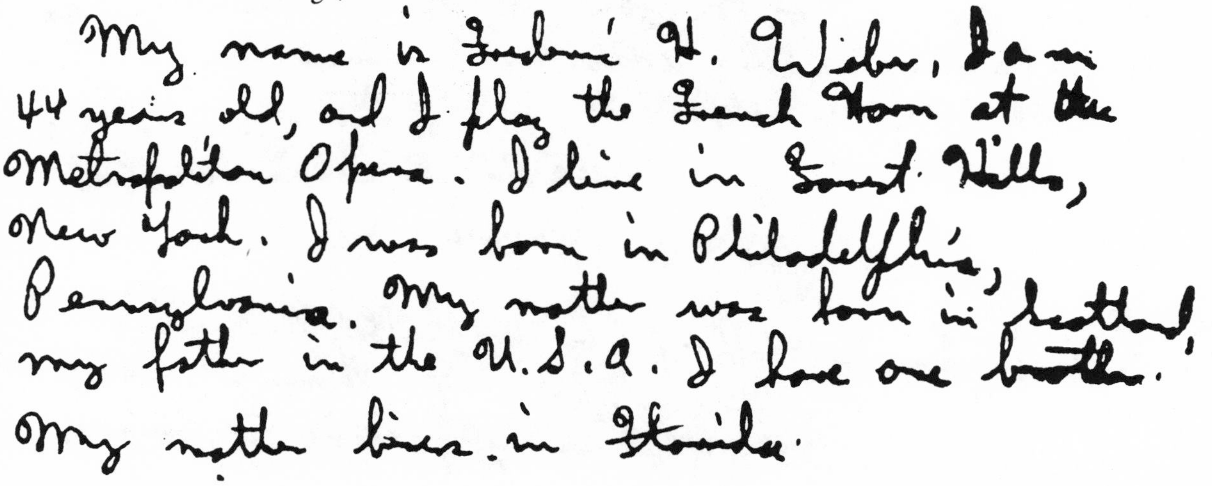
My name is Frederic H. Weber, I am
44 years old, and I play the French Horn at the
Metropolitan Opera. I live in Forest Hills,
New York. I was born in Philadelphia,
Pennsylvania. My mother was born in Scotland,
my father in the U.S.A. I have one brother.
My mother lives in Florida.

Franz Lehár (1870-1948), composer ot *Merry Widow*

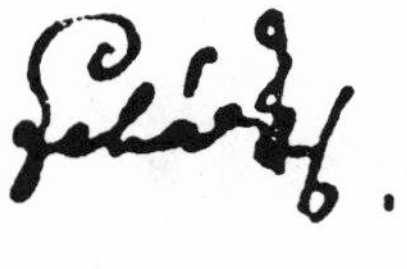

Franz von Suppé (1819-1895), composer of *Boccaccio*

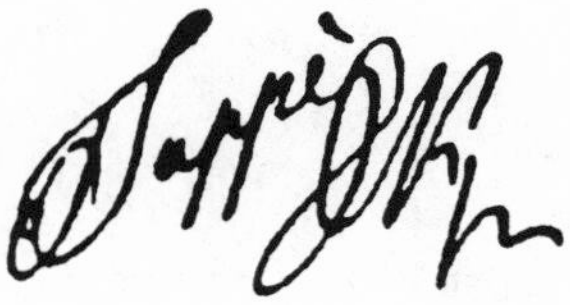

Obvious treble clef in Harry Belafonte's signature.

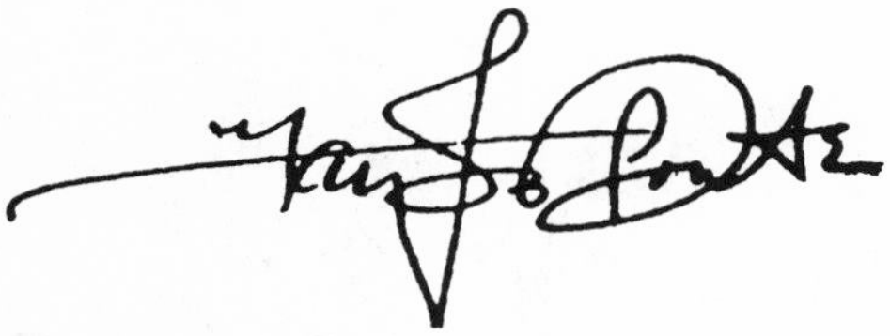

Isaac Stern draws his violin bow in his t-crossing and in the extra upper stroke above his signature.

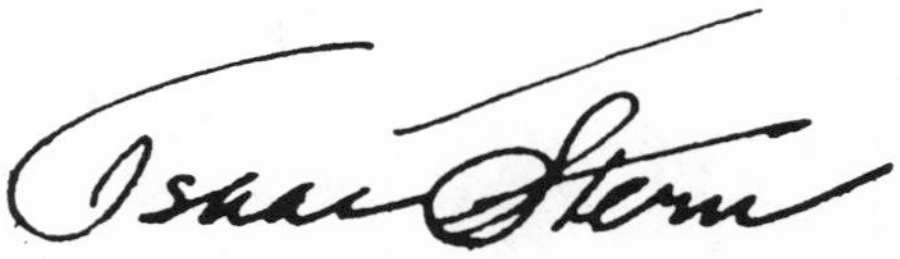

Van Cliburn's signature resembles a keyboard in the rectangular form of the white and black keys of a piano.

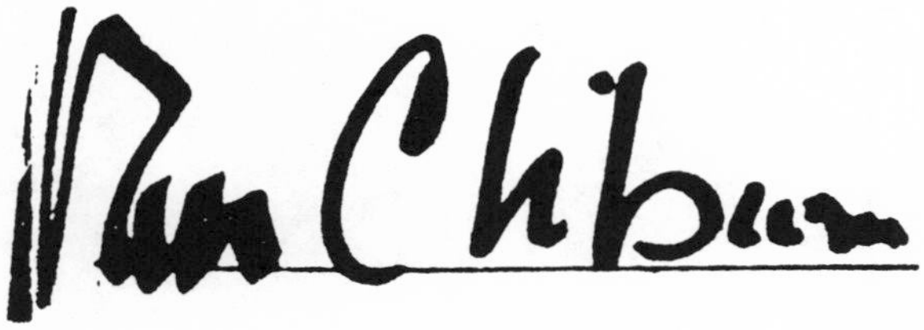

credeva che lui fosse cagione che non ebbe la permission di ballarin teatro. addio. non scordarvi di me io sono sempre il vostro

fedele fratello amadeo wolfgango Mozart

Mozart's writing consists of all kinds of notes, semibreves quavers, minims, crotchets and fermatas in the the to-the-left bent d's.

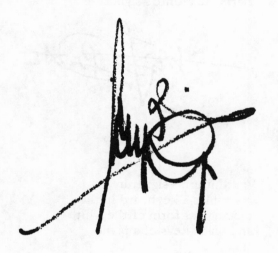

Victor Borge, the comic piano player, draws in his signature a fool's cap with bells.

PART ONE

MOVEMENT

The signature of the Austrian skier Annemarie Moser-Pröll
symbolizes a gliding down the track in circular movements,
interrupted by the halts necessary to maneuver around the poles.
(Note the spaces inside her signature.)

INTRODUCTION TO THE THREE PICTURES

Picture of Movement
Picture of Form
Picture of Arrangement

In the preceding chapters we have established that handwriting letter forms arise as symbols created in the unconscious. Let us look now at how we project our letter forms on paper.

Very young children will sit for hours putting crayon to paper. In Kindergarten they draw lines and circles according to their inherited temperament. Soft and kind children draw soft, more rounded and curved lines. Stubborn children create more angular and straighter lines. Later they learn the up-and-down strokes of letter forms and move them along side by side from left to right. This *movement* follows the *form*, which is drawn by the teacher on the blackboard. It has to be *arranged* on given lines in the copybook.

Thus the rules of handwriting are introduced to all of us, but then each of us adapts them to his unique personality. Handwriting formations are as individual as fingerprints.

The three elements—*movement, form,* and *arrangement*—together make up the unified overall first impression we receive of a person's handwriting. As we proceed through this study it may seem difficult to distinguish one from another, difficult to see a script as a whole structure or *Gestalt*, wherein the whole is greater than the sum of its parts. But if we concentrate we can separate them and receive from each its distinct message. Let us first concentrate on the *picture of movement*.

PICTURE OF MOVEMENT

The picture of movement is a faithful photograph of the way we move through life: running, gliding, swinging, dancing, hesitating. Here are some samples of different movement pictures: First, we see a strong, passionate driving movement in the script of a man propelled forward to reach his goal quickly. His superiors said: "We need a young general who is without fear, who can ride with his command straight into the heart of enemy country, and Custer is that man."

The famous boy-general G.A. Custer

This second sample of movement, that of a famous composer,
is so powerful that the form is almost dissolved. We see a strong
personality with leadership qualities.
(Ralph Maria Siegel)

Best wishes and kindest regards.
Love Elizabeth

This slow-moving, hesitant, cramped handwriting shows a person
who is inhibited, rigid, and a slow-poke.

Dear Mom & Dad:

Well, I just finished eating a tremendous Thanksgiving dinner. Sgt. price, one of the sergeants I work for, invited me over for a turkey dinner. we all eaten about two P.m. and finished about 3:30.

This is the writing of a disturbed young pilot of the British Royal Air Force. I would not advise anyone to sit in his plane. His movements in the air would be as unpredictable as those in his writing. The continuity of movement is interrupted by up-and-down-dancing, unrhythmical, uncontrolled and dangerous.

I am a poet and studying psychology in school at N.Y.U. changing to the New School in the fall

A lazy, dragging, uneven, weak, insecure movement
discloses inferior psychic energy.

PICTURE OF FORM

The second of the three pictures is *form*. As we said earlier, each of us develops his own individual letter forms after we have learned the rules of handwriting in childhood. Our script may become stylized, imitative, natural, inventive, creative, or even revolutionary. Our letter formations may be undeveloped or extremely individualized, as in the sample below. Here we see very rigid forms in the script, resulting from the influence of old-fashioned European tradition and principles.

Narrow, rigid, angular letter forms in a stiff movement

Simplified letter forms reveal a natural, intelligent, reliable individual.

Faithful school writing, à la Palmer method,
reveals a person who is faithful and obedient to law and order.

23

Lieber Sperber —

Montag

Einen schönen Dank für Ihre lieben Worte und für die Ankündigung Ihres und Frau Liebermanns Besuches!

Expansive, creative form of an artist.

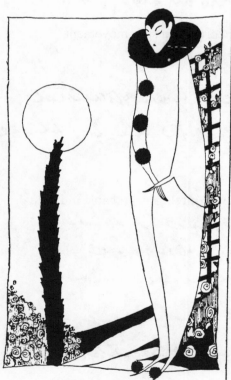

a colonnade, and the nine white columns of the colonnade are nine muses standing like votive candles before a blue mountain, they are nine candles flaming quiet circles . on the ceiling of a marble pavilion where a young man, surrounded by slaves, lies sleeping, and the sky behind the pavilion is a curtain of purple velvet painted with stars in heavy gold. Do you not see how the sky sags with the weight of the

William Faulkner's illustration and page from his manuscript
The Marionettes shows the refined poetic soul of the young writer.
Drawing and handwriting complement each other in their filigree forms.

PICTURE OF ARRANGEMENT

The way in which we react to space reveals our adaptability to the world and to society. We are all familiar with such extreme reactions to space as claustrophobia (fear of being closely confined), and acrophobia (fear of open places). We all react to space in daily life. Some people like small, cozy rooms. Others like an open uncluttered environment, needing to pace and take full strides from room to room. When we wake up in the morning, we like to stretch, yawn and feel the space of the room. Some people like to walk briskly down wide streets; others prefer narrow, winding streets.

The writing paper is the symbol of the given space where we arrange ourselves, according to our demand for "Lebensraum." Here are some samples of pictures of arrangement:

I have a lobster but no pot to boil it in. That is the reason for my coming down here

Free, independent, secure arrangement on the writing paper

This arrangement is completely confused, entangled like the thicket around Sleeping Beauty's castle. Adaptability to society has not yet been achieved.

25

RELATIONSHIP OF THE THREE PICTURES

[handwritten sample] which accounts for the hump on the camel, and the Sphinx's incredible smile.

Lillian R.

After receiving the first impression of the three pictures—movement, form, arrangement—we determine their relationship to each other. The sample above shows us harmony of all three pictures: the spontaneous movement leads to secure and individualistically-created forms and arranges them rhythmically and well-balanced on the paper.

[handwritten sample] in a few days. How have you been? I think about you a lot and haven't seen you look forward to getting together with you. Keep in touch.

Love John.

In this sample we have an insecure picture of movement, form and arrangement. It belongs to an immature person.

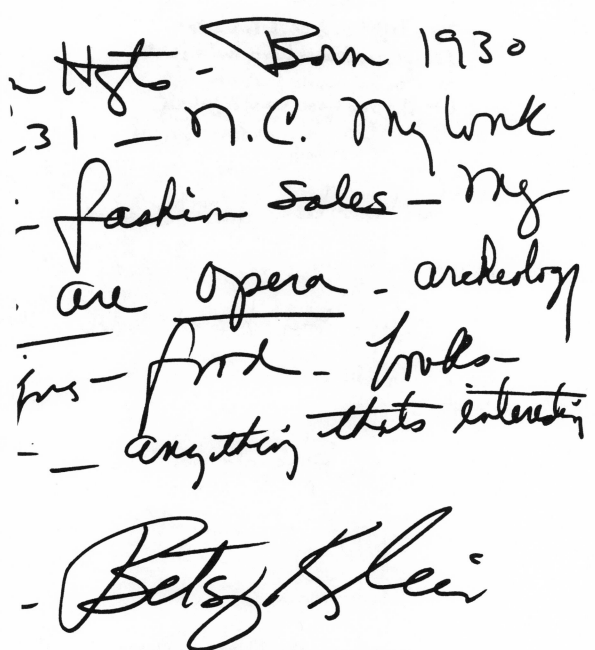

A strong picture of movement is dominant.

We can see how it sometimes crushes the letter forms—the form-picture—spreading all over the writing paper; this is a rather disturbed picture of arrangement.

Men left her a ship to sink;
They can leave her a hut as well,
And be but more free to think
For the one more cast off shell.
                    Robert Frost

Robert Frost

You have been most kind
to make all the changes I asked
for — I hope they haven't disturbed
you too much —

                    Sincerely

                    Jacqueline Kennedy

Jacqueline Kennedy

28

Camille Pissarro (1830-1903),
French impressionist painter

In these three samples of the American poet Robert Frost, of Jacqueline Kennedy and of the French impressionist painter Camille Pissarro, we see how the form picture dominates the picture of movement.

CONNECTIVE FORMS

Now that we have introduced the three pictures in general, in an overview, we can concentrate on the singular elements. We begin with the connective form, the way the small letters are connected in the middle zone. There are five main forms of connection in which the downstrokes within a word are connected to each other:

The Angle connects the downstrokes with angles on top and bottom.

The Garland connects the downstrokes with curves which are open at the top and have angles at the top.

The Arcade connects the downstrokes with an arching curve which rests on the baseline.

The Double Curve connects the downstrokes with curves at top and bottom.

The Thread, an undistinguished connection between downstrokes, may have garlands, washed-out angles, or simply wavering lines.

Besides these main forms of connection we also have:

Undefined Forms
School Writing
Disciplined Writing
Stylized Writing
Infantile or Child-like Writing

30

THE ANGLE

As a movement the angle may be regarded as a sudden change of direction in writing. These abrupt changes in the direction of the stroke demand sudden halts at the turning points, requiring a constant tension in writing the letters. Because this writing is *aimed* it does not permit any transitional, easy turns, which means the writer does not know how to compromise. He loves to find obstacles in his path. Like a tiger, he is always watching, ready to leap. Powerful of will, he is contemptuous of feeling and emotion, regarding them as attributes of the weak.

He has little capacity to relax, to loosen up. Actually, as he grows older, his conservatism strengthens, and he may become more tense and difficult. He lives by strongly developed principles, is persistent, stable, sober, and he is intensely active. This is seen in the sharp, pointed form of the angle, a perfect picture of the abrupt reactions of the angular writer. Whether or not we find positive or negative character indications will depend upon the evidences of energy and basic vitality in the script. One thing is clear, however—willpower is dominant; feeling plays only a secondary part in the writer's life.

The angular writing of German Foreign Minister von Ribbentrop during the Hitler Regime.

31

The sharp, angular handwriting of von Ribbentrop, Nazi Foreign Minister during the Third Reich, demonstrates all the virtues and vices of an angular writer. He is fanatic, without humor, dogmatic, uncompromising, inflexible and arrogant. He tries to present himself as a fighting spirit, masculine, virile, solid and correct. He is proud of his persistence and tenacity. He has prejudices and his active and passive willpower are constantly controlled. His fanaticism and dogmatic attitude make him unsuitable for diplomatic missions.

In this large, powerful handwriting of the movie star Pola Negri we see lack of adaptability, severe self-control and rigid class-consciousness. Her self-esteem is more a self-demonstration; she is ready to fight, to challenge her colleagues and directors, but with limited intellect. She loves to exercise power and cannot bear criticism or contradiction. Only she does the contradicting. As a dramatic angle writer she likes to show off with an almost masculine virility. Softness and yielding are alien to her. Her decision-making is without hesitation.

Sincerely,

Donald J. Trump
Dinner Chairman

The energetic angle writer, famous builder of New York's Trump Tower.

Pure angular writers are rare. Most people write mixed forms such as angular connective forms with softer garlands. This means the character remains virile and masculine but not as easily irritated or as stubborn as the pure angle writer. In this sample we have the more positive characteristics of the angular writer, such as responsibility, reliability, submission to duty and clean, exact, straight, objective thinking abilities. Vivacity and speedy intellect balance the otherwise rigid traits of the strict angular writer.

Special angular forms:

Soft angles = lack of firmness

an this continent

Behind sharp, angular writing is always a great amount of tension, as seen in the sample of von Ribbentrop. Whenever this tension gives in to relaxation the writer loosens his tight grip and the angles become soft. The sample above shows the gradual transition from an angle to a garland writer.

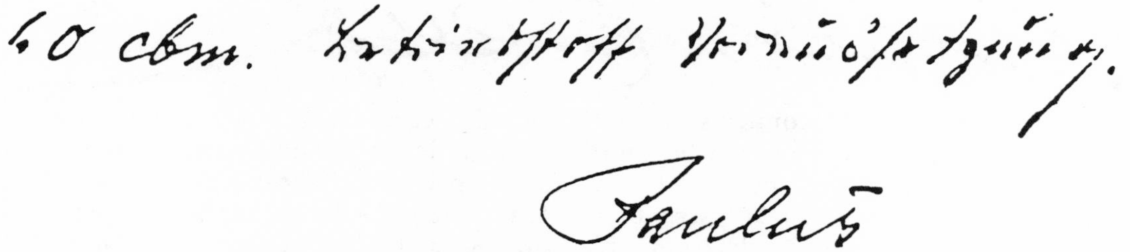

General Paulus, World War II

This transition occurred at a critical moment. Paulus lost Stalingrad when he surrendered his exhausted army to the Russians, contrary to the orders of his highest commander, Adolf Hitler. We can see the degree of his conflict—between a military oath and the humanitarian act of saving his soldiers—in the softened angles.

THE GARLAND

Bill Bell

The garland writer connects downstrokes with curves which are open at the top. The garland is like an open bowl, beginning from the left side and moving to the right, a friendly invitation to the world. The garland is open to receive from above, symbolic of love, receptivity, impressions, passivity and femininity. (A lovely example is the beautiful garlands of the George Washington Bridge glowing with their perfect curves against the night sky.) The movement of the garland is natural, relaxed, full of tolerance, amiability, conciliation and feeling. It signifies the spontaneous embracing of the YOU, an empathic affirmation of the other human being, a warmth for all humanity.

The garland writer makes contacts easily and is more practiced at adaptation. When we see an overlong, outswinging garland at the end of the signature (sample above), it implies communication.

The weaker the garland and the wider the distance between each singular garland, the easier the person is influenced, lacks independence, or tends to self-destructive self-sacrifice. Garland writers lead with their hearts, not with their heads.

I qu mtM

When all letters are written in curves, and even t-crossings and downstrokes are garlandically connected to the following letters, a conciliatory, warmhearted character is seen. When the writer begins with an initial curve as in the *m*, we speak of the initial garland. It reveals politeness, amiability and good manners.

and a ...

When the garlands are concealed, not free-swinging but rather creeping down the stem similarly to cover strokes, we see inhibition and often insincerity.

have never had my hand-writing

Déjeuners

When a garland sags down from the baseline, we speak of the *drooping garland*. The writer has not enough stamina to master his daily routine; he tends to melancholia and sentimentality. It is as if an invisible weight lies upon his shoulders, dropping his psychological burden deep down upon the baseline.

Wieland Wagner, grandson of Richard Wagner

These perpetually to-the-left looping garlands are symbols of the writer's constant connection with the past. This writing belongs to the grandson of Richard Wagner whose life goal is to honor the tradition of Bayreuth where a "temple" to Wagner's genius is dedicated.

Paramahansa Yogananda

The simplified, concentrated, narrowly-looped writing of Guru Paramahansa Yogananda shows continuous connection with the past, from which the old masters direct him.

35

The more a garland begins to look like a chalice, or like a goblet, as in these samples (p. 35), the more the warmth and receptivity of the garland will be suppressed. Tension and artificiality take over. We see the so-called *supported* garland where the up-and-down strokes flow together creating a narrow, limited form of a garland. It reveals an artificial, to-the-etiquette-chained, calculating, form-possessed writer full of pride, tradition, morals and self-control.

An anxiety complex hinders friendliness and openness. There will be convincing compulsive talking, persistent attempts to draw attention and to win the other over.

I love New York

The wider and rounder the garland, the more receptive the writer.

If we see a garland in a very regulated handwriting we know the writer is attempting to hide a fear of helplessness and inner weakness behind a kind of self-deception. His personal anxiety and fear are transformed into an ethical attitude of being especially kind, friendly and tolerent to his fellowmen.

Lucille Sabria

The narrower and higher the garlandic form, the more restricted, formal and ethical the behavior becomes.

Walter F. Mondale

Walter F. Mondale

The large and wide-swinging garlands of *Walter* in the signature reveal the receptive intellect of Walter Mondale. He is easily stimulated, likes to learn, has spontaneous ideas and can speak and act without inhibition. He carries his heart on his tongue. His first name (symbol of youth), Walter, is illegible and consists only of curves with the exception of the downstroke *t*, which is slightly curved, as are the downstrokes of the *d* and *l* in Mondale. Yet, one special stroke, the first stem of the *n* in *Mondale*, turns to the left in a kind of overcontrol, but soon the writer gets back to his rolling-along curves which demonstrate amiability, open-mindness and a comfortable, easygoing desire for harmony. His large middle zone displays inner pride and self-confidence, partly overshadowed by the wavering of the slant, which indicates ambivalence.

Special forms of garlands.

Mechanical, stiff garlands	= stiffness, cultural formality
Initial garlands	= politeness, amiability
Garland and large size	= noble soul
Garland & regularity & pressure	= ethical attitude
Garland & enforced regularity	= behind the mask of altruism lies egocentricity
Garland & pastosity	= courteous, unaffected, easy
Garland & vertical slant	= reserved, yet easily influenced
Garland & looping	= exaggerated politeness, superficial amiability
Garland & mixtures of angles and garlands	= camouflaging softness with discipline and harshness
Washed-out garlands (weak garlands)	= superficial sociability
Terminal garlands	= desire for communication
Garland and angle	= warmheartedness and strength

The English sculptor Henry Moore creates strong angular
and garlandic forms in his signature, which radiates the same
power as his sculptures.

The arcade is a kind of connective form occurring especially in the internal formation of *n* and *m*. It consists of a curving upstroke followed by a curving downstroke, both strokes connected at the top, leaving an opening at the bottom, like an inverted bowl. This movement seems to be a protective one, like constructing a roof, or holding an umbrella over one's head. The written *arcade* resembles the Roman aqueduct, as in the picture above.

The arcade is the opposite of the *garland*, which consists of curving strokes stretching out along the baseline, moving to the right, often at high speed.

If we turn the garland upside-down, we have the *arcade*, with the curve arching over the base line. The arcade also moves to the right but ends in a bending centripetal stroke, suddenly ending on the base line, in contrast to the ending of the garland which swings out in a round, conciliatory curve.

The arcade represents a shield against the influences of the world, as we can see in the accentuation of the downstroke. The downstroke accent in the arcade can signify caution, rational thinking, or even calculation.

The writer who prefers arcades is primarily interested in his own values and standards, his own roots and resources, his heritage and his family. The arcade writer is reserved, sometimes inhibited, is comfortable with convention, and occasionally acts out a lifestyle of self-deception. His guiding image is, accordingly, strongly subjective and may be somewhat rigid.

Arcade writers create architectural structures in their letter forms with varying degrees of aesthetical form feeling. Two forces combine in the creation of an arcade: the tendency to expand vertically and the tendency to limit expansion horizontally. In this sense, the arcade not only creates forms, it protects and preserves them.

The essential characteristics of the arcade writer are caution, reserve, concentration, condensation, and limitation. A model for a typical arcadic writer is the aristocrat who cultivates noble self-representation, keeps his distance from society and exercises self-discipline, denying natural impulses. His arcades testify to the formalism of his social taste.

Arcadic writing is symbolic of the inner conflicts between being and pretending. We can then easily understand that general insecurity leads the arcadic writer to hide behind solid architectural structure. We may find these writers cautious and possibly calculating.

Arcadic writing is often found in the script of children going through the turmoil of puberty and in the scripts of those who are too weak to deal with life and who tend to isolate themselves from the world. Their protecting, shielding arcadic letter forms may be built for defense.

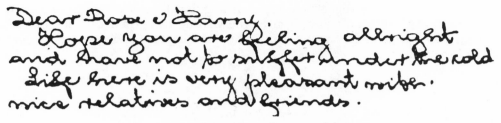

Arcadic forms in puberty writing

The so-called *meander-arcadic* writing (after the winding course of the ancient river in SW Asia Minor: Latin (meander), Greek (maindro); the ornamental pattern of winding or criss-crossing lines one sees on Greek vases and gowns, represents typical puberty letter formation.

In contrast to the garland which lies on its back, so to speak, and is filled with the world around it, supportive and carrying, the arcade stands on its feet and supports itself, setting up a resistance to intrusions on emotions and to depressing ordeals. We see in the arcade a symbol of the male principle.

The final downstroke of the arcade ends abruptly on the base line. If it were to continue in an imaginary curved line, it would curve to the left. This would imply qualities of introversion, such as a turning away from society, bonds to the past, love for tradition, power to resist, concentration and reserve, and in some cases deep insecurity.

If the arcade were constructed within a negative form niveau, then this imaginary continuation of the final stroke would imply insincerity, hypocrisy and deceit.

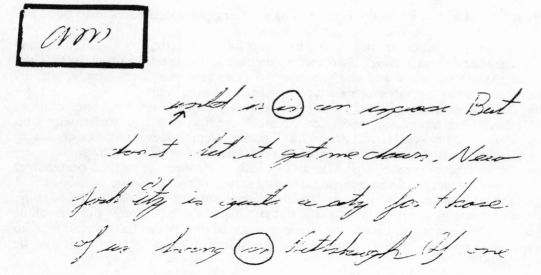

This terminal arcade with a slight to-the-left-turning arcadic movement is called the *shark-tooth*, coined by early graphologists; it gives the writing an extra deceitful look. When the form niveau is as low as in the sample above, the *shark tooth* underscores the negative characteristics of the writer.

The so-called *shark tooth*

The so-called *active arcade* in Thomas Jefferson's writing is built like a torpedo, shooting through the water, reaching its target with enormous energy and efficiency due to its ellipsoidal form. The same energy lies in the active arcade writer.

The *lateral supported arcade*, a perfect example of sacré coeur writing in the signature of the Spanish movie star Conchita Montenegro, expresses form rigidity, devotion to tradition, seclusion and formality.

Let's look at this odd lateral supported form: the first upstroke on its way down covers a part of its own upstroke and on its way up creeps along the preceding downstroke, but then changes direction. It is a kind of covering stroke, but each time the direction changes it symbolizes cunning, dishonest behavior.

Initial claw-like arcade

Terminal claw-arcade

The claw-like arcadic transforming of the terminal letter or of the initial letter shows hypocrisy, calculation and cautiousness.

This is the *supported arcade* which results in a narrow, stiff, mostly vertical writing. It reveals over-control, a forced effort to be efficient, strong willpower, the tendency to calculating, cunning, lying, insincere behavior. The supported arcade writer hides his true nature behind extremely good manners.

animals

The *looped arcade* with its unnecessary extra loops belongs to the hypocrite who wants to present himself as something he is not.

firmly

Bosgard

The soft-pressured arcade is the defense mechanism of a weak nature, a simulation of security and stability.

Brighton

Brooklyn.

The arcade with a right slant in sloppy writing reveals an extremely polite character, but when it appears in a script with high form niveau we see the right-slanted, active arcade as representing strong drive.

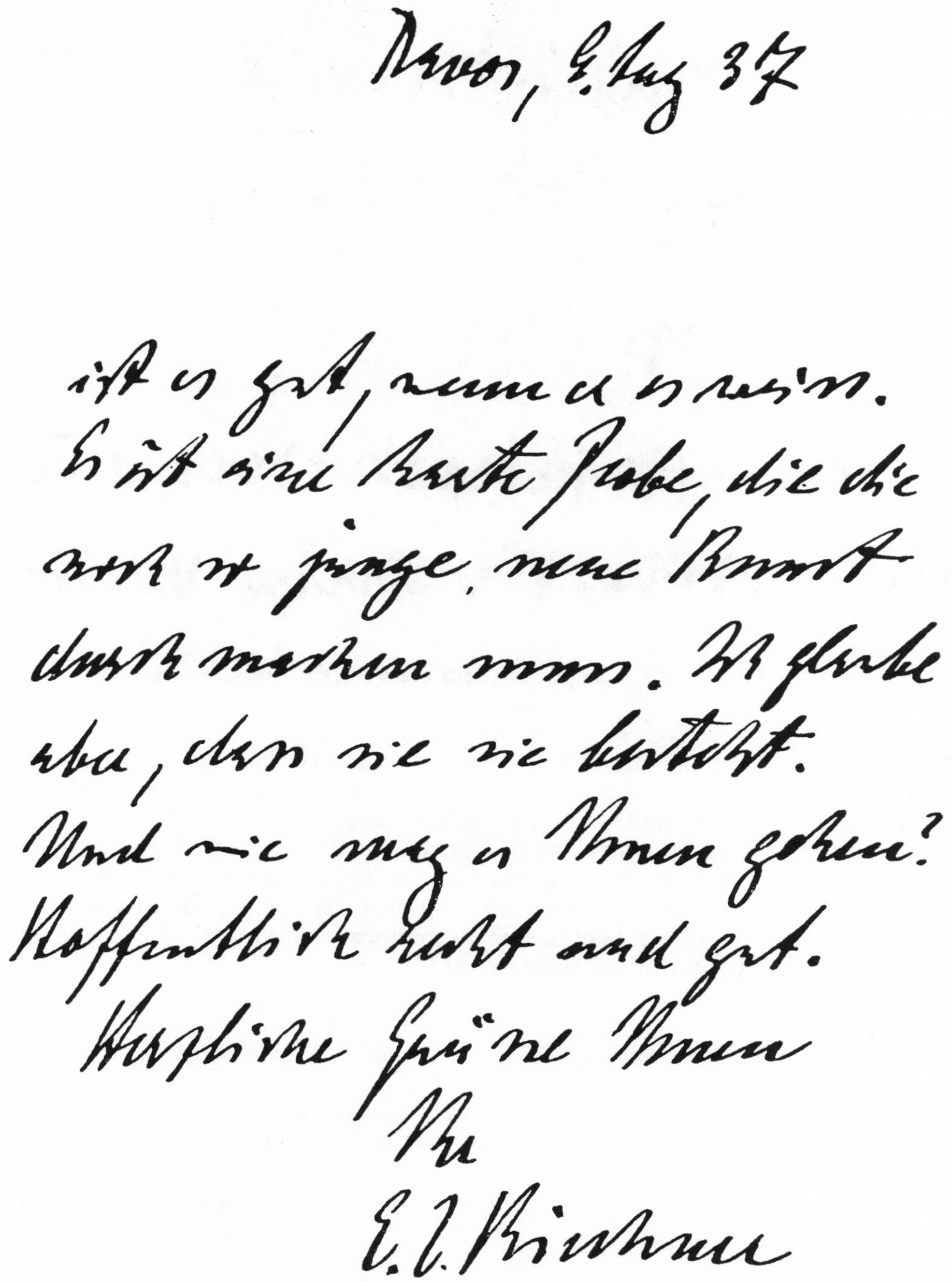
Davos, 8. Aug 37

ist es gut, wenn er es weiss.
Es ist eine harte Probe, die die
noch so junge, neue Kunst
durchmachen muss. Ich glaube
aber, dass sie sie besteht.
Und wie mag es Ihnen gehen?
Hoffentlich recht und gut.
Herzliche Grüsse Ihnen
Ihr
E. L. Kirchner

The German painter, E. L. Kirchner, expresses in this beautiful arcadic handwriting his great despair over the defamation of expressionism in Hitler's Germany. He was a fighter for the then new German art. We see in the active arcadic forms the determination to preserve the ideals of his colleagues. The even right slant shows deep feeling.

The angular arcade is a special form used by the angular writer.

While retaining the main characteristics of the construction of an angle, instead of curves in the connective form, the angular writer rounds off the upper parts of the angles, especially the tops of the *m*'s and *n*'s. This kind of arcadic transformation gives some extra politeness and reserve to the character of the writer, but it is more a superficial politeness because the main character of the angle writer remains, with its harshness, contradiction and iron willpower. It is difficult to imagine an American creating these arrogant, unnatural forms, where aggression is hidden behind elegant manners. (Script of Adolf Galland, one of the best-known German fighter pilots during World War II.)

Special forms: Arcadic transformations

Arcade & vertical slant	= reserve stemming from discretion
Arcade & large size	= need for self-representation
Initial arcade & garlands inside a word, cut-off finals	= very friendly in the beginning but abruptly cutting off later, insecurity, avoids responsibility
Narrowness at the word endings	= egotistic caution
Vertical endings	= mistrust
With enlarged word endings	= lack of self-confidence, despondence
With pressured, club-like endings	= affected behavior
With tapering word endings	= vulnerability, oversensitivity
With left-bent finals (shark-tooth)	= sly like a fox
Crippled word endings	= avoiding responsibility

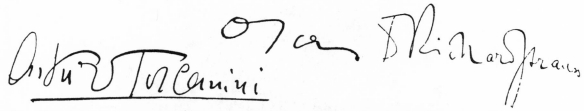

Arcadic transformations in the upper lengths are found among artists, conductors, actors, sculptors, those whose vision transforms.

The harmonious signature of lovely "Dynasty" star Linda Evans shows a predominant garlandic connective form, but the arcade of the η in Evans gives the writing a certain elegance, reserve and self-presentation in society. Her self-defense mechanism is inbuilt out of caution and calculation, but the wide swinging of the large flowing garlands conquers all rules and reason. Her emotions are stronger than her need to be aloof.

The *initial arcade* at the beginning of a word, as in this sample of a wide, arcadically formed upstroke, reveals a writer's feigned self-confidence. He wants to exhibit elegant manners, is circumstantial, ceremonious and formal.

THE DOUBLE CURVE

[handwriting sample]

The *double curve* is exactly that: two curves formed side by side in one flowing movement of arcade and garland. There are no sharp points in the gliding, smooth movement of the arcadic upstroke into the garlandic downstroke. The double curve or double bow, as some call it, is not a distinctive form since it has mixed characteristics of arcade and garland: the protective quality of the arcade and the receptive quality of the garland.

The double curve writer is an opportunist by instinct and behavior. He can slip from one situation quickly into another without losing his sense of security. For him there exists only adaptability at any price. He is as spineless as the double curve itself. He is a virtuoso at adaptability; he holds no opinion; and his main aim is never to be offensive, avoiding conflict at all costs.

[handwriting sample: Dominic's fingernails]

Table for the double curve character

Sympathetic & understanding
Extremely flexible
Adaptable at any price
Emotionally changeable & responsive
Opportunistic
Disregarding ethics and moral principles when self-interest is threatened

THE THREAD

The *thread* is so named simply because the connection between letters in the middle zone resembles a loose thread. The thread is a dissolved form because the letters and connections become one gliding line without the up and down movements of other connective forms. The thread may be the indicator of a writer in a great hurry. In these cases we speak of the *speed thread*.

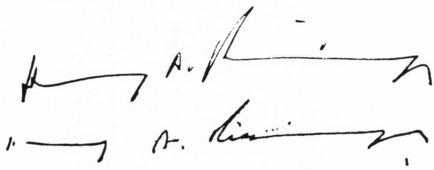

In Henry Kissinger's signature the long straight line is dominant. Occasionally the signature is graced by four legible letters: the capital *K,* sometimes a garlandic *i* as in the second signature and two angular blotted s'. The rest dissolves into a strong, stiff line, ending with the angular formation of a suggested *ger.* A powerful drive stands behind these daring simplifications.

When the thread is drawn with power we call it the *active* or *primary thread.* It appears in the writing of such creative natures as Picasso, Napoleon, Beethoven and Adolf Menzel, (see samples). Although the main characteristics of their threads appear in a higher form niveau, we see the typical traits of ambiguity, intellectual mobility, lability, security of instincts, unlimited adaptability.

In the primary thread of Picasso's signature we have two legible letters,
P and *i*; the rest is an illegible, creative thread-like form.

47

Napoleon's exploding, dynamic, primary thread
is recognizable in the energetic, sharp stroke.

Beethoven's rhythmical, fluctuating, illegible writing
consists more of primary, powerful threads
than distinctive, connective forms.

Adolf von Menzel (1815-1905), painter

In the brush-like forms of the Prussian painter Adolf von Menzel, best known for his historical painting of Frederick II, we see only threads except for the huge capital *M*.

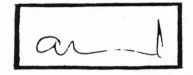

Secondary Thread

When the thread is drawn weakly we call it passive or *secondary thread*. If the secondary thread occurs in a lower form niveau, we see the more prevalent nature of the thread writer, a person who avoids permanent connections to things or people and is inclined towards ambiguity. He is generally unclear, indefinite, uncertain, vague, elusive, and indolent, lacking discipline. He finds it difficult to adjust, and unfolds his talents in circumstances of his own choosing. Because he often denies fixed norms of behavior, he may appear indecisive, unpredictable. If this secondary thread appears in a high form niveau, then his genius may prevail and bring success. But when it appears in a low form niveau we may expect a person capable of questionable compromises.

The limited legibility of thread writing certainly points to some lack of respect for the reader, as well as to the writer's own negligence, insincerity and dishonesty. However, now and then the thread writer will reveal sparkling potential, promising true artistry on the one hand and asocial attitudes on the other.

In Richard Nixon's handwriting we may study the character of a typical thread writer. It is a kind of adaptability at any price. The illegible, flat and undistinguished middle zone letters reveal inner insecurity and self-deception. He has to use all his diplomatic and intellectual capacities to confront the imaginary enemies he fears and tries to deter with exaggerated amiability.

Special forms of thread

Thread with pastosity (thick stroke)

This thread writer has charm and likes to question others continuously, without talking about himself.

49

Speed thread, as in this sample, is the most common way restless, impatient people write. They are changeable, vacillating, unstable, have occasional psychic insight and are diplomatic.

Powerful thread of Orson Welles

Elastic, rhythmic swinging of Richard Burton's thread writing

Thread writing of artists

Mystical and magic radiation of the artistic personality
Love of adventure
Impressiveness; appealing to people's emotions
Creative individualism
Improvisation talent
Intellectuality
Visions
Bohemian nature

THE UNDEFINED FORM

The mixed connective form (where all forms alternate at random, almost aimlessly) is called the *undefined form*. The writer who uses this form tries to adapt properly to each situation. Whether he achieves his purpose depends on his degree of intelligence, judgment and knowledge of human nature. In contrast to the writer who uses definite connective forms he is more flexible. In a hopeless situation he easily finds another dozen possibilities to escape and thus conquers obstacles with bravura.

Undefined form is related to thread writing. There is no faithful use of one distinguished connective form but instead a wild, haphazard, impetuous use of connective forms; it discloses the following characteristics:

Opportunism
Practicality
Change of attitudes
Capacity to respond objectively to new situations

51

Marlene Dietrich

The concentrated, yet manifold uses of connective forms are revealed in Marlene Dietrich's writing. Angles, garlands, arcades, and threads give color to this creative writing and reflect the many facets of Dietrich's strong personality.

SCHOOL WRITING

We call this kind of copybook writing *school writing*. In every country, elementary school teachers teach the specific method chosen for that country. Germany once preferred the angles; now, having turned more to the international scene, the rounder, softer Latin script is taught there. France prefers vertical slant, and England allows connectedness between words, and the melting pot of the United States, where immigrants of various nationalities and races are assimilated, choose a presentation which combines the different characteristics in a soft, round garlandic way.

Someone who uses faithful school writing after he has completed his formal education may not have had much occupational opportunity to write (farmers, for example); or he may not have enough artistic and creative drive to experiment with letter forms; or he may be a poet who likes to hide his shyness behind the stable form of school writing, like these German writers.

Hermann Hesse

Rainer Maria Rilke

Sometimes the hyper-sensitive, artistic person chooses school writing to protect easily-hurt emotions behind a shield of modest behavior.

One speaks of school writing only in reference to adults who have no difficulties with the technique of writing but whose connective forms reflect all the criteria of the copy-book. The person who uses school writing for connective form—for instance, the Palmer method in the United States—tends away from individualism and independent thinking and judgment. He completely acknowledges convention and tradition as guides for conduct and goes to great pains not to be "out of place."

haven't written like this in a very long.

Table of School Writing

Belief in authority
Love of tradition
Simplicity
Adaptability
Eagerness to be correct
Sometimes, masked
Sometimes, lack of individualism

CHILD-LIKE OR INFANTILE WRITING

Writing not only mirrors the physical growing and fading of the human being but also the strength and vitality of his psychic maturity. Psychological development is not dependent on age, for there are many writers who have traits of child-like quality—a wide range of genius naiveté. As Max Reinhardt, the famous German director said: The actor is a person who has put his childhood in his pocket to play." Great, rich, genius natures often display graphic signs of immaturity because they never seem to have accepted a completed inner development. "How happy to be a clown," wrote the internationally known Grock.

The child-like handwriting
of the clown Grock

The extremely simplified, teenage writing of the great German actor Werner Krauss, who played under Max Reinhardt in Berlin and at Vienna's Burg-Theater

DISCIPLINED WRITING

Related to school writing is the so-called disciplined writing. As the name implies, this writing is the result of self-discipline. Any individualism will be suppressed. All efforts will be made not to be different from others. Schoolteachers, clergymen, military personnel and public officials tend to create disciplined writing.

The highly disciplined writing of Marshal Ferdinand Foch (1851-1929).

When there is an artificial form, as taught in the convent of the European countries, we call it *sacré coeur* writing. It describes formality and reserve.

In an extreme, lateral-supported form we see only the appearance of character: disguise, pretense, hypocrisy, cunning are the reality.

Here we see writers who have cultivated their aesthetic natures
and their handwriting is stylized.

There are some writers however who are utterly devoted to the superfluous letter form. They enjoy ostentatious self-display and attention-getting ornamentation, as seen here:

Joan Fontaine

Olivia de Havilland

The stylized signatures of Academy Award-winning Joan Fontaine and her Academy Award-winning sister Olivia de Havilland

CONNECTEDNESS

Writing is a process of alternately moving and stopping. We are forced to interrupt the flow of our writing at the end of each word and at the end of each line. Some of us pause to breathe in the middle of words as well. And, of course, we have to lift the pen to dot *i*'s, cross *t*'s and make diacritical marks like the cedilla in *façade.*

Writers who connect three or more letters are using connected writing. Their pen glides over the paper in one connecting rhythm. Connected writing results from the unity of a twisting, entwining flow in the creation of the letters.

The connected writer associates ideas. He is usually realistic, reasonable, and logical. He strives for theoretical, practical, and ethical qualities of thought. If his connected writing springs from an inner vitality we say that his writing has *vital connectedness.* His script appears to flow lightly and easily.

However, if the connectedness in a writing seems to be washed out, the connections dissolved and neglected, we know the writer is not concerned with accuracy and detail. Mobile, restless, eager to associate with his fellowman, he is always on the go, curious, looking out for the next stimulation. He tends to think and act too quickly.

In this overconnected easyflowing
writing, we see an elegant flight
of ideas

59

Could you please tell me something about my business prospects, what would be

In a slow, elaborate handwriting the connectedness may have another source. The writer is afraid to leave his accustomed comfortable lifestyle. He is subservient to peoples' opinions and tends to conventional generalizations. He has no desire for independence and adapts obediently to society.

I didn't expect to meet you here this morning It's certainly a very pleasant surprise. So,

In spite of a high form niveau, we see an overconnected, too-easily-flowing writing, revealing the unrestrained flight of ideas and slight tendencies to hysteria.

Their flag to April's breeze unfurled,
Here once the embattled farmers stood,
And fired the shot heard round the world.
R.W. Emerson.

In the refined, high form niveau writing of the poet Ralph Waldo Emerson are overconnected, beautifully swinging forms—an expression of speedy imagination.

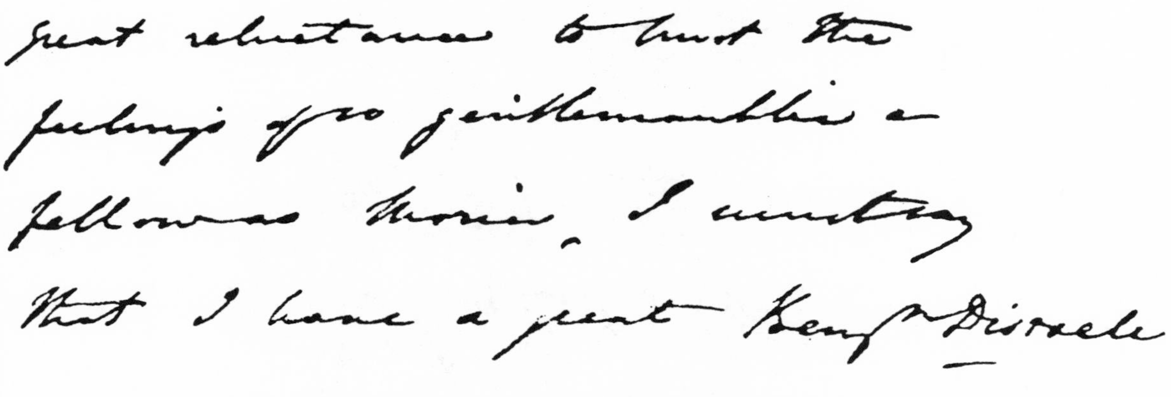

The elegantly connected handwriting above belongs to the British author and statesman Benjamin Disraeli. We can see intellectual capacity in this easily flowing, refined, simplified writing. Clarity of mind, wide intellectual horizon, methodical thinking, easy association, and logical combination of thought-processes are all revealed. On straight lines he speeds toward his goal with inner stability, looking neither right nor left.

There are some letters which tend to be easily connected with the following letters in a word. Note the capital *D* (in *Dear*) the combining of the i-dot into the following letter strokes, and making the t-crossing part of the *h* (in *the*)—when we see such signs of combining thought processes we know that the writer makes speedy associations.

DISCONNECTEDNESS

Salvador Dali, surrealistic painter

Disconnected writing is a kind of *juxtaposed writing* in which the letters are set side by side as in printing. The *disconnected writer* may draw his letter formations so carefully, with such fidelity to detail, that the flow of the movement is interrupted and the script appears perforated, pierced, or punctured. The *disconnected writer* is usually so reflective that he pauses often to "breathe," interrupting the flow of the script. It causes him to lift the pen often, to let a constant flow of new ideas enter his mind, striking like lightning, splintering connected writing. The pen chisels and burns the paper, as we see in the Salvador Dali lines and writing symbols which stand almost isolated, revealing the unpredictable, intuitive mind of the painter.

Robert Oppenheimer shows in his partly connected, partly *disconnected writing* how logical and analytical thinking work together to bring intuitive ideas into being.

One hundred and fifty years ago Michon divided writers into two categories: those who connected letters had a realistic, practical mind and a logical conception of the world. Those who juxtaposed letters had singular impulses and tended to be illogical as a result. Such a person might discover gold but would not know how to utilize it. Michon admired both logic and intuition, which we see in partly connected and partly disconnected writing.

Michon also spoke of *l'arrêt du penseur,* reflection before action, when the first letter of a word is isolated. He wrote: "The handwriting of Napoleon is typical. He stops after the first letter. His intuition works, he produces an idea, a plan. But as soon as the conception is fulfilled, he connects all letters to the very end. His practical reason does not lose a beat after the initial moment of reflection."

Napoleon Bonaparte (1769-1821)

Michon calls the isolated capital *B l'arrêt du penseur,* the reflection of a thinking man before he moves toward his goal.

The American novelist reveals her way of thinking:
reflecting for a moment before going on.

The higher the quality of the writing —high form niveau— the more positive the meaning of disconnectedness: richness of imagination and ideas; ability to think analytically; intuition; a high degree of individualism; a need for independence. The disconnected writer reacts more to stimulating moments. He lacks the ability to enter into committed relationships or associations. He clings more to immediate, concrete, singular things. His script is suddenly interrupted, much as the flow of a river is halted by a huge stone or tree in the water, and he is then forced to find a way around the obstacle.

The disconnected writer has to concentrate more upon single thoughts—the stones —in his forward movement. His writing does not flow as smoothly as the writing of the connected writer. But when the obstacle, the interruption by the new idea, has been overcome, the stream has become richer, the continuity of thinking has been reestablished— until the next interruption, the next intuition.

The airbridge

If in disconnected writing the pen is lifted for one moment and then continues in the same direction after the leap, we call this interruption an *airbridge.* This kind of writing is regarded as *connected writing.*

However, when the leap is not followed immediately by an apparent continuation, even in the air, then a real gap is created. We consider this *disconnected writing.*

63

phisiology

full 8

Oscar Wilde's artistic airbridges are imaginary lines
between the singular letters.

letter   *almost*

An imaginary line connects the last
e-stroke with the *t*-stroke and
continues to the end without
further interruption.

In the word *almost* the *s*-stroke
glides through the air and continues
at the downstroke of the *t*.

Skeleton writing

We see an extreme form of disconnectedness in *skeleton writing*. The writing elements are so greatly reduced that there remain only downstrokes, looking like pilings, standing in rows. Oversimplifying writing in this manner is a sign of essential thinking quality but indicates at the same time strong detachment from society.

Isaiah Berlin   *stage*   *reminded*   *hope*

Isaiah Berlin

Enclosed

picture and some negatives

In an irregular disconnected writing with low form niveau the writer's lack of concentration is visible. He is nervous, easily irritated, moody, forgetful and unpredictable.

*Comme je sais que tu correspond avec
(Anna) et qu'elle n'a pas l'habitude de te*

In an insecure, disturbed handwriting, disconnectedness is rooted in the writer's lack of vitality. He is anxious, inhibited and lacks mobility. The weak caved-in *t*-stem, *g* and *l*-stem show so-called directional pressure from the past, suffering in childhood, which results in weak writing.

[handwriting: I realize that you are extremely busy and may not yet have had]

If a script has wide gaps between words and lines, and sudden abrupt endings, the writer's adaptability to society is completely disturbed.

[handwriting sample in German]

The Swedish playwright August Strindberg was famous
for his misanthropic behavior. The wide gaps reveal loneliness.

Explorers, painters, inventors are likely to be disconnected writers. Observation and comprehension are their particular gifts. They may be theorists and may produce a torrent of ideas, but they lack practical judgment; they may be tireless investigators but fail to draw conclusions. They will discover a source of oil, but cannot bore through the layers of earth to release it.

Among disconnected writers we may find the butterfly collector, deeply immersed in arranging his colorful catches; or the stamp collector, so enchanted by the rarity of his *Mauritius* that he cares not at all for the rigors of associating ideas or for the world of logic.

[signature: Arturo Toscanini]

Toscanini's intuitive,
disconnected signature

Disconnectedness

Emily Dickinson's
handwritten poem, signed, "Emily"

This tender, disconnected writing with the large gaps between words belongs to the great poet Emily Dickinson. She needs a self-imposed solitude to express her highly artistic nature in the purest way possible.

STRONG PRESSURE

Jenny Jugo, a German movie star,
writes with such pressure
that her pen splits.

George Wallace has such strong
pressure that his pen splits.

Extreme pressure in handwriting opens a third dimension—besides height and width—because it creates both the illusion of depth and actual depth on the paper. Writers who use strong pressure are always intensely determined to overcome obstacles. The stronger the pressure, the more densely do the minute particles of ink adhere to the surface of the paper.

Handwriting pressure can be strong, weak, irregular, or mixed. If the writing surface impedes the flowing movement of the pen, personal energy will show up in the degree of pressure exerted. (See for example, the split nib in the samples above.)

A *compact pressure* symbolizes the vigorous vitality of the writer, whereas an *irregular pressure* reveals a flickering or flaring vitality. The primary significance of pressure is its revelation of the inherent strength of the writer. When pressure is applied with *regularity* we see willpower. If it is associated with *irregularity* we see instinctive impulses. When pressure is *regular and rhythmical* the upstrokes are not accentuated. It is the *downstroke* that will receive the emphasis.

If the direction of pressure is suddenly diverted, for instance, at the end of a word, we call it *displaced pressure*. This symbolizes diplaced libido, psychic energy, because pressure is directly related to psychic and sexual energy.

Displaced pressure — the emphasis is on the last,
horizontal, energetic stroke.

We can only judge or evaluate pressure when it is actually visible and significant. The quickest way to examine the violence of the stroke is by turning the page over and looking at the imprint on the backside.

In this sample of strong pressure we see the main ingredients of the pressure writer. He needs to feel his existence, to experience his own efficiency, to show off his courage, his virility, his zest for life, his aggressiveness (which we see in the end strokes, as in the number 5 on the second line, drawn with a hook and demonstrating combativeness). This is the writing of a successful patent lawyer in Europe, internationally known for his activity, energy, diligence, intellect and ambition. The intelligence lies also in the combination of thread and simplification of letter forms.

Klages introduced the concept of passive and active willpower in handwriting. We can prove the strength of our willpower by conquering the world or by conquering our-selves. Active willpower is more expansive, exploring the world with determination and energy, achieving success, whereas passive willpower is directed toward resistance and endur-ance. In the field of intellectual achievements we have the samples of two successful writers who conquer the world through the power of the mind.

Herman Wouk   Thornton Wilder

The powerful pressure of Herman Wouk and Thornton Wilder

1893

The strong pressure of the powerful statesman Prince Otto von Bismarck, Chancellor of the German Empire (1871-1890). The 'Iron Chancellor' unified the German Empire after the French-German War 1870-1871. Michon spoke about *Bismarck's club*, the last downstroke of the *k* in Bismar*ck*, which symbolizes the fighting spirit of the Iron Chancellor.

68

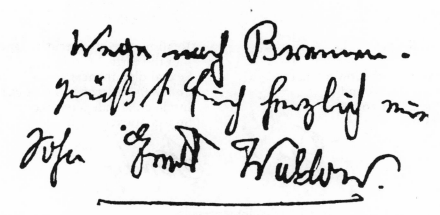

As soon as the form niveau sinks to a low primitive form, as in this sample of a 16-year-old murderer, we see in the rigid, club-like strokes the strong impulse to destroy. The violent pressure is probably due to the suppression of sexual urges and to primitive compulsions he cannot control.

Mahatma Gandhi (1869-1948)

In Gandhi's strong-pressured writing we see the inner struggle to maintain self-control and achieve *passive resistance*. His self-discipline was so strong that he gave up Western ways when he was only 36 years old and lived abstinently, according to Hindu ethic and dressed only in loincloth and blanket or shawl.

Pressure	*Interpretation*
Compact pressure	Strength or vitality
Pressure in the middle zone	Accent on the personal sphere
Pressure with angles	Soldier-like behavior
Pressure on baseline letters	Manual and technical gifts
Pressure on angular lower lengths	Suppressed emotions
Increasing pressure on downstrokes	Needing security
Pressure on lateral forms	Affected behavior
Sudden pressure on syllables	Sudden halt of emotions for ex-pression of power
Point-like pressure on initial strokes	
Horizontal pressure on word endings	Obstinacy, antisocial nature, love of bravura

Strong Pressure

Pressure (continued)   *Interpretation*

Pressure in the lower lengths   Realism, need for security, anchoring
                                                      in the earth

Irregular pressure in the lower lengths   Sexual disturbances
Pressure toward the ground   *Commander stroke* (Bismarck)
Pressure in the upper zone   Intellectual independence
Swelling pressure   Spurts of excitement
  (See sample)

Swelling pressure

Sudden blocking of pressure   Change in relationship to the partner,
                                                      sexual frustration

Alternating writing pressure   Irritated, unpredictable, unsteady
Flickering pressure   Restless impulses, fluctuating willpower,
                                                      quick enthusiasm, quickly dying

Pressure in the downstroke   Insecurity
Pressured impression visible on the backside
  of the paper   Putting on an act of vigor and power
Needle-like decreasing downstrokes   Not in touch with reality

John Hinckley's needle-like downstrokes disclose hesitation and fear of the world.

The fading, flickering pressure in the handwriting of mass-murderer
Charles Manson shows mental decay and insane, unpredictable impulses.

Displaced Pressure Sample

Notice the emphasis in the upper zone. It shows a domineering personality.

The so-called *flamed stroke* made for effect:
sudden swelling of pressure in the downstrokes.

The handwriting of a woman with disturbed blood circulation revealed by *flamed* or *swelling pressure.* These characteristics might appear with pregnancy, menopause, gall bladder problems, kidney ailments or certain heart conditions. In chronic alcoholism such swelling strokes are tremulous and appear in all three writing zones.

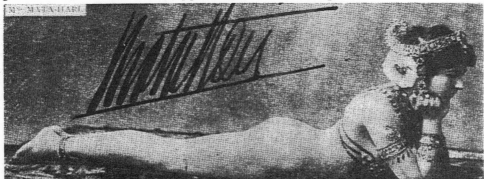

Courtesy of M. Wesley Marans
Mata Hari (1876-1917)

The notorious World War I spy must have been better at concealing secrets than is apparent here. The fence-like high middle zone, artificial ruler t-crossing, and straight edge underscoring her signature are drawn unconsciously, signifying prison bars.

In this sample of extreme irregularity in pressure and forms
we see bizarre forms of letters, which may be due to physical or mental disturbances.

The irregular pressure matches the "friendly" message.

WEAK PRESSURE

Whereas the strong-pressure-loving writer has bursts of energy, activity, vitality and often harshness, with lack of tact and sensibility, the writer with weak pressure shows refinement, tenderness, impressibility, vulnerability and sometimes even anxiety.

In this sample we see characteristics of weak pressure, such as lack of initiative, intensity, and determination. In the writing above, the gliding, soft movement exhibits the soft quality of the pressure, and in fact, most of these samples are by persons who rarely have the energy to overcome obstacles.

If weak pressure is found in connection with regularity, delicacy, tenderness and width, as in the sample below, it may reveal ethical purity, provided the writing has a high form niveau, as does this sample:

The tender, graceful handwriting and drawing of the dadaistic
and surrealistic painter, sculptor and poet Hans Arp (1887-1966)

[handwriting: Jerusalem is the most beautiful city in the world — Golda Meir]

Golda Meir, born 1898 in Kiev,
was 1969-1974 Prime Minister of Israel

In Golda Meir's delicate handwriting we see sudden strokes carrying more emphasis so that the whole writing seems to be interwoven as with iron threads in a carpet of silken embroidery. These strong threads are proof of inherent energy and determination which break through in times of crisis. The basic nature is feminine, modest and soft. But the t-crossings and some downstrokes (as in *t* in *most, beautiful, city*, the crossing of the capital *G* and the large curved initial *m*) show a power usually kept hidden, as the blotted vowel *o* in *world* and *Golda* reveal.

[handwriting: Auguste Rodin]

Auguste Rodin (1840-1917), the French sculptor, uses in his speedy, elegant writing the delicate stroke of the sensitive artist. The main ingredients of the weak pressure writer are sensibility, sensitivity, vulnerability, impressiveness, refinement (which might be the result of weaker vital instincts, weaker willpower or physical exhaustion).

Whereas the strong pressure writer shows off, with vitality, courage, vital tension, activity, energy, efficiency, ambition, aggression, toughness and sometimes absence of consideration, the weak pressure writer is refined and sensitive; depending upon the degree of the form niveau, the weak pressure writer may actually *be* weak and ineffectual.

The light, amusing text in this water color by the German painter Hans Fischer fits the light pressure of his drawing and defines the light and easy nature of a weak pressure writer. His is an "aesthetic nature who goes to bed late and creeps out of bed even later," he says. His weak pressure in drawing and writing reveals receptive, spiritual, artistic gifts, refined humor and lots of illusions and dreams.

THE THIRD DIMENSION: DEPTH

Auguste Rodin, the French sculptor, reminded a painter: "Ne vois jamais les formes étendues, mais toujours en profondeur." (Never concentrate only on extended forms, look always at their depth.") The painters who represent the extended style, the surface style, are Albrecht Dürer, Leonardo da Vinci, Raphael and Titian for instance. The painters who represent the third dimension with its dark, deep strokes are for instance, Rembrandt, Rubens and Goya.

At an international Graphological Convention in Lindau at the Swiss, Austrian and German border, Professor Böllinger from Zurich, spoke about the relationship between painting and writing: the less sharply defined the contours of the painting, the stronger is the visual impression of depth. The less sharply and broader the margin and letters in the writing, the stronger is the impression of a colorful carpet with intertwining forms and velvet texture.

Against the dark background Rembrandt's *Old Woman Cutting Her Nails,* holding the knife in her left hand, gives us the illusion of depth. The same depth we see in Rembrandt's handwriting (see next page).

Courtesy of The Metropolitan Museum of Art, Bequest of Benjamin Altman, 1913
Rembrandt's *Old Woman Cutting Her Nails*

76

The broad-wide-swinging initial curves of the capitals show the same depth of passion.

Courtesy of The National Gallery, London
Rembrandt's beloved *Hendrijke Stoffels.*
Her face is painted with an unmistakable depth of feeling which brings out
the gentleness of her character. The same depth we see in Rembrandt's signature.

The Third Dimension: Depth

Graphological elements:	*Significance:*
Broad, saturated, dark stroke	Deep passionate feeling
Absence of sharp contours	Heaviness of the soul
Pastosity of stroke	Dynamic emotions, sensualism
Black and white plastic reliefs	Sense for dramatic contrasts

Courtesy of The Albertina
Peter Paul Rubens' self-portait is done with the same depth
of feeling as the full, dark strokes of his signature.

78

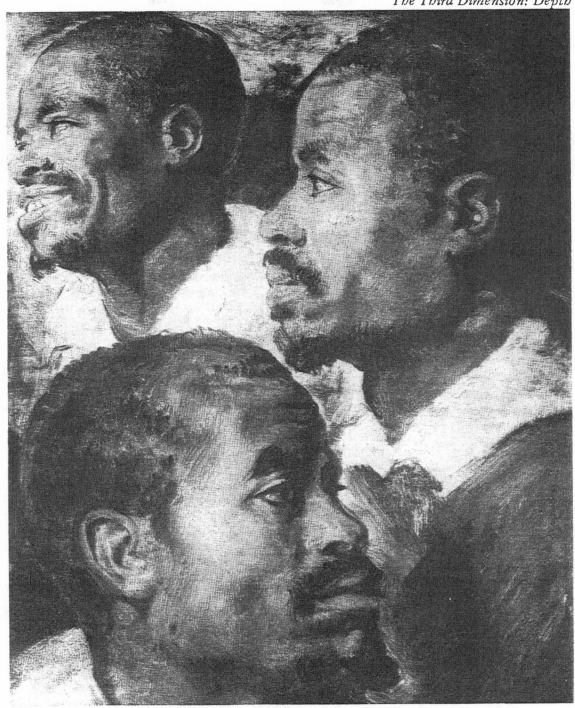

Courtesy of Musées Royaux des Beaux Arts
Peter Paul Rubens (1577-1640), *Têtes de nègres*, describes the contours and details
of this dramatic face. The compassionate, deep expression is mirrored in his handwriting.

79

Courtesy of The Metropolitan
Museum of Art, Harris Brisbane Dick
Fund, 1935
In Francisco de Goya's painting
"The Swing" we easily perceive the
third dimension of depth.   The movement goes from left foreground to
right background. The gallant
cavalier stands on the left,
initiating the movement of the swing.

Francisco de Goya, Spanish painter (1746-1828)

From the strong-pressured letters, standing side by side,
with the boat in the background, one easily experiences the illusion of depth.

Ezra Pound, US poet in Italy (1885-1972)   Giuseppe Verdi (1813-1901)

On the background of the white paper the broad and colorful stroke of Ezra Pound and
Giuseppe Verdi create a light and dark illusion of depth. The signatures show in their
deep-penetrating writing passion and depth of soul.

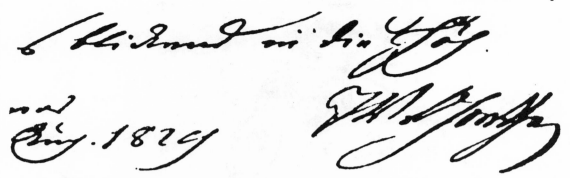

The same deep strokes of Rembrandt's and Ruben's art of painting we discover in some handwritings. A most beautiful sample of broad, full, wide-swinging strokes —to the left— to the right—upward-downward— which gives the illusion of depth, is seen in the hand-writing of the 80 year-old German poet and writer Johann Wolfgang von Goethe.

If the upswinging stroke bends to the left, the attitudes of the writer are influenced by the past and tradition. If the embracing curve in the lower zone is directed to the right, the qualities of empathy and humanity are found.

The capital letter *K*, swinging to the right in an arcadic form, has the character of reserve, distinction, secrecy, politeness and caution. The open bowl of the independently formed capital *J* deeply penetrates the darker regions of subconsciousness.

The depth writing of Joan Collins. Note the even, deep-reaching J-capital-lower loop into healthy anchoring in the soil and the even, beautifully swinging upper curve of the C-capital — a perfect inte-gration of body and mind, as shown by the 'depth' stroke. The strong garlandically curved middle zone and the powerfully penetrating stroke of the underscoring show strong self-esteem. The whole writing breathes efficiency, or-ganization and self-confidence.

Courtesy of The Albertina
Albrecht Dürer's self-portrait, at age 13. (1484)
It is the oldest self-portrait known in German art. It exemplifies surface painting.

Dürer's ambivalent handwriting shows white space between the letters.
This gives the impression of lightness and extended surface writing.

Courtesy of The Metropolitan
Museum of Art, Gift of
Junius S. Morgan, 1919
*The Riders on the Four Horses
from the Apocalypse*
by Albrecht Dürer.
Note the even surface,
extended style.

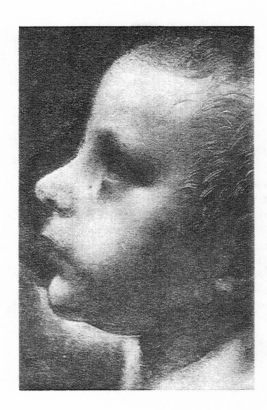

Courtesy of The Louvre, Paris
Leonardo da Vinci's
Virgin of the Rocks
Leonardo's technique involved a warm
brownish underpainting, followed by the
working of blues, purples, cool colors,
finishing with warm glazes. This detail
illustrates the bluish paint visible
through the flesh tones on the Christ
Child's nose. Leonardo's technique
also belongs to the extended, surface
style category.

Madame Curie's methodical, scientific clarity is a model of plane surface writing.

The harmonious, spiritual, simplified, pure, aethereal writing of the physicist Albert Einstein
is another example of surface-extended writing.

Graphological elements	*Significance*
Thin and pale strokes, Meagerness	Sensitivity, Predominance of objectivity
Exact and precise contours, Small margins	Clarity, quietness, Self-limitation
Regularity and stability of letters	Self-restraint
	Extended surface writing.

WARMTH AND PASTOSITY

Fullness and thick strokes (pasty strokes) are the ingredients of a three dimensional depth writing as we see it in Goethe's handwriting. Every painter knows that certain colors, like red and yellow, have a warm effect, and other colors, like green and blue, produce a cool impression. The same is true in handwriting. A thin, pale stroke will never radiate the warmth of a dark-colored velvety stroke; thin, meager forms will appear cool; and round, voluptuous forms are created by the affectionate type.

A thick stroke without tension, as in Balzac's sample, is called the pastose stroke and gives the script colorful richness and fullness. The texture of the stroke is like cake batter. The writer has to hold the pen loosely and flat to produce these broad, softly flowing, occasionally smeary strokes.

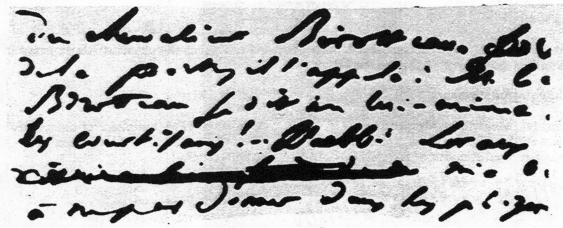

Honoré de Balzac (1799-1850),
French novelist who enjoyed the pleasures of life wholeheartedly.

84

People who love to write with a pasty stroke are fascinated by beauty. They are attracted to and sensually stimulated by colors and music. Many painters and musicians have this brush-like, pasty writing which radiates vital strength, originality, richness, awakened senses and a relaxed, unaffected nature.

Joan Miro (1893-1985), Spanish surrealist painter,
demonstrates in his pasty writing visual impressions
rather than abstract theoretical perceptions.

Aristide Maillol (1861-1944), French sculptor,
reveals in his handwriting the easygoing flexibility of a creative
artist who is not restricted by self-control and harsh self-discipline.
He needs time for decisions and yields to emotions.

The pastose, often smeary stroke in the sensuous writing
of Oscar Wilde (1854-1900), Irish playwright.
In this highly artistic writing we see smeary, dark spots,
which Jung called the dark spots in the character (degenerated shadows).

Il Vostro aff.mo amico

Nicolo Paganini

Parigi li 18 Decembre 1838

Nicolo Paganini (1784-1840)
shows all the strengths and weaknesses of the pastose writer.

We see sensuousness in the thick, pastose stroke; natural talent and musical genius in the voluptuously created letter forms, especially in the wild underscoring of his signature; vivacity and passion in the accent-like i-dots; and sense of rhythm in the round, sweeping lower loops.

diras-pas un mot, et que je le traiterai comme un être absolument étranger.

Marie Antoinette

We see the child-like charm of the fun-loving daughter of Maria Theresia of Austria. Marie Antoinette, given in marriage to the Dauphin of France, failed to recognize the threatening signs of the revolution, suggesting lightly to starving people: "Let them eat cake." Her pastose writing shows the pleasure-minded carelessness which brought her to an early end.

W. A. Mozart

Wolfgang Amadeus Mozart
(1756-1791)

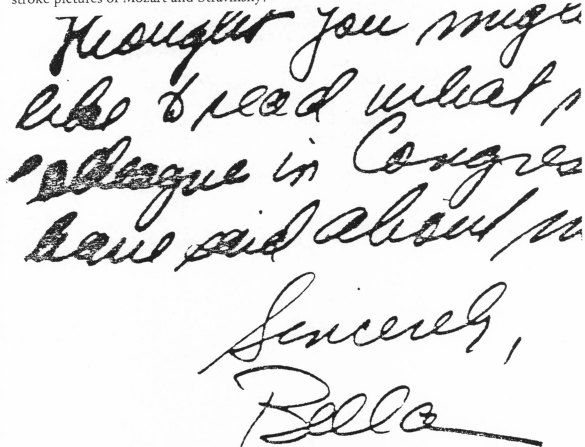

Igor Stravinsky
(1882-1971)

The deep feeling, artistic sensuality of composers is seen in the dark-colored, rich, pasty stroke pictures of Mozart and Stravinsky.

Bella Abzug's pastose writing

The pastose and smeary, ink-blotted, large handwriting of Bella Abzug reveals a social, altruistic personality, often tactless and loud, yet warmhearted and generous—as the large, swinging garlands show. Her club-like endstroke mirrors willpower and determination to reach her goals.

87

Warmth and Pastosity

Table of pastosity (thick stroke)

Vitality

Warmth

Sensuality

Love of colors

Lack of delicacy of feeling

Gourmet

Carefree, untroubled

Passion

Strength

Depth

Instinctual

Zest for life

Originality

Naturalness

The ink-blotted, dark, passionate writing
of Pablo Picasso reveals all the qualities and vices of a pastose writer.

SHARPNESS AND COOLNESS

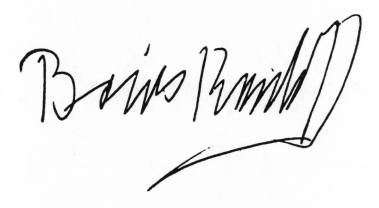

We consider a writing sharp when the stroke is tense and thin. The writer usually takes the pen strongly between his thumb and the third fingers. The pen is almost upright and can create careful and well-distinguished letter forms. The width of the stroke remains consistently thin. The sharpness will be supported by pointed finals as in the sample above.

The sharp stroke visualizes the relationship between strength and tension. We speak of domineering, sharp intellects in contrast to those who think with their hearts and are sensual. People who write with sharp strokes shield their emotions, have self-discipline, goal-orientation and a harsh intensity. They are precise in their thoughts and their actions.

Boris Karloff

If the stroke is not pointed, has only a thin quality, the usual aggressiveness of the sharp writer is subdued and we see only the cool, sober character of the sharp writer.

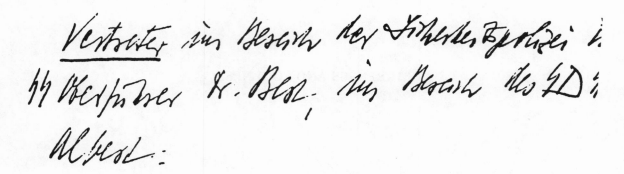

Heydrich's dagger-like finals.

The sharp, aggressive, pointed writing of Gestapo chief Heydrich, "Hangman of Europe."

Graphologists of old categorized handwriting not only by pastosity and sharpness but also by heaviness and lightness. The *delicate* writer with his sensitivity and easy irritability suffers a great deal throughout his life from loud noises, certain odors and changes of temperature. He is marked by great sensitivity, excitability and a high susceptibility and sense of impression. He depends heavily on sympathy. He is highly susceptible in matters of cleanliness. He is easily enraptured and quickly disillusioned. He has an aversion to vulgarity, toughness and brutality.

Table for the delicate writer.

Sensibility	Tact
Refinement, delicacy	Feet not on the ground
Touchiness, tenderness	Absence of sensuality
Susceptibility	Irresoluteness
Enthusiasm	Cautiousness

Table for the delicate writer (continued)

Excitability
Extreme cleanliness
Abstract mind
Impressionability
Inhibitions
Psychological and physical fragility
Tendency to asceticism
Accuracy of detail

Hesitation
Modesty
Anxiety
Spiritual lightness
Sharp intellect
Criticism
Reserve, discretion

RIGHT TREND

When we say that our writing moves forward on the real or imaginary line we are actually describing its movement to the *right*. Bows and curves may appear within this forward movement, tending back to the left, like the lower g-loop in the sample of Serge Prokofieff, although here the to-the-right-striving *S* and *f* crossings give the writing the *right trend*.

Serge Prokofieff (1891-1953), Russian composer,
with to-the-right-turning note symbols in his *f's*

We might also describe the right trend forward movement as an expression coming from the *ego* to the *you,* to the world, to the future, all of which lie symbolically to the right. Right trend writing is a gesture of attack, activity, extraversion, giving and altruism.

In a low form niveau, right trend can show such negative characteristics as absence of contemplation or independence. In these writings we often find weak will and an easily influenced personality.

Right trend means future-oriented, goal-oriented. *Right trend upwards* into the higher spiritual regions shows the writer's longing for spiritual stimulation and development.

The high-grasping strokes in this sample are "antennae" to the universe.

Right trend downward (with pressure) is a sign of depression and negative activity.

92

Christopher Columbus
(1451-1506)

The right-trend writing of Christopher Columbus, driven forward to explore the world.

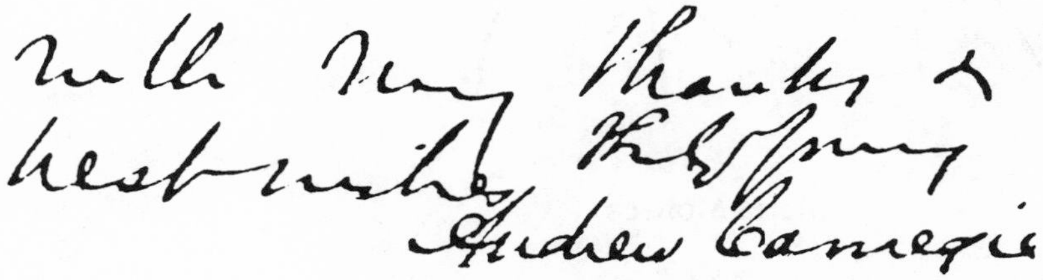

Andrew Carnegie
(1835-1919)

In Andrew Carnegie's right-trend letter forms
we see the altruistic, future-oriented spirit which guided him.

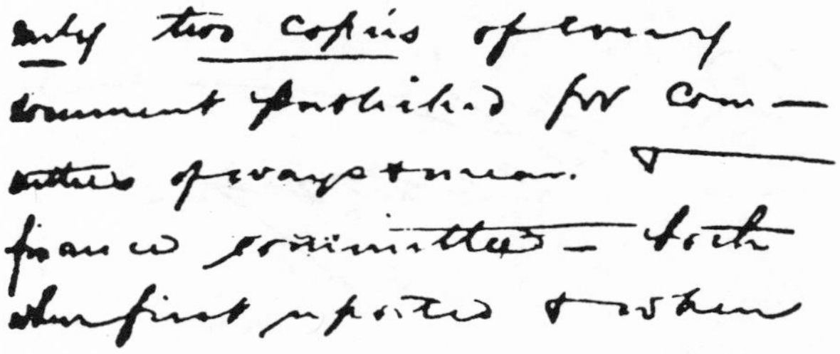

John Pierpont Morgan
(1837-1913)

John Pierpont Morgan's to-the-right extended endstrokes show long-range planning ability and generosity. He donated huge sums to the Metropolitan Museum of Art, which received a valuable portion of his collection.

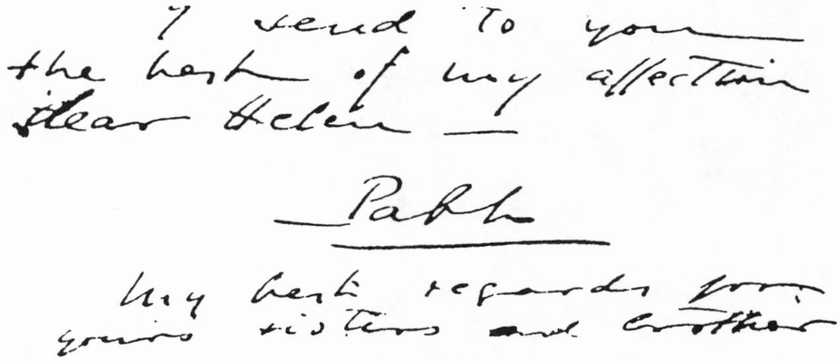

Pablo Casals
(1876-1973),
world's greatest cellist,
shows in his widely
extended endings all the
qualities of the right-
trend writer:

Tendency to expansiveness
Altruism
Turned to the world
Forward striving into the future
Activity
Openness; does not need earthly possessions

Maria Montez

Right trend with width shows generosity
altruism with pressure, strong willpower.

Philip Kearny

In this rightward-flying signature of Brigadier General Philip Kearny we see the born leader
who storms toward the future with·
Security
Decisive judgment
Determination
Tenacity
Independence

LEFT TREND

Unlike right-trend writing which is future oriented, the trend to the left is a continuous turning back upon the ego, upon the past, upon one's history. Symbolically it is the gesture of egocentricity, tucking things behind one's back to conceal them. The left trend may thus signify:

Self-interest
Acquisitive nature
Selfishness
Egocentricity

We see pure egocentricity when the left trend stroke aims
downward as in this sample.

When the left trend is directed *upward* as with the lyrical *d* in Mozart's, Edison's and Walt Whitman's writing it signifies turning back from the future, from the world, to contemplation, meditation and introspection. All left trend movements show the tendencies to preserve, to save, to maintain. The scale ranges from egocentric aims to concentration, introspection.

Lyrical *d*'s of Edison

Whitman

Mozart

95

Sir Isaac Newton (1642-1727), English physicist and philosopher, combined right and left trend in his handwriting. To explore, to discover the laws of motion, he had first to return to the past (left) to proceed into the future (right).

The lyrical *d* in *obliged* has left trend,
the combination of *w* and *t* in *Newton* has right trend.

If the head of the left-bound *d* is very large it shows the huge amount of fantasy and poetry in the writer. When the *d* is toppled over to the left we find this poetic person disappointed in life; he is hyper-sensitive and buries himself in memories and resignation, and he becomes a sad dreamer of his lost past.

In this huge, left-bound crossing through the signature and then turning back to cut even more through the signature, one sees a crossing-out of disappointment.

96

Many left-trend enrollments, spirals, show the writer's egotistic character traits and self-preservative instincts.

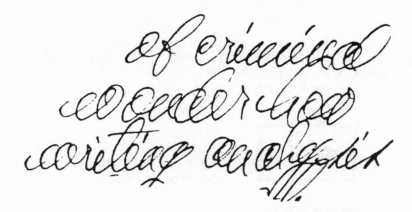

The looped garland with its continuously rolling backward curves in the middle zone, also belongs to left trend.

Spoon-*e*   Spoon-*e* with spirals

Spiral forms of some middle zone letters, like the *spoon-e*, are a symbol of ambitious, efficient passion which belongs to people who are not afraid to fight or who intrigue to reach their goals. These enrollments in the middle zone to the left show insincerity, secretiveness and suppressed lust for power.

In the to-the-left-swinging open bowls instead of lower loops
we see Goethe's receptivity to the culture of the past.

Vuzina

Any my

New York.

The to-the-left-swinging bent-in downstrokes with the to-the-left-swinging lower loops in a weak handwriting are one of the signs that the writer has not freed himself from his early attachment to his mother. It may indicate latent homosexuality.

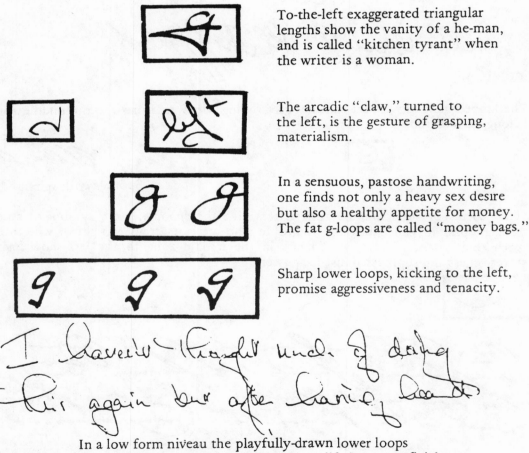

To-the-left exaggerated triangular lengths show the vanity of a he-man, and is called "kitchen tyrant" when the writer is a woman.

The arcadic "claw," turned to the left, is the gesture of grasping, materialism.

In a sensuous, pastose handwriting, one finds not only a heavy sex desire but also a healthy appetite for money. The fat g-loops are called "money bags."

Sharp lower loops, kicking to the left, promise aggressiveness and tenacity.

In a low form niveau the playfully-drawn lower loops
show a talking, chattering individual who enjoys life in a superficial way.

To-the-left trend is similar to the so-called shark tooth—a to-the-left-bent final stem of the *m* or *n* in an arcadic form. Its special significance is only to be judged in the *Gestalt* impression of the script. It always belies a contradiction between inherent character and acquired life experience and reveals hypocrisy and insincerity.

Shark tooth = to-the-left,
bent-in last stroke of the *m*.

SPEED

Camillo Baldi, professor of medicine at Bologna's University, published in 1625, *How to recognize the nature and character of a writer.* He said:

"Fast writing speed reveals intensity of feeling, impulsiveness, passion, violence, inconstancy and sometimes fickleness. Slowness in handwriting shows laziness, apathy, clumsiness, sensual desire for pleasure and lack of clarity. If the writing is quick and uneven, the writer shows fast-changing moods and actions. Even his judgment suffers from inconstancy."

In 1812 the graphologist Hocquart said:

"An impulsive and strong handwriting radiates energy. The writer who never makes an error in his letter formations, inspite of his tremendous speed, has power of concentration." Hocquart describes Pascal's speedy almost illegible handwriting: "Pascal's mind is impatient and powerful. It works so quickly that his pen cannot follow." And Preyer observed in his *Psychology of Writing,* 1911: "It is natural that a scientist like Pascal, who is completely devoted to the solution of his theoretical task, neglects unimportant traits in his writing. His letters are the result of his fast, almost eruptive thinking process. Probably only he himself could decipher his skeleton handwriting."

Blaise Pascal (1623-1662),
French mathematician, physicist and philosopher.
(Pascal's words say: "La synagogue a précédé l'église.
Les Juifs, les patriarches, les prophètes ont existé avant Christianisme.)

Charles Darwin's thoughts flashed across his mind so quickly that he could not form clear, distinctive letters. The speed of his mind was quicker than the speed of his pen.

100

Speed is, besides pressure, one of the most important features of personality characteristics found in handwriting. We might say that the higher the agitation level of a person, the faster and more expansive are the movements of the entire body. Thus, vivacious people not only walk fast, they dislike sitting down and gesticulate lavishly when they speak.

At the beginning of this century, the German psychiatrist Georg Meyer published in the *Wissenschaftlichen Grundlagen der Graphologie* (Scientific Basis of Graphology) studies of his patients. They suffered from a form of psychosis which was characterized by excited feeling, delusions of grandeur, elevation of mood, overproduction of ideas and psychomotor hyper-activity. In a happy, euphoric mood the patients would dance, sing, and clap their hands, day and night, accompanied by wild movements. Meyer studied the handwriting of these manic patients in the euphoric mood. The i-dots were transformed into commas and accents; initial and terminal strokes were drawn with a kind of hyperkinetic movement and widely extended. The to-the-right-movement was dominant.

Then Meyer compared these results with those of highly vivacious persons who also had hyperkinetic movements. Their handwriting was similar. It was characterized by large back-and-forth movements, originating in the elbow and the wrist. The pen was held by slightly stretched fingers.

This writer has the typical "pen-speed" described by Meyer and Pophal.
Before he begins to write with extraordinary speed,
he loosens his wrist by shaking his hand wildly in the air.

"A writer's speed is determined by his innate nervous organization. The rate of nerve conduction and the speed of associative progress as well as of motor responses, regardless of how they are influenced by endocrine, nutritional or other factors that determine the functional state of the nervous system, all contribute to the personal speed.

"A thorough examination of the stroke may reveal how quickly it was written. A straight line is not only the shortest distance between two points, but also the quickest traversed; and the line quality will indicate the speed and freedom with which it was produced." (Osborn)

"Thus a straight, smooth writing line reflects firm, quick movements; a limp, wavering

101

stroke, a slowly executed one. The shaping of an angular letter form needs an abrupt stop at each turning point. For this reason the curved, swinging stroke has been made the basis of most systems of *shorthand*, with angular symbols reduced to a minimum." (Saudek)

A spontaneous, speedy handwriting usually tilts toward the right; with haste or acceleration of pace, the slant grows more pronounced. Speed tends, furthermore, to reduce whatever left trend may be in a person's handwriting. It also distorts the i-dots, which may be stretched into streaks or commas pulled forward by the speedy movement. In a slow handwriting the i-dot is usually placed accurately above the letter *i* or lags behind it.

As Georg Meyer points out, the inner state of mind greatly affects the speed of writing. A happy mood releases and increases the flow of movement whereas an anxious mood, inner tension, or depression slows down the movement and restrains it.

Speed   Slowness

Relatively constant, regular speed characterizes the well-organized person whose thinking, acting and feeling are controlled. The writing speed becomes irregular when the movement is affected by emotional stress and when attempts to check such reactions are effective. Fluctuations in speed due to emotional influences can be detected by abrupt stops, headlong haste, occasional acceleration or slowing down.

Moreover, speed in writing, like speed in any other function, increases with practice. There is the natural development from the painstaking, slow, insecure tracing of a child to the automatized, sure fluency of the adult. Apart from certain fluctuations during puberty, writing speed changes little during the years. Usually at the age fourteen a child has reached his normal writing speed.

Some characteristics of speed writing

Increased right slant
Large difference between upper and lower lengths
The strokes appear slim, stretched, intense and gliding
The pressure is even
The connective form in the middle zone is mostly curved
The initial and terminal strokes are widely extended

102

Symbol of Speed
We distinguish between action speed and pen speed.
In this sample by Napoleon we see both.

Enormous speed, originating in dynamic back-and-forth-movement, is called *pen speed*. Short-cut, simplified, reduced letters with their tendency to threads and flying-ahead i-dots show *action speed*. The pen-speed writer and the action- speed writer have this in common: strong motivation.

The pen-speed-writer is vivacious, spontaneous, impulsive, lacks inhibition and is easily overwhelmed by emotions.

Pen-speed writer

The action-speed writer is dominated by the will to have success balanced by an economical overview. He thinks quickly, associates easily, knows what he wants, is ruled by his intellect and by reason.

103

[handwritten sample]

Action-speed writer Erich Fromm, psychologist and author

Another type of speed writer is the one who is compulsively *hasty*. Whereas the natural, spontaneous speed writer likes to move fast, enjoying his quick writing movements, the hasty person rushes along without being quick by nature. He tries to speed up his inherent tempo. The saying: "The more haste, the less speed," fits these writers.

[handwritten sample]

The hasty writer becomes nervous about catching trains or delivering reports on a deadline. He tries for top performance at top speed. The willpower required for these exaggerated efforts to hurry makes him tense, worried, and he may feel hunted.

The *natural-speedy writer* uses back-and-forth movements coming from the elbow and the wrist. The *hasty person* writes with a stiff wrist. To improve his speed, he increases the movement of his fingers. In the effort to increase speed, his right slanted letters fall flat on the base line, almost tilting over, as in the sample above. The size of his writing gets smaller, the difference in upper and lower lengths decreases and the i-dots fly wildly forward.

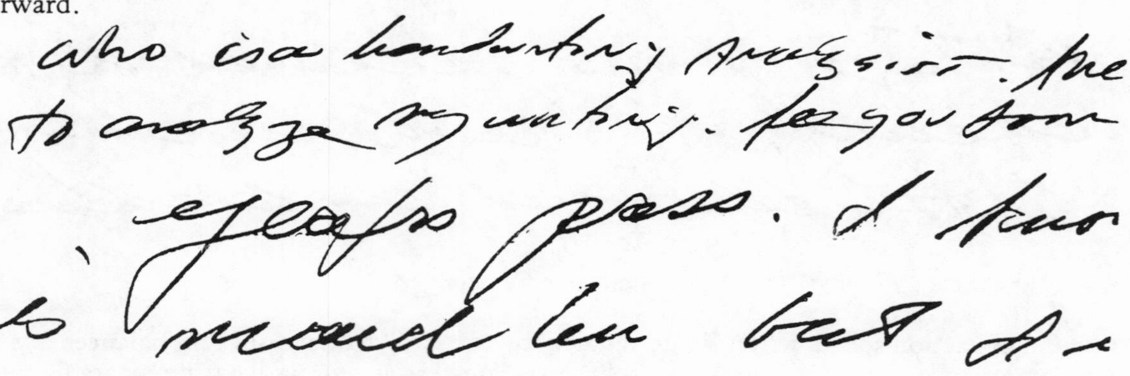

[handwritten sample]

If the speed is voluntarily exaggerated it becomes *haste;* despite natural spontaneity, we find restlessness, lack of inhibition. The hasty person is nervous, feels hunted and driven.

Sometimes we see in a hasty writing so-called *flamed strokes* with sudden pressure, indicating an explosion of temper due to uncontrolled passion. Psychologically we must therefore distinguish between the dynamic *action speed writer* (Napoleon) and the hasty writer who is driven by compulsive fear of failing.

Pen Speed

Graphic elements	Interpretation
Right Slant	Extraversion
Average size	Emotion
Richness of movement	Temperament, joy of living
Slim, even stroke	Elasticity, freshness
Curved connective form (garlands)	Easy reaction, receptivity
Connectedness	Continuous thinking ability
Fast hand and arm movements	Driving power, spontaneity

Action Speed

Graphic elements	Interpretation
Disregard for accuracy	Fast thinking of an independent person
Width	Expansion, easy comprehension
Simplified forms	Intelligent, goal oriented
Elastic finger and hand movements	Economical efficiency
Small size of writing	Abstract thinking ability
i-dots flying forward	Fast thinking ability
Diacritical signs connected to the following letters	Ability to combine thought processes; intellectual
Terminal thread	Speedy thinking ability

Haste

Graphic elements	Interpretation
Often dynamic impression of writing	Stubbornness, energy in action
Width	Eagerness to reach goals
Curved connected form	Less resistance to speed
Flaming, irregular pressure	Outbreaks of temper
Comma-like, flying-ahead i-dots	Impatience
Speed thread	Restlessness
Often rigidity in the writing	Stiffness of overworked wrist from tenseness
Dissolved writing forms	Rushing
Often rhythmical disturbances	Due to rigidity and stiffness

105

Speed

Summary

The natural speed writer is generally secure, impulsive, spontaneous. He is expansive, likes to explore. He enjoys his fast thinking mind, complementary movements. Speed is a movement which can be regarded as an expression of motivation and reaction. It is a method of arriving quickly at a goal. Continuous concentration on the goal can be so strong that even the formation of the letters in the script can be regarded as an obstacle to getting there. Remember the writings of Pascal, Darwin and Napoleon.

The most significant symptoms	*Character traits*
Inexactly-dotted i's	Spontaneous activity
Thread-like endings	Impulsiveness
Increasing width	Vivacity
Connectedness	Industriousness
Enlarged endings	Excitement
Increased curves	Restlessness
Right trend traits	Haste
Increased final letters	Carelessness
Enlarged left margin	Eager to finish everything

Special cases

If the speed is restrained by pressure it shows energetic initiative.
Speed and rigidity show violence, irritation and explosion.
With enormous speed we see hunted, worried persons with psychic disturbances.

The speedy writing of G. Gordon Liddy

Gordon Liddy radiates a dynamic personality and leadership. He is changeable, needs constant stimulation, has blind devotion. He is always ready to go, continuously forward striving. There is never enough time. He never sits still. There is danger of superficiality. He is used to immediate reactions, is quick with judgment and his impulsive actions can become dangerous, ruthless, almost fanatical.

106

If the handwriting is *speedy* but imprecise, without restraint, we see

Spontaneity
Impulsiveness
Hyperactivity
Need for new projects
Irritability
Adventurousness
Talkativeness

If the handwriting is *hasty,* neglected, has irritated word-impulses and hasty strokes, we see

Mobility
Taste
Anxiety
Restlessness
Carelessness
Inconstancy
Need for change
Frivolity
Fickleness

If the handwriting is *balanced* and has *vital connectedness*, we see

Connectedness
Naturalness
Activity
An impelling, driving inner force

Edouard Manet, painter

In a high degree of speed with elegant combinations and short-cuts and simplifications we see

Fast comprehension
Broad, intellectual horizon
Capacity for abstract thinking
Ambition

Nikola Tesla, inventor

SLOWNESS

The person who writes slowly also works slowly toward goals. He needs time and takes steps carefully. The graphic indications of slowness are:

Exact i-dots
Exact connections
Mostly vertical slant
Disconnectedness (juxtaposed)
Small differences between upper and lower lengths
Tendency toward conventional writing
Increased upstrokes
Increased left trend movements
Increasing narrowness

[handwritten sample]

The slow writer radiates an impression of quietude, contemplation and self-control.

If we have a writing with lower form niveau we can assume that the writer is phlegmatic, passive, clumsy, heavy, dull; if slowness is paired with pressure we see a quiet, solid and careful person. If slowness is paired with rigidity or stiffness, the writer is full of inhibition, anxiety, hesitation and is unable to take chances.

How do we recognize slow writing?

A sure sign of slow handwriting is the stability of the writing slant, especially when the vertical or left slant dominates. In a slow writing we have more disconnected letters and less reduced "short-cut" letter formations.

[handwritten sample]

One takes time to produce angular formations and sharp rectangular strokes, as in this sample above.

I hope you are having a very good time while

An initial exaggerated ornamental letter capital is primarily a sign of elaboration in a leisurely written note. (All to-the-left-swinging upper and lower loops are a sign of left trend which hinders the forward movement and produces slow writing.) The slow writer appears self-controlled. He is cautious; he thinks before he acts; he is mostly reserved; he is conscious of his responsibilities. When he writes to authorities he prefers the vertical slant.

fact, waiting to hear you I am, in tell me about me.

The exact dotting of the *i* is easily managed because of the slow tempo.

Frieden gefunden hat, kann er daran gehen, ihn in der ganzen Welt zu suchen

Martin Buber

Martin Buber (1878-1965),
theologian and philosopher.

Contemplation, harmony of inner thoughts, is reflected in a slow, quiet, philosophical writing.

Apologies for lateness.
I am on a plane to
Madison for a few days,

An easygoing, uninteresting writing, too lazy to dot the *i*'s

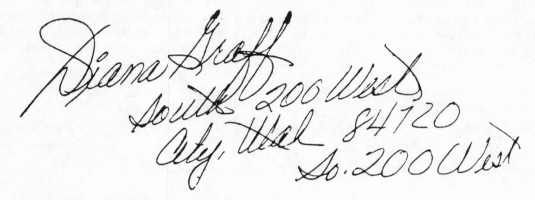

Space-demanding, slow-moving writing shows a person who is abundantly self-involved; circles for i-dots, angry downstrokes on t-crossings and overlarge numerals take time to write.

I am the greatest Banquet
Manager in the world. I enjoy
my work and do the best
possible for everyone.

When a slow handwriting has ugly letter forms, as well as misspellings and partly blotted and corrected letters, one sees the low form niveau of an uneducated mind without self-confidence or guilt-feelings.

My name is Shelley Annette

I recently moved and

my new address is   Stree

my birthday is November 9, 1

kes me a ~~Scorpio~~ Scorpio.

Slow writing comprises as well the handwritings of persons with cerebral or spinal disturbances, alcoholics and drug addicts. One calls this kind of writing *ataxia* (Greek: ataktos = disorderly).   It means   the total or partial inability to coordinate voluntary body-movements, as in controlling wrist and finger movements.

it sending as I've been looking for an.

for a couple of weeks since I've heard what

For contrast, look at this simplified, slow, healthy handwriting of a mechanic who repairs with great accuracy. Striving ambition is seen in the high upper loops and exactly dotted i's. The initial fanciful garlandic curve of the capitals shows love of ornamentation and detail work.

NEED CLEANER Lamp.   *Marie Bernard*
Cleaned Developer Bearings   *340 E 55 St*
Cleaned Cleaner Lamp + Filter   *NY   NY*

PARTS BILLED SEPARATELY ON
INVOICE/# _____
Samuel L Mayl

Here is another ataxic, uncontrollable handwriting, due to physical impairment: the muscles no longer obey the brain. The letter formations are involuntarily misshaped and deteriorated. Coordination is lost.

> I am a bank president
> married with two small
> children. I have two teenage
> from an earlier marriage
> I enjoy reading and sports
> and am a fairly
> self conscious person
>
> 10/22/78

The handwriting below could also be a result of a kind of Parkinson's disease, characterized by a rhythmic tremor and muscular rigidity caused by degeneration in the basal ganglia of the brain.

> between state therefore
> the state had the right
> to declare null and void
> certain Fed. laws.
> § 225 My condemnation of
> violence was in it

112

Summary

The graphic elements of slowness

Emotionally-dominated slowness

Concentration
Quietness
Indolence
Indecision
Passivity
Even-tempered
Aesthetical

Reason-dominated slowness

Slow thinking ability
Slow comprehension
Slow in combining thoughts
Lack of associative ability
Love of detail

Compulsive slowness

No drive
No motivation
No ambition
Lack of striving
Fatigue

Sample for all three kinds of slowness

In a slow, elaborated handwriting we often see insecurity and hesitating, welded strokes or heavy, regulated strokes.
The slow-moving writer prefers:
    Angles, supported forms
    Concealed or double curves
    Precisely dotted i-dots or circles
    Tendency to vertical and left slant to-the-left-bent terminal endings
    Falling lines
    Correct left margin

113

Sample for all three kinds of slowness (continued)

Narrowing of the script
Heavy stroke-disturbances (tremor or ataxia due to inner disturbances)
Hardly any difference in strength of upstrokes and downstrokes
Disconnectedness
Ornamental, exaggerated initials

POPHAL'S BIOTYPES

Pophal related a person's handwriting to the predominant motor centers of the brain. We know that most left-handers have the writing center in the right hemisphere of the brain, whereas the right-hander's writing center is in the left hemisphere of the brain. Pophal speaks about the oldest and most primitive movement—the *back-and-forth movement* (climbing, running, swimming, scratching, flying). These movements consist of tension and relaxation, a rhythmical exchange of the agonist and the antagonist muscles. The *agonist* muscle is directly engaged in contraction, as distinguished from muscles which have to relax at the same time. Thus, in bending the elbow the biceps brachii is the *agonist* and the triceps the *antagonist*. In our body there is always a tension and a relaxation of the agonist and the antagonist muscles, a so-called *reciprocal innervation*.

There are also the *elasticity vibrations*. These are passive powers which form an interval between back-and-forth movement, creating rhythm. These elasticity vibrations occur in breathing, swimming (the glide between strokes).

Pophal reminds us that 2000 years ago the Romans enjoyed a game which demonstrates elasticity vibrations. They forced ostriches to run through the arena, then shot arrows through their heads. The tormented creatures kept running, the arrows in their heads, until these elasticity vibrations died out. The rhythmical reflexes of the old brain persisted after death.

All back-and-forth movement belongs to the oldest phylogenetic development. The phylogenetic law says that the human individual goes through a recapitulation from the egg-cell to the last stage of human development.

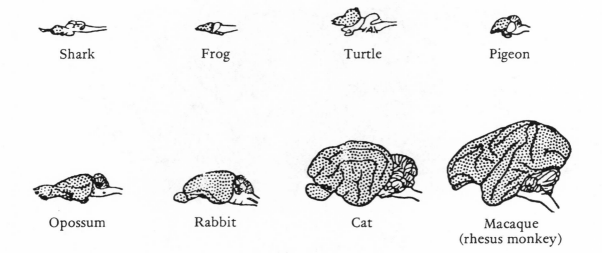

| Shark | Frog | Turtle | Pigeon |

| Opossum | Rabbit | Cat | Macaque (rhesus monkey) |

115

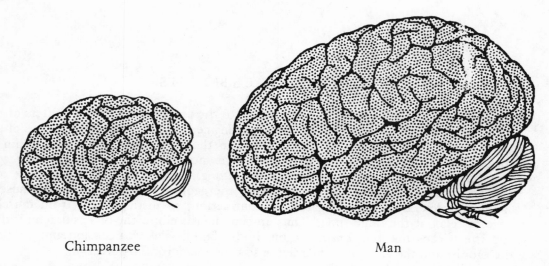

Chimpanzee   Man

The palae-encephalon, the oldest primitive brain, is found in all vertebrates from fishes, amphibians, reptiles and birds to mammals. The new brain (cortex) developed in small degree in the three hundred million year-old shark. The lizard has a larger brain, the rabbit even larger, and the human has the largest new brain.

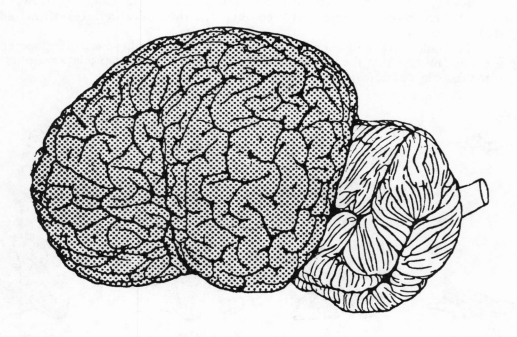

Minke whale

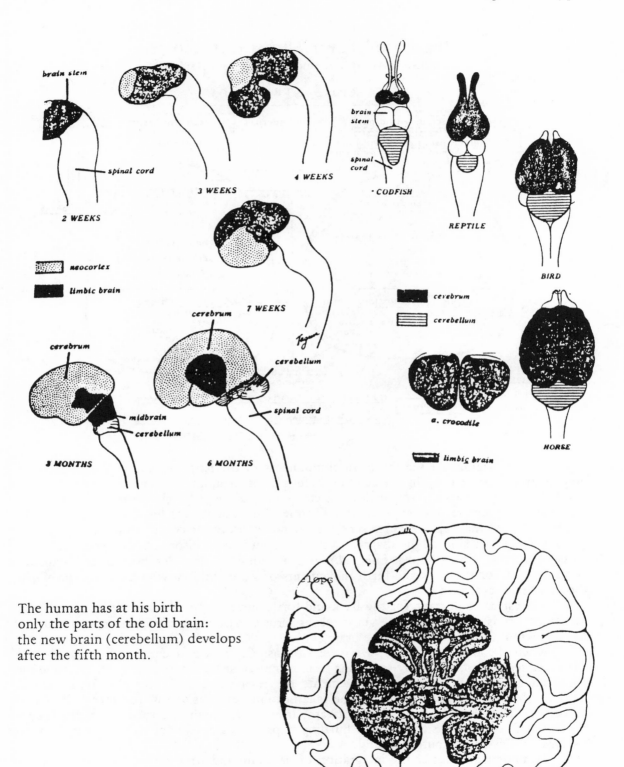

The human has at his birth
only the parts of the old brain:
the new brain (cerebellum) develops
after the fifth month.

Completed Human Brain

117

Die motorischen Hirnstammzentren — Basalganglien und Anhangsgebilde

In this diagram we see the main components of the *basal ganglia,* the four masses of gray matter located deep in the cerebral hemispheres - caudate nucleus (possessing a tail), lentiform (lentil shaped), amygdaloid nuclei (almond shaped), claustrum (thin layer of gray matter) which separates the internal capsule. The caudate and lentiform nuclei and the fibers of the internal capsule which separate them constitute the *corpus striatum.*

On the left side of the diagram we see the nucleus lentiform, which consists of the *globus pallidum,* which Pophal calls *pallidum.* Pallidum is the oldest part of the brain and is responsible for the back-and-forth movements of little children who have not developed the new brain, the cortex.

Almost as important for the back-and-forth movement is the *nucleus ruber.* If this motor center is out of order we get cerebrosclerosis (hardening of the brain, especially of the cerebrum, the largest part of the brain).

When the pallidum is hurt we have Parkinson's disease, a chronic, nervous disease characterized by a fine, slowly-spreading tremor, muscular weakness and rigidity; we see the "pill-rolling" tremor, alternating movements of flexing and extending the fingers which produce this characteristic tremor. The face becomes expressionless, the speech slow and measured. The head is bowed, bent forward, arms flexed, thumbs turned into palms, knees slightly bent. One walks with short, shuffling steps. The arms do not swing in rhythm with the legs, as they should automatically.

To understand better the integration of pallidum and striatum we have to study the wild, tempestuous writing movements we see so often in scripts without the steering influence of the striatum.

118

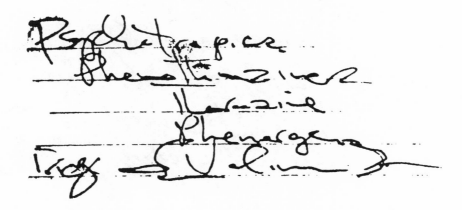

In this handwriting with low form niveau we see the uncontrolled back-and-forth movement of a primitive pallidum influence:

Interruption of strokes	= Irritability, restlessness
Thread-like connective form	= Instability
Great differences in lengths	= Desire to expand horizons
Ligatures	= Association of ideas
Illegibility	= Unconventional

The signature of Anton Walbrook (1900-1968)
who fled from Nazi Germany and started anew in England.

In the wide, expanding, aimlessly dancing movements we see the influence of pallidum without the steering influence of striatum.

119

[handwriting sample — Horace Greeley]

The wild pallidum writing of Horace Greeley (1811-1872), founder of the *New York Tribune*, a political journalist with great influence during the Civil War; he died insane.

[handwriting sample — Adolf von Menzel]

The pallidum writing of painter
Adolf von Menzel (1815-1905), Berlin

Adolf von Menzel's pallidum writing:

Hyperkinesis
Increased movement
Centrifugality
Large differences in lengths
Extensions of beginning and endstrokes
Fullness = fantasy, originality
Pressure = vitality, activity, tension
Fluctuations of slant = restlessness, emotional disturbances
Dissolving of connective form = creativity, many-faceted talent

In the rhythmical curves of a
genius like Beethoven one
sees the predominance of a
valuable pallidum,
the mystical elements which
form the creative power
of a human being. From the up-
and-down of these swinging.
curves one can imagine the heavenly
sound waves flowing through
mind and body.

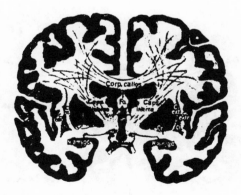

The two hemispheres with the corpus callosum separating them;
below, capsula interna, separating nucleus lentiform and
nucleus caudate (see diagram on page 122).

121

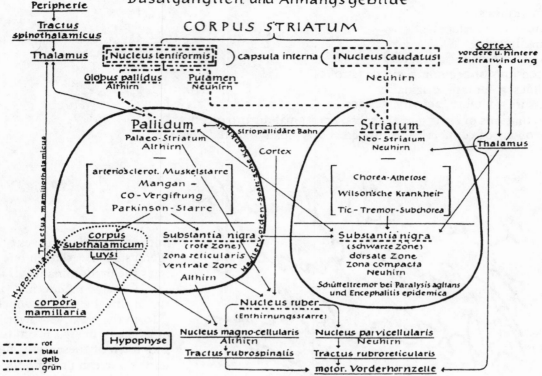

Die motorischen Hirnstammzentren
Basalganglien und Anhangsgebilde

Peripherie

Tractus spinothalamicus

Thalamus

CORPUS STRIATUM

Nucleus lentiformis) capsula interna (Nucleus caudatus

Cortex vordere u. hintere Zentralwindung

Globus pallidus Althirn

Putamen Neuhirn

Neuhirn

Pallidum
Palaeo-Striatum Althirn

striopallidäre Bahn

Striatum
Neo-Striatum Neuhirn

Thalamus

[arteriosclerot. Muskelstarre
Mangan –
CO-Vergiftung
Parkinson-Starre]

Cortex

[Chorea-Athetose
Wilson'sche Krankheit
Tic-Tremor-Subchorea]

corpus subthalamicum Luysi

Substantia nigra (rote Zone)
Zona reticularis
Ventrale Zone
Althirn

Substantia nigra (schwarze Zone)
dorsale Zone
Zona compacta
Neuhirn

Schütteltremor bei Paralysis agitans und Encephalitis epidemica

corpora mamillaria

Nucleus ruber (Enthirnungsstarre)

Hypophyse

Nucleus magno-cellularis Althirn

Tractus rubrospinalis

Nucleus parvicellularis Neuhirn

Tractus rubroreticularis

motor. Vorderhornzelle

–·–·– rot
– – – blau
·········· gelb
–··–··– grün

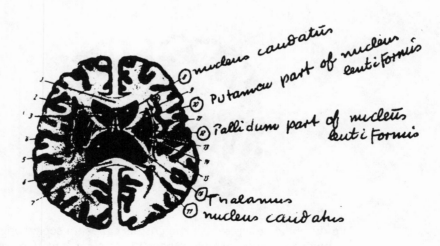

nucleus caudatus

Putamen part of nucleus lentiformis

Pallidum part of nucleus lentiformis

Thalamus

nucleus caudatus

Abb. 5

Corpus striatum und Thalamus.

Horizontalschnitt. (8 und 17 Schweifkern, 10 Putamen, 12 Pallidum, 16 Thalamus.)

122

The *striatum* consists of the nucleus caudate (tailshaped kernel) and the *putamen,* a part of the nucleus lentiform (lentil shaped). Both are separated by the *capsula interna,* which has a striped tissue, therefore the name *striatum.* The striatum is the controlling element, like the brake in a car. If the striatum is hurt, the pallidum takes over and sudden, involuntary movements occur: facial grimaces, quick, jerky and purposeless (St. Vitus' Dance), *chorea,* (Greek = dance) a nervous affliction marked by muscular twitching of limbs or facial muscles. St. Vitus' Dance is also a functional nervous disorder, causing muscular spasms.

When the striatum is hurt, slow, irregular, twisting, snakelike muscular movements are seen mostly in the upper extremities, especially in hands and fingers. It is easy to imagine how the handwriting is affected. This disease is called athetosis (Greek: not a fixed condition).

Another disease caused by the malfunction of striatum is *hemichorea* or *hemiballism,* (Greek: half jumping); jerking and twitching movements appear on one side of the body. If the striatum acted alone and ceased to function, it would stop movement (*akinesia:* Greek: no movement). We observe this in beetle bugs, which lie motionless in times of danger.

Striatum handwriting

In contrast to pallidum writing, striatum writing is dry, boring, without youthful élan and mostly without intellect. The striatum writer misses the freshness, the naiveté, the instinctive powers of the pallidum writer. He has no depth, no unconscious sources. He is only the brake in the car. The whole script looks monotonous, stiff, rigid, without rhythmical or flowing movements. There is no spontaneity, no initial activity, no elasticity; there is only psychic slowness and fatigue.

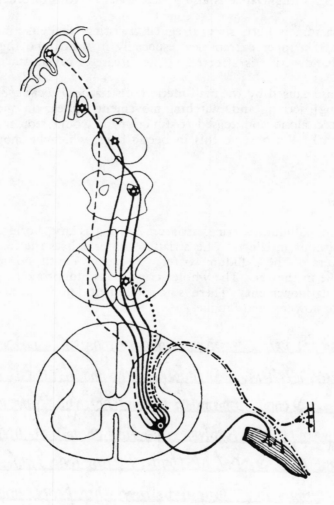

The extra-pyramidal tract system carries the impulses of the back-and-forth movements, the *involuntary movement of the old brain (brainstem, substantia nigra, nucleus ruber, pallidum, striatum)*. If the pallidum is hurt (the oldest part of the brain), we have Parkinson's disease, a tremor which is most likely worse in a position of relaxation than when a voluntary movement is carried out. Alternating movements of flexing and extending the fingers produce a characteristic pill-rolling tremor.

The pyramidal tract and the extra-pyramidal tract, carrying the voluntary and the involuntary movement impulses, are united at the end in the cells of the ventral horn, like two rivers, and flow together from the muscles into the spine. This system was named the pyramidal tract because of its passage through the medulla pyramid, a compact bundle of nerves shaped like a pyramid in the medulla oblongata, part of the end brain.

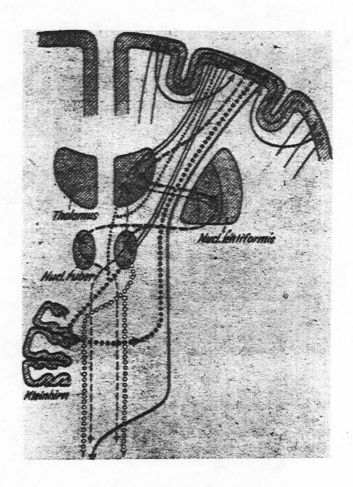

The voluntary and involuntary movements of the pyramidal tract system

Cortico-spinal tract or pyramidal tract, one of three descending tracts of the spinal cord, leads the impulses from the cerebral cortex, the thin five layers consisting of cell bodies of neurons in the cerebral hemispheres, into the spine, into the gray matter of the spinal cord. These giant pyramidal cells were named by Russian anatomist Betz (1834-1894). They are present in the motor area of the cerebral cortex. They carry the individual movement impulses for the *voluntary* movements of hand and fingers.

If the flow here is suddenly interrupted, we have the paralytical stroke. After a stroke, fine voluntary movements such as writing and piano playing are no longer possible. Sudden death can occur when a cerebral hemorrhage happens as a result of a rupture of a sclerosed or diseased blood vessel in the brain—often associated with high blood pressure.

125

Courtesy of The Louvre, Paris

Pophal's *cortical handwriting* is best mirrored in the sharp, simplified, meager writing of the great "Schoolmaster of Europe," Erasmus of Rotterdam (1466-1536). The clear structure of his script shows typographic forms, *connected* and *disconnected writing*. It shows a flexibility of mind and short, singular, aimed movements, not out-swinging terminals as we have with pallidum writings.

126

The brainstem is the oldest part of the brain. With evolutionary changes over millions of years, additional layers of gray and white matter have been added. Here we observe the growth of the cerebrum, the seat of all sensory impulses, all voluntary muscular activities. Our cerebrum is the seat of the conscious and the center of the higher mental faculties of memory, learning, reasoning, judgment, intelligence and emotions. If the cerebrum or cortex, as we call both the outer layer plus the cerebrum, is hurt, there is no possibility of bringing kinetic impulses to the brainstem. All the conceptions in the pre-programmed single movements are destroyed. A human being without cortex cannot exist. Sometimes there are only parts which do not function, as expressed in *agraphia* (a = not, graphein = write), a loss of ability to express oneself in writing due to a central lesion (wound) or to muscular incoordination. Copying or writing from dictation may still be possible. Partial injury of the cortex leads to so-called *alexia,* the inability to read, due to central lesion, also called word-blindness.

Brainstem handwriting

Brainstem handwriting is the most natural and most harmonious of all brain-influenced handwritings. Here is the natural rhythm, the pulsating swinging, flowing, the elastic, speedy movement. We have soft, round curves, rhythmical flowing back-and-forth movements, vital connectedness, garlands, genuine natural pressure, diminished differences in lengths.

Je marche sur ton âme
Sur ton ventre
Je bois le restant de tes années
J'ai avalé ta lune
le rêve de ton innocence
Pour devenir ton ange
Et te protéger à nouveau

Marc Chagall

127

Rhythmical flowing movement	= Vital security, easy adaptability, psychic elasticity, naturalness
True, genuine pressure	= Joy of living, looking for contact, warmheartedness
Diminished differences of lengths	= Maturity, contentment
Legible garlands, open and pure	= Altruistic, warm feelings

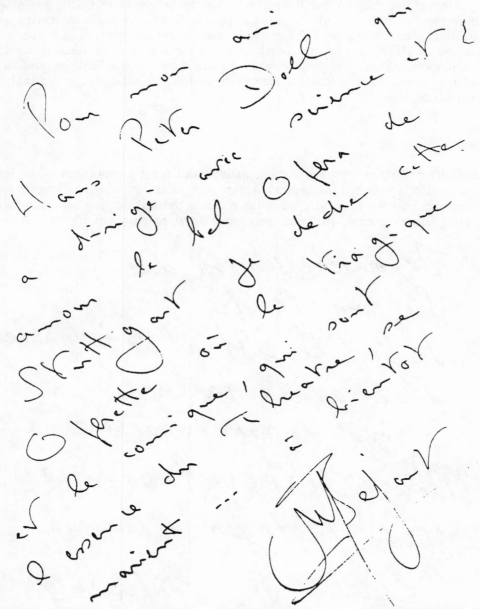

A most beautiful sample of the rhythmical flowing of Pophal's brainstem writing is the script of Belgian choreographer Maurice Béjart with the main qualities of the brainstem writing: natural rhythmical pressure, vital security, feeling of power, joie de vivre, warmheartedness and harmony. The emphasis on the lower loops shows Béjart's anchoring in the depth of unconsciousness, his security of instincts and originality.

The spinal cord is the center of reflex action containing the conducting paths to and from the brain, so that all are integrated. Yet, there is still a hierarchy, as in Egypt's ancient history. The highest class, the priests, rule the king; the king rules the landowners; the scribe works for the landowners; and at the bottom are the ordinary people. The priest is the *cortex* which controls the cerebrum (the king). The *cerebrum* controls the *brainstem* (the landowner). The *brainstem* controls the *striatum* (the scribe). And the scribe stands above the ordinary people — the *pallidum* with their mobility, their emotions and vitality.

Pophal says that all psychic and emotional development depends on the structure of the brain. The awareness of pain originates there. Plato regarded the brain as the divine and dominating power of the body. Therefore the gods put the brain into the globe-like form of the skull. In the brain lies embodied the soul with its finest and most differentiated traits. It carries the secrets of the human personality.

Pophal's merit was to talk about the predominance of four different brain centers and their influence on handwriting: *pallidum, striatum, brainstem* and *cortex*.

The purest type of cortical writer is the *theoretical-scientific* person. Striving for discovery, for knowledge, is his main aim. His joy of learning is playful curiosity, a play with principles, reason, logic, and dialectic. Socrates said: "The true philosopher does not know the way to the market nor the offices of the city. If he cares for money and goods it is only because he is afraid of the future, where illness and poverty may prevent him from enjoying the fruits of his spirit. His weapons are polemic, criticism. The theoretical person is a radical thinker."

Max Planck, physicist (1858-1947), Nobel prize, 1918

Pophal's Biotypes

Graphic ingredients

Controlled arrangement
Natural rhythmical balance
Polymorphic letter forms
Highly diversified singular movements
Cortical coordination
Reduced forms
Clarity of script
Small lower loops
Vertical slant

Interpretation:

Objectivity
Spiritual laws
Logic
Playful curiosity
Dialectic
Scepticism
Radical thinker
No materialistic interests
Reason-dominated

The Scientific-Theoretical Type

Erasmus of Rotterdam (1497-1543)

Dr. Alfred Adler (1870-1937)

Dr. Jonas Salk (1914-)

Ingredients of the Scientific-Theoretical Type.
All cortex writings through the centuries have the same ingredients:
regularity of movement, form and organization (moral, ethical values).
Singular movements preferring:
angles, arcades, garlands, double curves, small, slow, coordination, simplification
shortening of ways, connectedness and disconnectedness, printed forms,
vertical and left slant, regularity, stiff, mechanical rhythm
Signification of the single movement:
independence, freedom, individuality, analytical, abstract thinking,
observation, consciousness, realism
Regularity and stiffness of movement:
self-control, concentration, attention, love for organization, obedient to the law,
ethical, modest, moral, self-discipline

The Ethical Type
Graphic Ingredients

Moderate tension
Creativity (original forms)
Aesthetic regularity
Tasteful arrangement, humility
Longing for knowledge and truth
(seen in the extended, high t-crossings)

Albert Schweitzer (1875-1965)

The Religious Type

Graphic Ingredients	*Interpretation*
Smallness	Humility
Leftward bendings	Contemplation
Angles, garlands	Warmth and strength
Harmony of arrangement	Striving for perfection
Regularity	Asceticism

Joannes Paulus, pp II

The Pope's handwriting shows spiritual love, asceticism, simplicity, humility, idealism, striving for self-perfection, purity as seen in the clarity of his harmonious writing.

The Aesthetic Type

Graphic Ingredients	*Interpretation*
Differentiated singular movements	Cultural sensitivity
Moderate Tension	Simplification
Cortical Coordination	Independence
Creativity in Forms	Longing for style and beauty
Tasteful Arrangements	Striving for harmony
Aesthetical Regularity	Cortically controlled form

Henri Matisse (1869-1954), French painter
131

Pophal's Biotypes

The Aesthetic Type is an advancing, searching human being. The writing is creative, tastefully arranged, aesthetically regulated with differentiated singular movements. Matisse's graphic ingredients are typical for the Aesthetic Type.

The Self-Representative Type

The vivacious handwriting of *Sir Laurence Olivier* mirrors the self-representative type of the Pophal-Spranger types. This type is full of self-admiration, pride, originality, arrogance, distinguished taste and culture and is creative, as seen in the extended t-strokes and imaginative signature.

The Economical Type

Friedrich Engels (1820-1895), socialist writer, banker, propagandist for Karl Marx.

Graphic ingredients	Interpretation
Speed, right slant	Speedy intellect
Connectedness	Logical thinking
Initial and terminal strokes	Practical organization
Spiral number symbols (zero, six)	Financial interests dominate
Smaller endings	Diplomatic

132

The Political Type

Franklin Roosevelt (1882-1945)

ю 50-тн летнего юбилея со дня

Joseph Stalin (1879-1953)

Graphic ingredients	*Interpretation*
Rigidity	Intolerance
Vital strokes	Power hungry
High pressure	Strong will
Angles, arcades, threads	Many faces
Club-like terminals	Determination
Powerful crossing strokes	Sometimes cruelty
Large size	High self-demonstration
Initial accentuation	High self-esteem

POPHAL'S TENSION DEGREES

Pophal's introduction of the tension degrees is a necessary result of the relationship of the brain centers to the kind of tension or looseness we use in our handwriting. We know that *pallidum* gives a kind of uncontrolled, large, expansive movement to the writing. Pophal called the influence of pallidum tension degree number 1.

Low form niveau with a biologically low-quality pallidum

High form niveau with a biologically high-quality pallidum

In both samples we find illegibility, back-and forth movement, hyperkinetically increased long strokes, thread-like connective forms, irregularity of the connective form, fluctuation of the slant and restlessness, lack of resistance. In the first sample we have a better form niveau, therefore we find creative letter forms and a harmoniously swinging rhythm, whereas the second sample shows a person without order, discipline, planning, a victim of his own contradictory moods. The first sample looks like an untamed animal, moving in many directions, defending itself, fighting: an unharmonious creature.

Tension degree number 1 (illegible, weak, without structure)

In Darwin's elastically swinging handwriting we see the mixture of pallidum and cortex in rhythmical harmony. Not too loose and not too restrained, just the right mixture to create out of the abundance of pallidum the source of natural fullness, health and vitality.

There is back-and-forth movement, light pressure, graceful, vibrant letter formations, together with elegant, combinatory thought processes. Number II of Pophal's tension degrees seems to be the nearest to perfection.

The same can be said about Jean Houston's handwriting (page 136). It swings rhythmically, with large upper and lower loops, expressing reaches to the heights and the depths, graphologically seen as centrifugality. There is no stylization; every letter swings gracefully, light and harmonious.

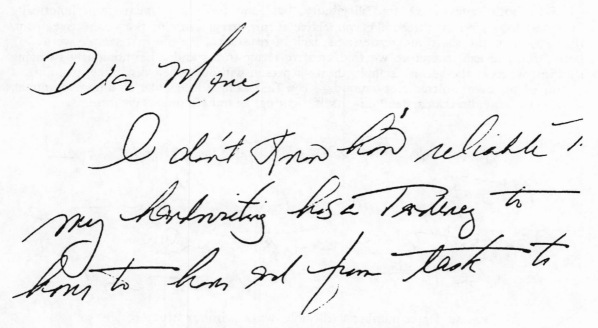

Jean Houston, Tension degree number II

Tension number III is a controlled brainstem-writing with a little more striatum (brake) than number II. It has useful inhibition (posture), tension with strength.
The graphic ingredients

Firm, determined stroke, elasticity, dynamic pressure (but not overpowering), almost even, moderate width, garlands, angles, security in movement, rhythm is a little too regular, moderate speed.
Character

Concentration, initiative, self-esteem, good coordination, economical, law abiding.

The active, emotional, secure handwriting of Jack London (1876-1916),
U.S. novelist and short-story writer

Tension degree number III
The firm, realistic but warmhearted, vital, rhythmical handwriting
of the French painter Paul Signac (1863-1935),
shows the concentration and depth of the true brainstem writer.

Tension degree number IV shows us *striatum writing: tense, rigid, monotonous, stiff, insecure, inhibited.*
The graphic ingredients

Inelastic strokes, rigidity, brittle angles, arcades, narrowness, meagerness, sharpness, slowness; cortical coordination is arhythmical. At work: dutiful, without vitality or enthusiasm, pedantic, subaltern, insecure, defensive, obstinate, stubborn.

(looking at and sometimes buying gives me much pleasure) and only opera unless it's by Mozart or a Handel Oratorio.

it would lead to mistakes by the compositor. at that time, hearing of my plight someone showed me a page from a graphology expert analyzing the many ways of dotting i's and interpreting them in terms of character There I saw all the i's I'd ever seen in my life – and more. one could, if one were a poet, make a poem about it. If one were a painter, one could paint a picture about i-dotting. A choreographer could do a ballet on it. Alas, I am only an editor who must write legibly for the compositor

I am completing a career of college teaching & look forward to doing more of things which I do now I do actively: — opera, concerts, global political movements, special friends, nature some travel (to mediterranean countries). So what are we waiting for: give me an affirmative signal & let us meet over supper & talk & get to know one another soon.

Tension degree number IV

The striatum influence is even higher in this *tension degree IVa* writing.

138

IVa

This unnaturally stiff writing is brittle, lame, cramped, monotonous, mechanical, completely comprised of angular arcades. It is a mask-writing, disclosing dishonesty, pedantry and compulsiveness.

The same rigidity appears in this striatum writing with a higher cortical influence, visible in the simplified, abstract, proud letter formations, full of security and sharp cruelty. The harshness of the character is only covered up by excellent manners and upbringing, education and critical intellect; the writer is easily irritated, as the sharp to-the-left-kicking of the small s-letters show. Arrogance and aristocratic pride cannot replace the lack of warmth in this demonstration of class-consciousness.

139

[handwritten samples]

The two samples belong to youngsters. The tension in their writing
is overstrong. The chaos in the handwriting mirrors failed hopes.

Tension degree number V is the over-cramped stiffness of adolescent writing. Out of weakness, stubbornness, revolt the inner insecurity comes a rhythmical fluctuation of all writing elements: the stroke is trembling or broken, has tremor or ataxia, is pointed or angular.

Other graphic ingredients

Illegibility
Unformed letters
Thread-like, weak connective forms
No coordination
Back-and-forth movements are wild and irregular
Changing width
Irregularity of lines
Fluctuating slant

At *work* such writers are negligent, easily tired, unstable, have choleric temper, cannot concentrate, and are unreliable, imprecise.

LOOSENESS

Having studied Pophal's tension degrees, let us summarize the graphological and psychological character of looseness in handwriting. Looseness stands at the lower point of the tension scale, between stiff and dangerously loose, which we find in the writing of some drug addicts. Such writers have no backbone and are without moral force and resolution, and this is reflected in the script.

The loose script is marked by softness of movement, especially in the middle zone.

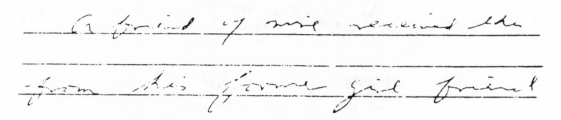

This sample of a loose writing looks coordinated and rhythmical. We are able to see immediately the easiness of the movement. In a positive form niveau it generally reveals a relaxed person with a flexible and conciliating attitude. In this special sample above, the writer has chosen lined paper to give his script some backbone, some frame for the smoothly flowing letters, without giving the impression of being too weightless.

Oskar Kokoschka (1885-)

In the handwriting of an artist like Kokoschka,
looseness shows an impressive, easily inspired psyche.

RIGIDITY

To find pure forms of rigidity we need only look at the handwritings of the Third Reich. Here we see excessive harshness and cruelty, a maximum of self-control and self-denial, pedantic obedience to the forced 'ethics' of the Third Reich, where such mediocre natures as Heydrich and Himmler could climb the ladder to the top of the National Movement.

The capitals, shaped like scourging whips, show the brutal force with which the writers drive themselves. Dangerous willpower is seen in the dagger-like strokes with which they cut the paper (and others) to pieces. The narrowness of the middle zone with its supported, retraced *m*'s, *n*'s, and *c*'s, show how ruthlessly the writers worked to suppress their feelings, until nothing was left but the mechanics of both robot-like script and character.

The angular, narrow handwriting of the minister of propaganda, Dr. Joseph Goebbels, includes fence-like strokes, letter chains of rigid, linear, vertical up-and-down strokes. The illegibility mirrors Goebbels' secretiveness and forced willpower, perseverance, and his fanatic faith in his "Führer." The covering strokes belie honesty. He also tries to hide his birth defect, a clubfoot, which made him in the eyes of the German people "the Devil's Advocate." His signature is subconsciously written *"Fuss,"* which means foot.

When a disciplined, sharply-chiseled, rigid writing is softened by pastóse strokes, we discover a balance between harshness and warmheartedness and a sense of pleasure.

142

cordial Thanks

Again, in this writing rigid traits are softened by a vital and healthy pastosity and the abrupt, angular, sharp writing becomes more human. We see conscious creativity, intellectual independence, and in the slight interruptions intuitive ideas splitting the logical, continuous flow of thoughts, like lightning. The writer is not easily influenced and cultivates strong resistance.

Irma Wright

When the form niveau sinks to primitivity, we see a cruel, brutal individual in the rigid, inflexible letter forms. One cannot disrupt the inner resistance or expect tolerance. This writing shows fanaticism of the most extreme kind. There is no intellect weighing decisions.

As we recall, the low form niveau of Pophal's tension degree number V samples showed the same vital disturbances: excessive inner anarchy and absence of control, with an equally rigid, stiff stroke picture.

RHYTHM OF MOVEMENT

There is a relationship between the inner rhythm of movement and the various degrees of tension in a handwriting, because the rhythm of movement can be weak, disturbed or perfect, according to the inherent degrees of tension. It is almost as if we might try to measure the movement of incoming ocean waves. They all differ depending on weather conditions. In Hawaii I saw 35 foot waves in stormy weather, calm on sunny days, and changed seas when a hurricane was brewing.

In handwriting we have unconscious movements which shed light on the writer's personality. Between explosive, wild movements we have harmonious or cramped, inelastic movements, which we must recognize when we look at a writing. Evenness and unevenness are the key factors. Interpretations range from vital harmony to controlled, strong will-power, to inner restlessness, to disturbance, to cheap affectedness, and finally to inner chaos.

The writing of Henri de Toulouse-Lautrec (1864-1901)
shows wild, revolutionary rhythm. Look at the impatient capital *B*
with its double, added wider upper loop. His eye, accustomed to
voluptuous forms, could not allow a shorter version of a capital *B*.
Look at the original way he combines HTL (initials) into one letter

144

The dancer Cha-U-Kao
of Moulin Rouge

Everyone remembers Marilyn Monroe's undulating hips.
In her writing-movement we see the same rhythmical swinging.

145

[handwritten signature]

This flexible, rhythmical writing radiates wise tolerance,
refined humor, and charm.

Perfect balance in movement

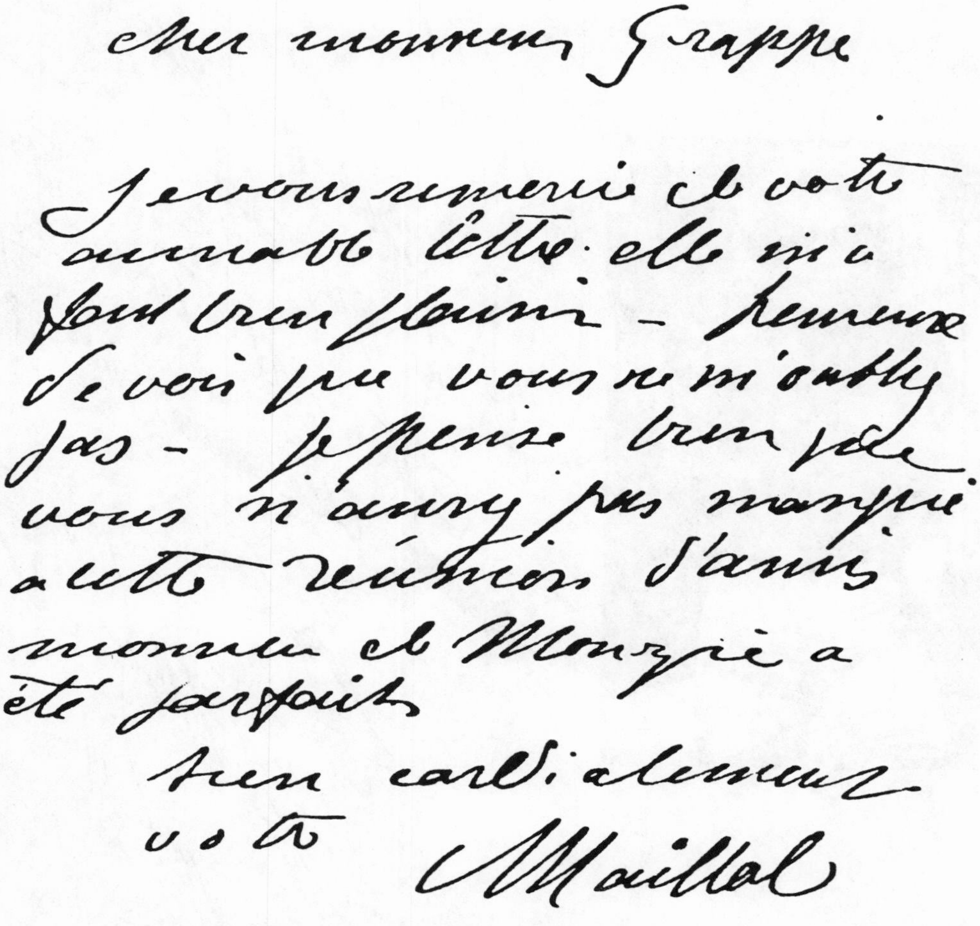

[handwritten letter in French]

Letter of Aristide Maillol (1861-1944)
written 21st of November, 1932 at Banyuls sur Mer

Maillol: Leda

Maillol is famous for his female sculptures.

    In the harmonious, beautifully swinging writing of Maillol we see the perfect, optimistic conception of life, a togetherness of stability and new experience—unconscious and conscious forces. His flowing movement guarantees adaptability, a grateful acceptance of life's gifts and pleasures, his desire to develop, to go from one phase in his life to the next, from one experience to the next. In this perfect swinging we understand the soul of the great artist who is himself a part of the cosmos, never seeing himself as the center of the world, as the simplified signature reveals. Emotions, even temperament and vitality are united. He is able to adapt and to assimilate.

Handwriting of the Italian writer Marinetti

147

The Italian writer Emilio Filippo Tommaso Marinetti (1876-1944) was the founder of Italian futurism. In his first manifesto (1909) he praises speed and the machine, he glorifies war, the destruction of culture and preaches hate against women; living powers are aeroplanes and trains. He speaks of creating a new virtue which is *speed* and destroys the old evil, slowness. Speed is the synthesis of courage in action, aggressive and warlike. Slowness is stagnant, cautious, passive and pacifistic. Ultimate speed is like prayer. The ecstasy of speeding cars is nothing other than union with God. Athletes were to be the first pupils of this religion. "We have to destroy houses, cities, to create new airports." (2nd manifesto, 1910)

With his new "religion of speed," Marinetti gave a vision to all new supermen and was with Picasso and Appolinaire one of the most important pioneers of modern art. Marinetti's handwriting shows us what power of speed he idolized in his manifestos, which influenced both fascism and Nazism.

Accentuation of movement

Vitality in achieving an aim dominates
Guided by immediate, powerful motivation
Belief in the strength of willpower, demanding everything of oneself
Self-esteem, self-assurance; because of the accentuation of willpower, psychic energy flags.
Instinctual values are also dominant.

Pierre Auguste Renoir (1841-1919),
the main representative of French impressionism

The Swing

Accentuation of movement in aethereal, spiritual rhythmic writing

Nervous self-control
Sensitive taste, refinement
Delicate, thin-skinned, fragile
Vulnerable, easily irritated
Emotional
Receptive, impressionable, sensible
Empathetic
Sensitive restlessness

Vivaciously driving inner rhythm
Impulsive
Effective
Unpredictable
Jumpy
Explosive
Difficulty in concentrating

Compulsive movement, driving force, compelled action

Difficulty in concentrating
Distracted
No controlled strength
No inner hold
Missing inner stabilization
Irrational impulse to move on
Fluctuating intensity
Too hasty

mother. I am going
something for 3-4 days which n
hospitals offer. Then I'll be abl
spend more time on greyhole
I am not seeing Victor &
there is no chance of marri
you were correct. He wa !

Disturbed rhythm of movement

Deteriorating psychophysical condition, deep-seated disturbances of self-confidence, un-happiness, feeling of incompetence, a loser, conflicts, irritation, abnormal excitability, tendency to destroy, impossible to work well; pessimistic moods are dominant.

ILLUSTRATING THE RHYTHM OF MOVEMENT

Without going into detail we can visualize the way a person moves along the lines as he writes. He walks through life the same way, in step with his inner rhythm.

I

Number one is strong and generous, he likes to give with full hands
and he likes to enjoy life with all his senses.

II

Number two is a light, elegant person who dances through life in an easy, swinging style

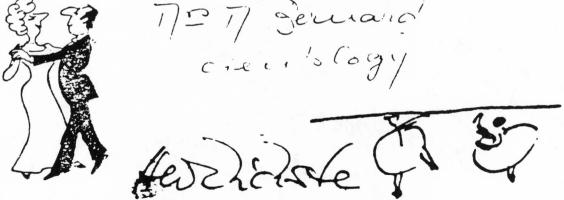

The inner rhythm is seen in the swinging curves of a graceful writing.

151

III

Number three is a sober, narrow-minded person who rarely shows feeling.

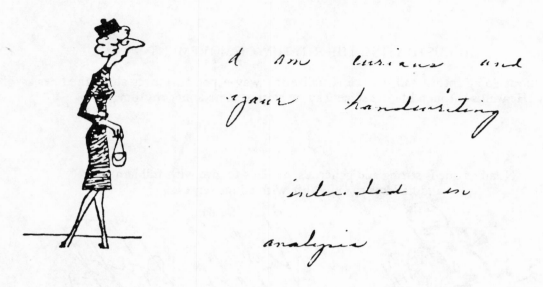

The writing is as sharp as the lines of a meager body.

IV

Number four is at one moment excited and enthusiastic,
and at the next, depressed and downhearted.

V

Number five is an upright, rather pedantic person, correct and reliable at all times.

Merry Christmas tommorrow.
Have a happy New Year,

I want to make my career

mari et moi pour Zürich. Là

VI

Number six is a confused person, torn by conflict.

Handwriting. I always feel

great in your party

if I go to Sydney we,

marie Bernard.

VII

Number seven is full of organization, planning, reliability, and makes a nice cozy home.

I know myself!
personality but I

Warmhearted, orderly, a good homemaker

VIII

Number eight is so confused that his whole house is down;
he can't pay his mortgage or his debts. He lacks organization.

Torn inside, unfocused, nervous

PART TWO

FORM PICTURE

INTRODUCTION

In the preceding section, *Movement,* we learned about the manifold demonstrations of movement in writing. These are the true gestures of the writer's expressive movements in life, which are involuntarily fixed, forever 'frozen' in the writing. We are able to see how a person's motivation, his impulses, his strivings are reflected in the movement of his writing. We discover the unconscious, involuntary impulses which are deeply anchored in the vital sources of the writing person, the element of spontaneity.

In the picture of form we see a more consciously and voluntarily created writing, born of an individual's love of or disregard for form. It may become a product of art and nature, façade, stylization or individuality. Form refers to the shape and construction of the individual letters. To learn more about the form picture and its elements we must study them separately.

Michon, who founded the first Institute of Graphology in Paris in 1875, paid special attention to the characteristics of 'signs' in handwriting. He prepared tables of the most important signs, the so-called *signes fixes.* Every comma, every curve, every hook in a letter was a symbol — an aspect of the writer's character.

As the science of graphology developed, however, writing analysis came to see that character is not only expressed by the *signes fixes,* those signs which recur regularly in a writing and help to build the foundation of the analysis, but also by other elements such as rhythm, individuality, simplification, distribution and tension degrees.

First there is the so-called *acquired form,* born out of respect for tradition. A child tries to imitate his father's way of writing, especially of the family name.

Then there is school writing, the faithful, obedient, copybook letter form construction wherein *adults* write as they were taught in school. The sense of individuality is either suppressed or non-existent.

Yet another form is *persona writing,* a form of artificiality, a façade behind which true character hides. (Even a murderer may 'hide' unconsciously behind this neutral form. David Berkowitz writes in the manner of school writing and so appears innocent and pure to the average observer. In the appendix there is a complete analysis of his unconsciously "chosen" school writing.)

There are also full and meager handwritings, enriched and ascetic forms, disciplined writing created with the utmost self-control, regular and irregular writing, and the initial and terminal accentuations and their special forms. There are the myriad ways to dot an *i*, to cross a *t*. There is evenness and unevenness and the rhythm of creative forms, some of which are born in the unconscious.

We will further discuss here the three stroke qualities: *the homogeneous, the amorphous, the granulated,* which were classified by the neurologist Rudolph Pophal.

As we discover in the handwritings of the great scientists, however, an analytical mind shows itself in simplicity. "Genius is diligence," says Goethe. Gifts and talents are not enough to make an inventor like Edison. He had to restrain an overflow of ideas by strong discipline, persistence and patience. Edison is in fact the personification of diligence: one percent inspiration, ninety-nine percent perspiration must have been his motto. His strongly controlled handwriting shows it.

alike await the inevitable hour

the paths of glory leads but to the grave

Thomas A Edison

Edison's powerful will is visible in the regular,
reason-dominated, self-disciplined vertical letter forms.

The dynamic process — the sum of all influences — education, upbringing, background, destiny — is mirrored in the form of the handwriting and enables us to penetrate the personality. Sometimes the propelling forces of the movement submit to the form and create an interesting picture; for example, what is stronger, the zest for life or the will to create?

Drive (movement) and self-realization (form) show their individualistic faces on paper (arrangement). Let us now explore the form picture — its stability, its softness, its lability, its sureness.

FORM NIVEAU

In 1625, Camillo Baldi, medical doctor in Bologna, wrote about form niveau in his publication, *Trattato come da una lettera missiva si conoscano la natura e qualità dello scrittore*. He said that every person has an individual quality which does not appear in anyone else's writing.

Three hundred years later Crépieux Jamin enlarged the concept of the form niveau by saying: "To create a graphological character portrait one has to find a place for the writer in the hierarchy of intellect and inner rhythm. One has to separate superior handwritings from mediocre handwritings as one separates the strong from the weak." Every writing element is then seen in relationship to the level of development of the writer, e.g., a curve may add beauty to a "high rank" writer, whereas it may add weakness to an already submissive nature.

Klages elaborated on Crépieux Jamin's thinking: "The life of a handwriting lies in the strength of its form. The higher the degree of originality in a writing, the more positive the value; and vice-versa — the higher the degree of monotony in a handwriting the more negative appear the same writing elements." To determine the degree of the high or low form niveau he proposes the following questions: "Ask yourself what kind of impression you get from the first look at writing: is it deep or flat, is it full or meager, is it rich or poor, warm or cold, harsh or soft, is it noble or vulgar, is it passionate or lukewarm, and so on." He proposed five degrees of form niveau, which are taught in all graphological institutes and universities in Europe.

For our purposes it is sufficient to learn to discriminate between high and low form niveau and to learn by experience from the first overall impression of a handwriting. Crépieux Jamin named the superior qualities, which he also attributed to high form niveau:

Intellectual capacities
Harmony and evenness
Genius and talent
Individuality
Originality

People without originality he thought boring and conventional, and he assigned them to the inferior categories of form — those showing monotony and no depth.

High form niveau: The refined, differentiated,
ingenious writing of Friedrich W. Nietzsche (1844-1900), German philosopher

159

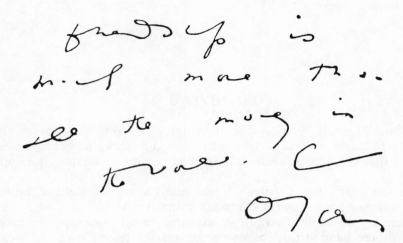

The soft, strange, beautifully swinging, original curves
of Oscar Wilde (1854-1900), Irish playwright

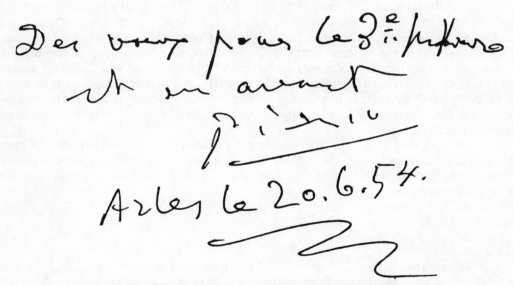

The explosive, dynamic, unpredictable, ingenious writing
of Pablo Picasso (1881-1973), Spanish painter and sculptor

Fresh, extraverted, vivacious, but without differentiation in form

Full of enthusiasm but bursting with vanity

Entanglements of lines: inconsiderate

Onset of senility

Pathological case

Low form niveau: smeary, illegible, clumsy capital *E*.

These samples ranging from high to low form niveau provide an overall view of Klages' degrees. With experience one learns to recognize them immediately. In the school-child's or uneducated person's writing, where the pen is not yet easily controlled, an analyst must consider the slowly and clumsily drawn lines in light of the degree of writing practice. With further education the processes of writing and thinking become more unified, almost second nature to the writer. One tries to simplify the letter formations, tries to find short cuts by combining *i*-dots and *t*-strokes with the following letters by creating new, tasteful, original letter formations (for instance, replacing the normal *e* with the Greek epsilon, avoiding extreme ornamentations, and striving for harmony between the three pictures of movement, form and arrangement). It is not necessary to analyze all writing elements to

161

determine the main character traits of a writer. Okakura, the Japanese aesthetician (1862-1913), saw in each writing line and curve the whole life of the writer. Taki, the Japanese artist, regarded the art of writing as true mysticism, sharing its secrets only with the dedicated few. Lavater could profile the writer from a splinter of his script.

In the following chapters we will learn to separate the writing elements from the three pictures. As we progress we will be training our eyes to spot the difference between high and low form niveau.

The main characteristic of high or low form niveau is referred to as the inner form rhythm. In these chapters we will concentrate on the various kinds of forms, with pulsating rhythm, with weak inner rhythm, and gradually we will train our eyes to see the difference.

This sample shows form-rigidity rooted in tradition and principles.

Healthy form-strength together with slow movement

Form-strength with simplified letters and flowing speedy movement

Palmer Method

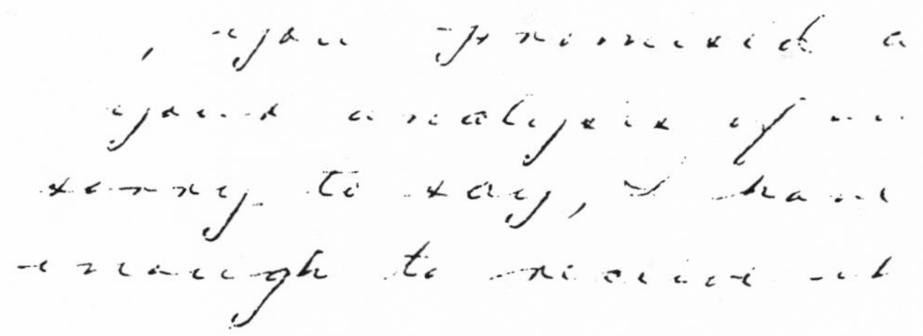

[handwritten sample]

Faithful School Writing

[handwritten sample — Kündigung Ihres und Frau Liebermanns Besuches!]

The powerful, individualistic letter forms of the true artist

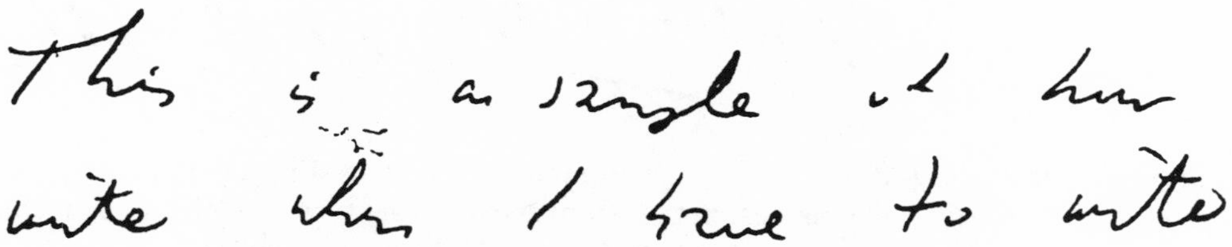

[handwritten sample — This is a sample of how I write when I have to write]

Dissolved, illegible form (also poor movement and arrangement)

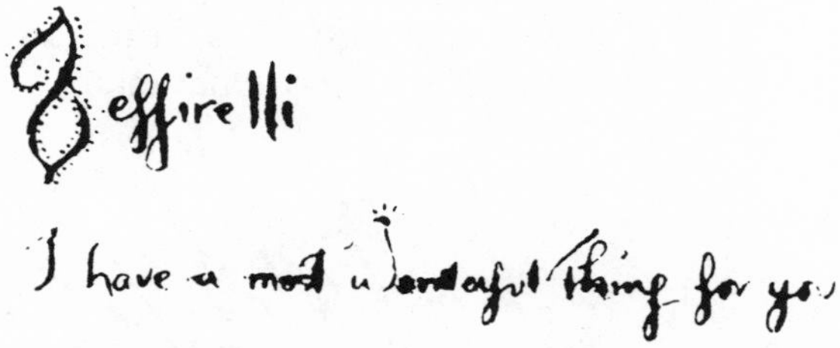

[handwritten sample — Zeffirelli]

[handwritten sample — I have a most wonderful thing for you]

A great admirer of the Italian movie director, Zefirelli,
pours her adoration into a Renaissance-type, stylized writing.

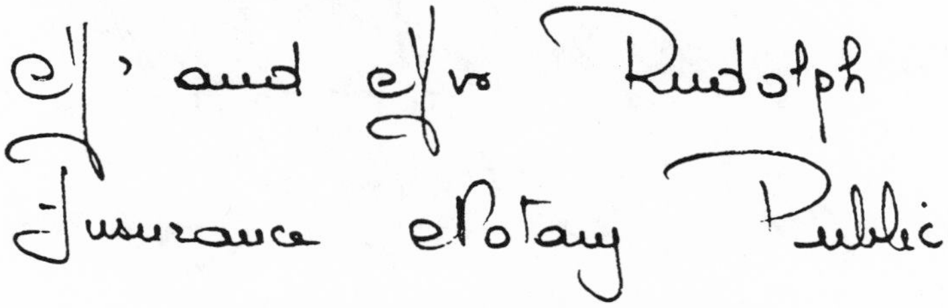

[handwritten sample — Mr. and Mrs. Rudolph; Insurance; Notary Public]

Restricted, artificial form picture.

PERSONA WRITING

The expression *persona writing* derives from the Greek theater. Actors wore masks to present different characters in a stage performance. Like the ancient stage actor, the persona writer shows a stylized façade to the outer world, be he soldier, priest, aristrocrat or lady of society, as in the writing below.

This style was learned by daughters of European nobility in French convents, and was named *sacré coeur* writing. This restricted, repressed writing is like the corset that constricts tender organs. The display of emotions was not allowed. The persona writer wears a mask behind which the genuine natural personality can be hidden and which remains undeveloped and suffocated. Often, however, persona writers have a need for wearing a social, official mask. Bismarck, the Iron Chancellor, known as an inflexible, uncompromising statesman, suffered deep depressions and cried in private. We see two samples: on the left the correct statesman, on the right the emotional man.

Controlled handwriting
of the Iron Chancellor

The emotional Bismarck,
persona mask absent

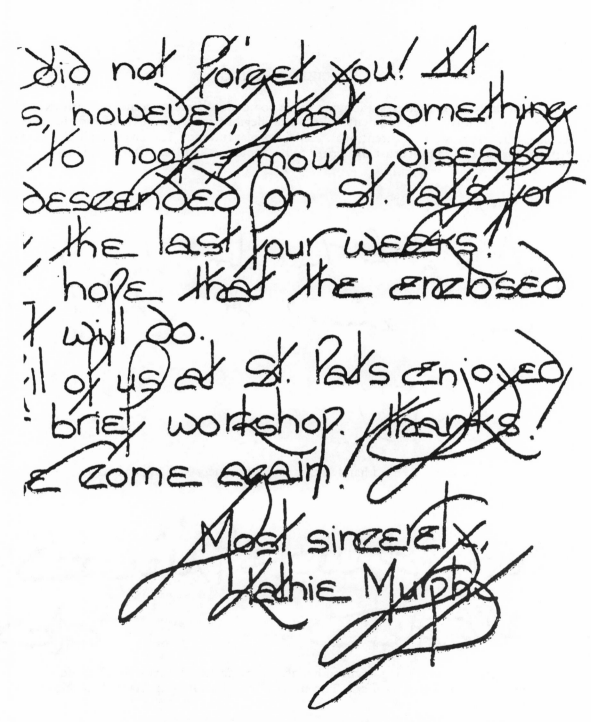

An extreme sample of persona writing wherein the natural behavioral impulse is completely suppressed and the script becomes a labyrinth of stylized fantasies.

STYLIZED WRITING

A stylized script reflects a longing to be someone different, someone with exclusive taste and originality. The moment it becomes illegible, vanity is obvious and the writing becomes the expression of intentional, contrived playfulness. The character hides behind artificial forms; one cannot trust the writer to be impulsive, natural or spontaneous.

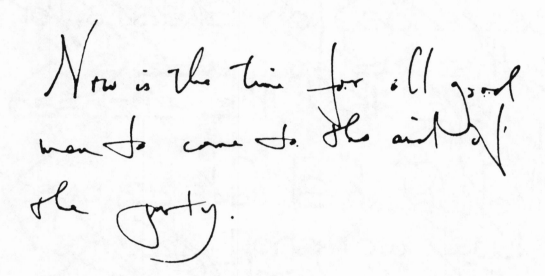

A beautifully stylized handwriting with extremely high upper lengths

In this creative, daring, stylized handwriting one sees the artificial attitude which the French call *l'art pour l'art*. The effect (form) is more important than the content.

REGULARITY

A writing is regular when the fluctuations of the letter formations are small, almost invisible. Regularity is therefore a characteristic of willpower. The writer tries to create a rule, a system to keep thoughts and writing in order. For this, absolute willpower is required. To regularity in handwriting belong: slant, large size, width, pressure and the direction of lines.

It is primarily the slant in the middle zone and upper zones which demonstrates the degree of regularity. Regular writing comprises a monotonous, motoric movement (a strong and persistent will, a striving for rationalism and intellectualism).

Sample of the regular handwriting of Pope Pius XII

Regularity, when exaggerated, can become rigidity, formalization, a support for a weak character. In this case, the stereotyped, mechanical writing mirrors façade, meaningless conformity. Even with such an elaborate mask, however, one can learn to see the degree of willpower of the writer.

Sample of an unnatural, mechanical, over-regulated writing.

Immanuel Kant (1724-1804), German metaphysician, discussed the regularity of the human face. "A measured regularity usually shows a very ordinary person who has little intellect. Even if we say that harmony and evenness are the main principles of classic beauty, it is this evenness which presents beauty, because beauty demands something with character. When regularity is too complete, individuality and character are missing."

W. Preyer wrote in his *Psychology of Writing* (1928) that the most regular writing looks plain because it is not creative. There is a difference between regularity of movement in writing and regularity of form. Usually we see in the narrowing of the movements during writing an attempt to simplify, and to dominate the Ego by willpower, as in this sample:

*he american wiew of time
and kindly to the lady
a service, for I am neither
for a gest of justice.
have something to tell*

By *trying* to create regular writing forms one serves an aesthetic form principle, namely order, from the desire to create something beautiful. The regular movement is done with self-discipline, resistance, tenacity, ethical willpower, tension, and it is done rather unemotionally, as in the sample above. The writing which is controlled by a desire to create a visual impression of regulated forms is the result of a wish to appear inconspicuous, servile, modest.

*The Sea is a bonus to all people, soothing
climates, feeding animals and human beings,
connecting nations together; the Sea is pregnant*

Jean Jacques Cousteau

The regulated, strong-willed high form niveau of Cousteau. Everything is regulated—the i-dots are accurately set, the lines are straight, the slant is even, the letter forms are even; his whole life is planned and regulated.

*the material I sent you, and I do
look forward to seeing the book. Please
note that my address; after June 1st,
will be Portland, Connecticut.
Sincerely,
Richard Wilbur.*

In this sample of inner regularity we see strong self-control,
strong ethics and morals, reliability and consideration, respect for the fellowman.

168

[handwriting sample]

In a lower form niveau we call unexpressive, primitive handwriting *drilled handwriting*.

It masks aggression and inner insecurity despite the picture of enormous willpower. The writing is stiff, rigid and drilled; individuality is suppressed.

[handwriting sample]

This regulated sample of exaggerated smallness is almost illegible and does not serve to communicate. Such microscopic writing reflects a kind of inner detachment from society; it forces us to use a magnifying glass to read the letters. It belongs to a special form of regularity called *compulsive handwriting*.

Table for the special form of regularity

Mechanized	Rigid regularity
Monotonous	Breaks, welded strokes
Exaggeratedly small	Sacré coeur writing
Illegible	Supported angles
Very narrow	Supported arcades
Very meager	Pedantically-drawn
Overconnected small writing	Horizontal lines
Narrow, blotted, smeary writing	

Special Forms of Regularity

[handwriting sample]

Regularity and accentuation of upper-lengths shows ethical striving,
desire for perfection and intellectual development. The writer can be a dreamer.

belongs to someone else.

Regularity and connectedness show willingness to accept consequences.

the nation's Capital. This is the first time attended the convention of the I.P.A

Regularity in a lower form niveau shows pedantic formalism.

Regularity and right slant and good structure,
coupled with large differences in lengths, show organizational talent.

(I'm) used to writing

Regularity and rhythmical pressure show aptitude for demanding professions
due to tenacity and persistence.

I love to travel

Regularity and width reveals activity, the love of exploration.

170

My husband is difficult to

Regularity, slowness and connectedness show lack of initiative,
slowness in decision-making, the inability to adapt to new environments.

., his dedication to his
it was really touching. Something

This regularity reveals neurotic compulsion. The downstrokes
are strangely misformed, as in *touching*.

IRREGULARITY

Klages said: "The writer who delivers a regular script is dominated by will power. The writer who gives us an irregular script is dominated by emotions." The irregular-writing person is impulsive, spontaneous, has little inhibition, wants to be free to explore, to develop, to realize his dream. He hates standardizing conformity.

Graphically we see irregularity in fluctuation of slant, size, width, pressure and direction of lines. In a good form niveau we have impulsiveness, love of freedom, individuality, originality, and an inventive life style. In an irregular writing with low form niveau we have lack of self-control, lack of security, changeability and sloppiness.

The main reason for irregularity is disgust with discipline coupled with lack of the willpower which might otherwise tame an abundance of emotions seeking experience. Irregularity is therefore a sign that full development of the personality has not been a-chieved.

Among the many things
I have learned from you, one
sticks out: miracles are achieved
only if you work hard enough.
Work seems to be the answer.
But so many of us hate to work.
So, I suppose character is the
answer.

Much love,

Tony Randall

Tony Randall's irregular writing: the high form niveau shows us that he is an individualist, an artist with originality. He is fresh, alive, loves variety, is often an *enfant terrible*, is easily excited and impressed, is spontaneous, and has multiple interests.

172

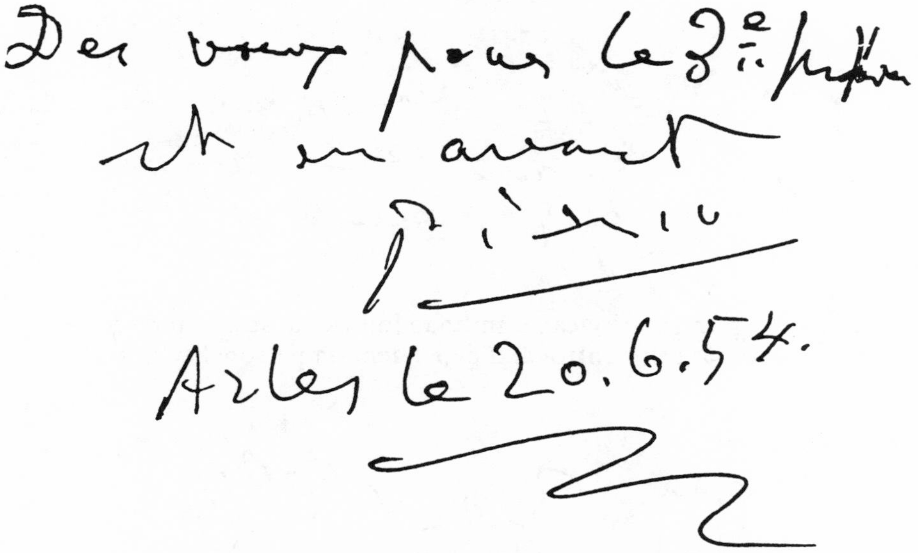

This irregular, powerful, unpredictable handwriting mirrors Picasso's wild zest for life, abundant creativity, anti-bourgeois lifestyle, constant longing for new development, new horizons. He is easily irritated and explodes from time to time like a volcano.

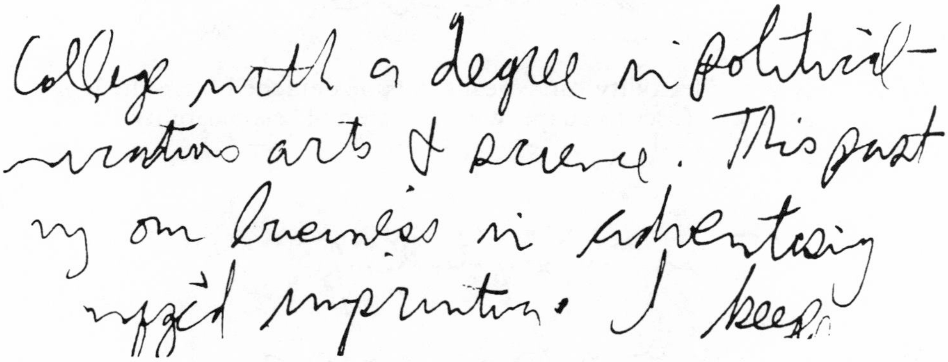

In contrast, this handwriting is merely irregular and sloppy. The forms are not clear, not original, they are simply wild, without creative form.

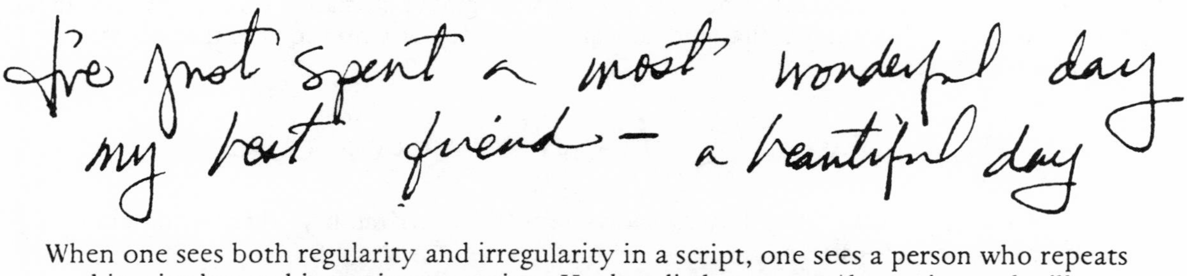

When one sees both regularity and irregularity in a script, one sees a person who repeats his mistakes and is not introspective. He does little to control emotion and will.

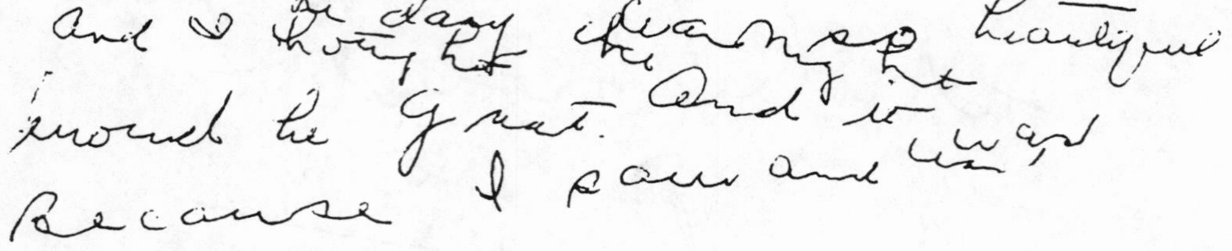

[handwritten text]

Strong irregularity can signify an individual still in puberty
or one without self-control and dependent—a personality in turmoil.

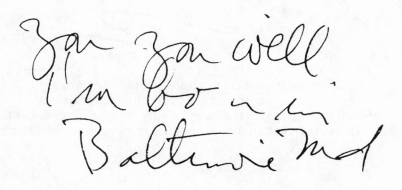

Irregularity with illegibility can reveal someone detached from the world,
one who refuses to adapt, with no sense of responsibility.

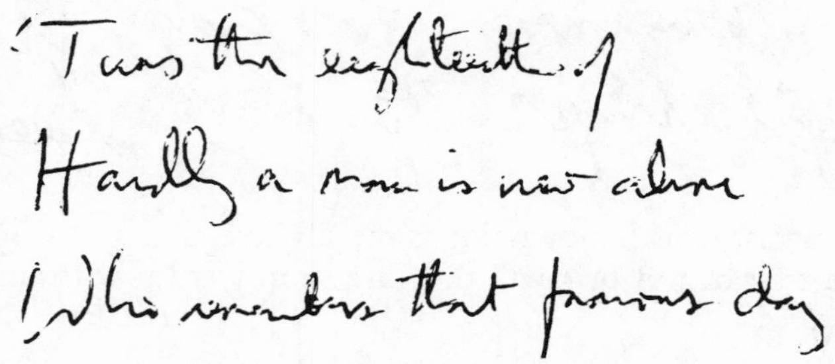

[handwritten text]

Irregularity with some legibility shows a person who makes demands on his environment, as for instance a highly intellectual and demanding professor who requires that his students attend all his lectures.

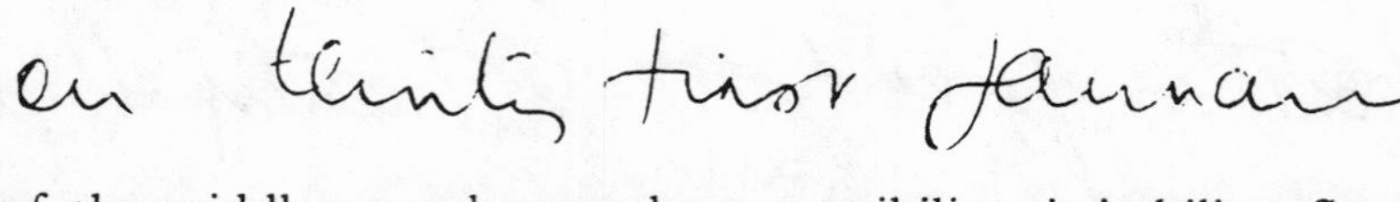

[handwritten text]

Irregularity of the middle zone letters shows sensibility, irritability, fluctuating emotions and disturbances of self-esteem.

[handwriting sample]

Irregularity of width shows an unbalanced attitude toward society —
continual fluctuations between impulsive approaches and sudden reserve.

[handwriting sample]

Irregularity in the slant means that the person is not mature;
the desire for human contact alternates with doubts about it.

[handwriting sample]

In this irregular writing we see the impressionable adventurer,
still in puberty, without conscience.

[handwriting sample]

Irregularity and pressure reveals irritability and a high degree of excitability.

[handwriting sample]

Irregularity and weak pressure shows lack of will power;
the writer is easily seduced.

175

ENRICHMENT

There are two reasons for enrichment: to embellish the handwriting out of vanity, playfulness, flamboyant self-demonstration; or to express creativity and an artistic impulse.

Enrico Caruso's self-drawn caricature: his embellishment consists only of a softly bound loop, an underscoring which mirrors in its garlandic curves his own warm heartedness.

In the prominent underscoring of Milton Berle's "space" we see a love of variety, a show-off attitude, a longing for approval.

His warmheartedness is seen in the flowing, soft garlands and the simplicity of the writing reveals a high sense of humanity.

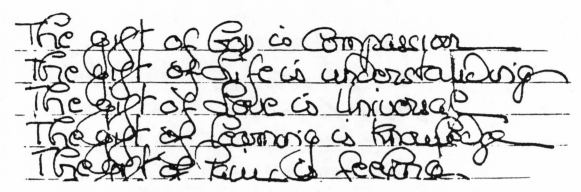

The visible introversion/involution of a poet with the enrichment of lower loops, stereotyped left movements and odd-enrolled letter formations. (Were it not for its stiffness, this writing would be considered full. The curls here are made deliberately.)

In this handwriting, overloaded with ornamentation, we see bad taste, pedantry and verbosity. One cannot easily recognize the words because so much "happens" around the letters. It shows egocentricity, the self-admiration of a phrase-monger.

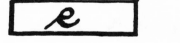

Singular enrichments, especially curled-inward middle zone letters reveal stubbornness, obstinacy, egocentricity, pedantry. In the enrichment of the middle zone we sometimes see the so-called *spoon e,* which is constructed with an extra little *'spoon'* after the first upstroke of the letter *e*, as if it were to be a *c*.

The *spoon e* is such a rare letter-form that I was able to prove that the signature of a client was forged. The forger did not use the *spoon-e* as he tried to imitate the name *Weber,* (sample on left side of page 177), and forgery was apparent. The circular enrollment of the *e* reveals exaggerated self-control and egocentricity.

Overemphasized forms in the middle zone, like claws, enrollments and spirals reveal insincerity. (See arrangement: *Insincerity in writing.*) In the samples above, the writer creates spiral vowels in the middle zone: a, o, e, as well as in the *d* and *g* heads.

This is an encapsulation which shows possessiveness, as do all closed spirals. The construction of such complicated spiral forms demands skill and is usually done by accomplished liars. The writer circles the truth like a cat circles a too-hot plate of food. He makes detours and excuses with great showmanship.

These are enrichments in a negative form, the sacré coeur.

The other negative enriched form is the terminal arcade, which reveals calculation, dishonesty.

With pressure the terminal arcade shows brutality.

SIMPLIFICATION

In both simplification and negligence (in both high and low form niveau), the writer shortens his letter formations. Everything that seems superfluous will be eliminated, reducing letters to the most abstract form possible, hardly legible. Those who write shortened, abstract forms think and act quickly, in a matter-of-fact way.

When in the process of simplification necessary parts of letter forms are omitted, negligence begins. Neglected forms show unreliability, lack of goal orientation, unpunctuality and a tendency to conceal things. A person who neglects writing forms is also hasty, superficial, not-persistent, impatient, not good at detail work, weak and untrustworthy. One who simplifies words shows the ability to reduce thought processes — he is rational, pragmatic, and so precise his style may border on mechanical, empty formalism.

Sample of intellectual simplification

Sample of intellectual negligence

Aesthetic, basic, intellectual; the simplicity of a great writer

In this writing we see systematic thinking with pragmatism.
The writer's excellent mind prefers practicality, and rational thinking will be emphasized.

[handwriting sample]

This writer prefers a simple lifestyle and likes the essential things; he is rational, efficient.

[handwriting sample]

This writer belongs to a type who thinks he has a genius touch: he is sloppy, unpunctual and without conscience. The high upper lengths show longing for greatness.

[handwriting sample]

The more intelligent a writer, the more he tries to unite his inner thinking speed with his ability to create reduced and simplified forms. In this sample we see that all letter forms are stripped of all superfluous ornamentation, yet the distinctiveness and legibility remain. In the sample above, the shortened simplification is born out of dynamic movement.

[handwriting sample]

But even more inconsiderate, illegible, is this writing of a well-organized genius who dances elegantly in space; alas, few can read it easily.

[handwritten sample]

This kind of writing shows more negligence than simplification. Most of the letter forms are washed out, equalized, not distinctive. The *m* and *n* are both equally constructed, the *i* and *e* are similar, the *e* and *l* have almost the same height (see: *myself*, the last word).

[handwritten sample]

Another simplification is the ligature, which is often used in England: the mind works so quickly in simplifying the construction that the pen glides from one word to the other, if possible never lifting.

[handwritten sample]

Unnecessary letters or letter parts omitted give this sample a sense of being incomplete and means the writer is imprecise and not good at detail work.

[handwritten sample]

This consciously created simplification approaches stylization and is done artfully, with decorative self-presentation. Because the letters are so exaggerated, reduced to the pure downstroke, one calls it *skeleton writing*. The *k* in *Doktor* (first line) becomes an enlarged *n*. This kind of writing is done mostly out of vanity, to appear different from others, and to produce an abstract art image.

Simplification: Special Forms

Both Simplification and Enrichment in the same handwriting:

Wouldn't it be nice if we were older

Simplification in the text and ornamentation in the signature indicates that the writer wishes to create an impressive image of what is in fact a modest, ordinary, everyday life-style. It shows the discrepancy between who he is and who he would like to be.

Summing-up Table for Simplification and Enrichment

Simplification	Enrichment
Basic thinking	Creativity
Aestheticism	Desire for self-demonstration
Taste	Sense of beauty
Architectural talent	Cheerfulness
Technical sense	Verbosity
Realist	Sense of tradition, culture
Sobriety	Ceremonial, pedantry
Sharp intellect	Emphasis on formality

Negligence	*Excessive Ornamentation*
Carelessness	Mannerisms
Bohemian nature	Show-off
Insincerity	Self-admiration
Ambiguity	Lack of taste
Without scruples	Vanity
Without principles	Playfulness
Unreliability	

FULLNESS

Fullness in handwriting is demonstrated by upper zone curves stretching into space; large, voluptuous forms in the middle zone; and lower-zone anchors with wide, round strokes. The full upper zone shows richness of fantasy; the full middle zone reveals richness of feeling and emotions and strong Ego image and self-involvement; and the richly developed curves of the lower zone reveal sexual and materialistic aims.

Circular movements in all three zones imply a circling around the self. It is not so much the forward or backward movement that is important here but a sense of a centripetal force resulting from deep concentration and self-absorption.

Fullness—round, soft and gliding movements—indicates fantasy, soul, illusion, feeling, an inflated Ego, images, dreams, imprecise thinking. These are the characteristics of a real feeling type whose life is dominated mainly by love and emotions and the desire for all the pleasures life has to offer.

In this simplified writing with voluptuous forms we see the writer's wide-open soul, strong, optimistic willpower, inner happiness. She lives to discover the beauties of the world; she "thinks" with her heart. She is a visual type, she learns and thinks in pictures. Her emotions are more important than reason.

It is easy to see in this full handwriting the richness of soul, the creativity and originality in the slow-moving letter forms. The joy of life, the enchantment of seeing the treasures of the world radiate from such voluptuous forms. They are created so differently from others and have their own life, yet they are legible, although a bit daring (like the *r*, a pure arcadic form from an old language). The Greek *epsilon* fits perfectly in this combination of antique and modern letter formations, symbolizing that the writer lives in both worlds. There is a certain phlegmatic sensuality in the heavy, deep-rooted letter forms, as the long penetrating anchor of the capital *M* shows. There is a healthy earthiness in the round, strong, pastose strokes, and every movement is done with intuitive knowledge; this is not a theoretical mind at work but a contemplative person who sees concrete pictures, who is bound by logic, as the continuity of the script proves. Klages once complained that we no longer have such deep-feeling Renaissance personalities as Pope Alexander.

Alexander III, Pope (1159-1181),
one of the great medieval Popes.

Pope Alexander III was one of the most distinguished champions of ecclesiastical independence in the Middle Ages. In this writing we see a Renaissance man, skilled and well-versed in all of the arts and sciences.

These two samples of fullness, although written 800 years apart, are so similar—as if they were created in the same century. They show the same pastose stroke picture, the large size of the middle zone, the slowness of movements, the voluptuousness and richness of letter formations, and a deep anchoring in the earth.

Some fullness in a meager handwriting shows more soul and warmheartedness than there is in reality.

This handwriting shows heavy 'money bags' in the inflated lower loops, a symbol of dominating materialistic (financial) interests, whereas the middle zone, seat of soul and heart, is meager.

Fullness of side parts indicates phrases, cliché, empty talk, unnecessary emphasis on unimportant things, as in this sample:

When upper loops are fuller than the middle zone, general interests predominate.

184

Middle zone fuller than lower lengths shows that personal interests predominate.

additional days

Fullness in *d*-heads, suddenly inflated in comparison with a small middle zone, shows egocentricity and boasting.

dog

Isolated fullness always shows exaggerated emotions which explode suddenly, then die.

wonderful

Inflated middle zone is vanity

love

MEAGERNESS

The writer who prefers meagerness in his script avoids feeling, emotions; his reason dominates his heart. The more we discover angular letter formations together with a thin stroke the more criticism and sharp-mindedness we can expect. The whole range, from eminent abstract intellect in a high form niveau to an empty formalism in a low form niveau, may be observed in meager handwriting. To be sure, a meager writing is not a juicy one which breathes life, richness and often voluptuousness with a rich libido, but is instead a bloodless, cool one, directed by a reason-dominated brain.

Robespierre's sharphy-chiselled meager writing
shows cruelty and sharp intellect.

The essence of his character is: objective
cool, sober, abstract,
simplified, cautious,
reserved, ascetic.

The abstract, intellectual writing of Dr. Jonas Salk

The main ingredients in the writing with high form niveau:
    intellectual clarity,
    strict, logical, scientifically oriented thinking,
    precision, rationalism, formal thinking.

Meager writing with suppressed, not open or round vowels *a* or *o*, reflects anxieties and inhibitions. It is not a sign of strength but of insecurity and lack of warmheartedness.

In this meager and dry, *juxtaposed handwriting* of Erich von Däniken, one discovers the inner solitude and the inner ascetic life standard of this writer. All his emotions seem to be suppressed by the power of self-discipline and control of instinctual urges. He may be a fanatic.

Marquis de Montcalm, military maneuvers

French General Louis Joseph de Montcalm (1712-1759) was sent to defend Canada in the French and Indian War. He captured Fort Ontario, restored control of Lake Ontario to France, and besieged and captured Fort William Henry. He lost his life in 1759. His small, meager, simplified, *juxtaposed writing* shows goal-oriented ambition, strict determination. The cool, reserved letter forms are softened by the emotional right slant. He was an active servant of the land for which he died.

When a meager handwriting with a low form niveau is penetrated by harsh,
dagger-like strokes, one sees fanaticism and cruelty.

There is no softness, no mercy. Such rigorous writing is typical of the leaders of the Third Reich.

David Rice Atchison

   This lawyer, politician and U.S. Senator (1806-1886) was a pro-slavery democrat; he was instrumental in the enactment of the Kansas-Nebraska Bill, which left the decision concerning slavery to the settlers. In his handwriting we see cruelty and heartlessness.

   John F. Kennedy's sharp, meager, abstract handwriting reveals an intuitive intellect. The illegibility of his *skeleton writing* with its over-high-striving upper loops reveals sky-high ambition and genuine idealism.

INITIAL ACCENTUATION

The first letter of a word—not necessarily a capital letter—is the self-representation of the writer, how he presents himself when he enters a room, or withdraws and stands forlornly and shy while waiting for someone to approach him. When the writer consciously neglects a first letter we see a modest, often servile, submissive person who has little courage or who has been maltreated. If the first letter is emphasized, the writer expresses his need for admiration, his desire to lead, his enthusiasm for life, and often, vanity or arrogance. The initial letter tells the world what is most important to the writer. If he emphasizes the pronoun I - the Ego - we know at once the degree of his self-admiration.

A German sculptor

The enrolled *P* of the German actor Max Pallenberg.

The writer of this sample with the enlarged I radiates security. When he enters a room he needs immediate recognition, acknowledgment; he tries to make a good impression with acting talent, unconventional, amiable behavior, or he shocks with an unnatural, boasting arrogance. Such a writer is interested only in appearances.

Franz Kafka's overexaggerated capitals hide insecurity. Such overexaggeration is a form of compensation.

189

The high capital *L* in Liberace
symbolizes the importance of the Ego.

Despite Liberace's excessive self-admiration we acknowledge his artistic showmanship, his need for personal esteem, his conviction that he is infallible. There is a naive, uncritical need for importance; he is playful like a child, open-hearted; his is an unrestrained enthusiasm.

The higher the initial letters, the stronger the conviction of superiority. There is self-admiration here, combined with self-deception.

The lower the form niveau, as in these wide-spread, uninteresting letter forms, the more we can expect all talk and no action.

Someone who hates limelight, likes solitude and modesty, concentrates on objective facts, prefers work with words, and prefers a small world, writes small and without the enthusiasm of the expansive, adventurous person. Anxiety and an inferiority complex can be behind this lack of initiative. People who write in this manner tend to stay in the background, believe in authority, are often servile and submissive, and are wary of the unknown. They often shy away from responsibility. Here we have the gamut of introverted types, from the self-absorption of the great scientists to the reticence of more fearful

190

individuals who do not dare to ask too much of life.

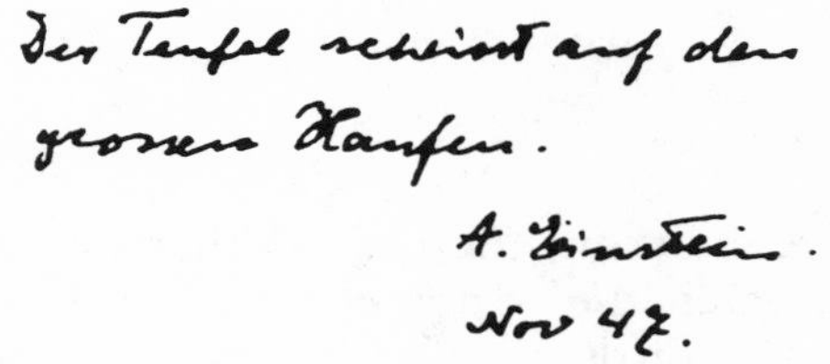

Der Teufel scheint auf den grossen Haufen.

A. Einstein.

Nov 47.

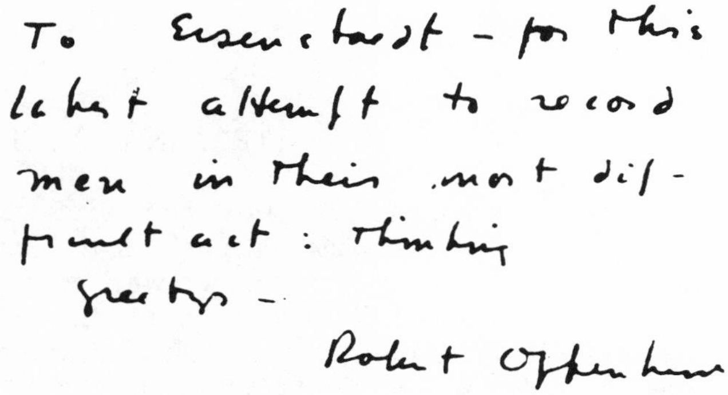

To Eisenhardt — for this latest attempt to record men in their most difficult act: thinking

greetings —

Robert Oppenheimer

The unpretentious, small, modest handwriting
of our great scientists, Einstein and Oppenheimer.

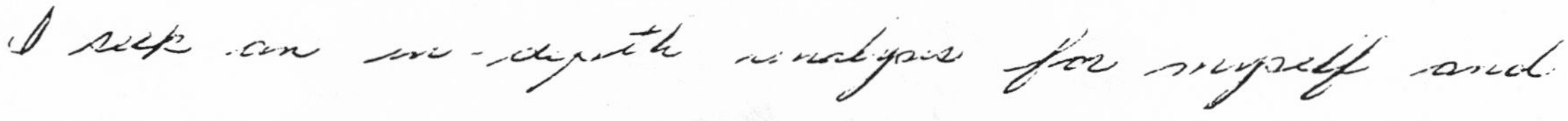

I seek an in-depth analysis for myself and

Behind this insignificant, small handwriting hides an anxious, shy person who likes to stay in the background; he worships heroes from afar.

TERMINAL ACCENTUATION

While *Initial Accentuation* symbolizes self-representation, the desired first impression, *Terminal Accentuation* symbolizes the moment when the writer meets his environment, when he comes into contact with people. Not only do the last letters of a word describe the relationship to the "you" but they also demonstrate the ability to turn expectations into reality or to escape into illusions and dreams.

Terminal accentuations show the writer's conscientiousness, his determination, his need for people, but also obstinacy, recklessness, or the ability to mislead by bluffing. Decreases in word-endings show the clever diplomat with psychic insight or the cautious one, the coward who resigns himself to circumstances.

Emphasized Terminals

Sense of justice
Determination
Solidity, stability
Terminal hook (as in the sample)
Tenacity
Stubbornness

Pointed Terminals

In a refined, intellectual writing
Sharp critical wit

In a more aggressive writing:
Biting humor, criticism, sharpness

Edward I. Koch, Mayor

In a heavy sharp writing
Determination, aggression

John D. Rockefeller IV

192

When the final elements of words are constructed larger than those at the beginning we recognize naiveté, indiscreet openness and some thoughtlessness. Children usually write with larger word endings. Clever, cunning, deceitful and diplomatic persons never dream of enlarging their word endings, yet the open-hearted person quite instinctively blurts out opinions, which we then see in enlarged terminals.

Decreased Word Endings

When the final elements of words are constructed larger than those at the beginning

Increased Word Endings	*Decreased Word Endings*
No reserve	Caution
No inhibitions	Mistrust
Thoughtlessness	Taciturnity
Childishness	Cunning
Love of truth	Hypocrisy
Lack of adaptability	Sophistry
Lack of psychic insight	Psychic insight
Enthusiasm	Intellectual flexibility
Audacity	Wit and humor
Impudence	Adaptability
No understanding	Impatience
Indiscretion	Exhaustion and fatigue
No tact	Self-control
Naiveté	Diplomacy
Always voicing opinions	

Terminal Accentuation

Terminals Widely Extended:

dealer

George Bernard Shaw (1856-1950)
British Dramatist

Harry S. Truman (1884-1972)

Lyndon B. Johnson (1908-1973)

Interpretation

Tenacity
Determination
Willpower
Self-esteem

Claw-like arcadic terminals

Eager for financial security

having my handwriting meeting

Vertical, high-striving terminals

Quarrelsome, verbose, ambitious

career

Dr. Hans Lammers, Chief of Reich Chancery

Fieldmarshal Keitel

High striving, curved terminals in a soft writing,
the so-called religious curve, signifies belief in a higher power.

Terminal Threads
Hurry, impatience, negligence, indifference to small things;
in a high intellect, diplomacy

Katherine Hepburn

Henry Kissinger

29. 4. 1945

Adolf Hitler
(terminal falling lines:
suicidal tendencies)

Horizontally extended terminals
show displaced pressure when exaggerated in strength and pressure.
Displaced pressure means that the *libido* is diverted into other channels, sublimated.

195

Terminal Accentuation

Terminal downstrokes
signify strong anchoring and tenacity.

O. Henry (1862-1910), short story writer

Cut-off Terminals
are those last letters which do not swing in curves but are cut off when they reach the base line. See sample below — John Hinckley's pointed, cut-off downstrokes — he tends to sever relationships abruptly.

The Terminal Arcade
is a kind of protecting wall against intruders;
it signifies caution, calculation and sometimes embarrassment, inhibition.

The Terminal Arcade
formed elliptically, bent to the left, is called *shark tooth* — a symbol of insincerity, cunning, 'sly like a fox,' dishonesty

196

The so-called *Oral Hooks* at the end of a word, turning to the left
(a symbolic return to the past), show a lack of mother love during
the baby's oral phase, in the sucking period, usually replaced by oral pleasures
like kissing, candy, smoking and verbosity later in life.

Terminal Garlands
continue the traditional character of the garland, moving to the right out of altruism, grace, and feeling for other people; they also show lack of independence and passive acceptance of "fate."

The so-called *elevated letter* at the end of a word (lettre suspendue), suspended in the air, means the writer tries to avoid reality by escaping into dreams and illusions.

Sudden vertical or left-slant-turning terminals are called *counterstrokes* because they represent turning against society: skeptical, revolutionary judgment, caution and mistrust in relationships, sudden hostility, sudden self-protection against emotions, forceful taming of instincts.

197

Terminal Accentuation

Terminal back-lash strokes
crossing the preceding letters, show a certain self-destructive tendency,
a kind of self-flagellation.

i-DOTS

Before we continue with a review of the variations of elements in handwriting we must remember that all the components into which we separate handwriting for analysis belong to the total picture, which has a well-defined contour, solidity and depth.

In 1912, Max Wertheimer introduced the concept of the 'Gestalt' — the whole is greater than the sum of its parts. In handwriting analysis this means that we must be aware that the dissection is only for the purpose of learning. We must not forget the complicated 'Gestalt' which is the *Overall Impression* put on the first line of the worksheet when beginning an analysis. All the variations in a handwriting should be measured, noted, and examined, with the aim of putting the puzzle together later, when the analysis is completed.

Let us now begin with an examination of the variations of the *i-dot*. As small and unimportant as these seem, they are of enormous value in analyzing a handwriting. Because the i-dots are created primarily in the unconscious, they belong to those writing elements which will be free of deception. They tell us more about the writer than any other letter, when for instance they appear light in a strong pressure script or strong in a light writing. A forger can be detected when he forgets to disguise the i-dots.

i-dots in variation

i-dots exactly set

Conscientiousness
Concentration
Good at detail work
Exactness, precision
Punctuality
Pedantry

i-Dots

This is a very nice

i-dots written immediately after writing the i-body, set and isolated

Correctness
Each new thought will be carefully executed lest something be forgotten
Accomplishing the task at once
Immediate reaction
Conscientiousness
Exactness bordering on pedantry

find a solution

To-the-right-flying i-dots

Impatience
Future-oriented
Illusions and dreams

This is

Wisconsin

To the-left-flying i-dots

Procrastination
Likes to think of the past
Hesitation

Roda

Roda Wieser, renowned Viennese graphologist connects i-dots with the following letter

Mental flexibility
Gift for quick thinking
Fluid thought processes

thinking
silver line

Double set i-dots (one combined with the next letter, second added)

Lack of confidence in one's efficiency
Fear of having forgotten something
Better doing too much than too little
Doubts own reliability
Insecurity; does not trust self

High-flying i-dots (isolated)

High flying ideas
Lack of sense of reality
Enthusiasm
Carelessness in small things

life is Doris

Low-set i-dots

Powers of observation
Practicality, pedantry
Realist
Need for stability
Sober, abstract thinking

intuition creativity

Inexactly set i-dots

Carelessness
No concentration
Impatience, inexactness
Speed, no love of detail

flight.

Flying-forward and high

Adventurous
Curious
Impulsive
Thoughtless

Horing

Flying-forward and low

Impulsiveness combined with pedantry
Tendency to deception

Livonia

Changing between forward set i-dots and backward set i-dots

Fluctuating between impulsive and restricted attitudes

personality

Exactly set i-dots

Despite speed, means excellent concentration

David

Comma-like i-dots

Vivacity
Eagerness
Energy
Temperament

Switzerland   Zürich

Accent-like i-dots

Vivacity
Humor

job is boring

Absence of i-dots

Feeling one is above "small" things
Disorder, not good at detail work
Disorganized
Unreliability

enjoy being

Weak i-dots in a relatively strong writing

Strength is not genuine
Weak character

The i-dots in each of the three pictures

Movement (dotted softly or powerfully)
Form (round or stroke-like)
Arrangement (high or low)

It is possible to set i-dots precisely, despite a quick-moving writing. The dotting then happens automatically in the rhythmical back and forth movement.

A) *i-dots in the movement picture*

Light, tender, suggested i-dots

Sensitivity
Gentleness
Weakness   *impose*
Sensibility
Tenderness

i-dots set heavily and forcefully

Powerful nature
Energy
Roughness   *interesting*
Clumsiness
Inconsiderateness

203

i-Dots

i-dots accent-like

Vivacity
Impatience
Tenacity
Determination
Willpower
Rebellion
Persistence

This is is handwriting

B) **i-dots in the form picture**

Beautifully rounded

Consideration
Teenager mentality in adulthood
Slowness

first time in Williams

i-dots formed like a curve

Humor (laughing mouth)

in having meaningful

Jesse Jackson's humorous *i-dots*

Circular i-dots (Old Egyptian sign for protecting the souls of the dead against evil spirits)

Desire to be different
Secrecy
Extravagance
Deception
Self-involvement

Hildegarde, the famous pianist singer

C) *Distribution of i-dots according to arrangement*

High-dotted
Intellectual interests
Idealistic tendencies
Religious, metaphysical interests
Desire to do extra-perfect work
In a heavy, materialistic writing,
high i-dots are an attempt to persuade
that the writer has high aspiration and
spiritual thoughts.

Low-dotted

Depressed state of mind
Thoroughness leads to pedantry
Precision
When emphasis on lower loops primitive:
   practical character
Realist
Gift for observation
  (when precisely dotted and in a small writing)
In quick, wide script, low dotting means that one knows what he wants

High and light

Enthusiasm
Excitability
Fancifulness
Cheerfulness
Resilience of spirit
Fast recuperation

High and heavy

Powerful vitality
Desire to be independent
Wish for dominance
Pretentious, superior attitude

Alternation between high and low

Content with the given situation
Adaptability
Inconsistency

Low and light

Shyness
Weakness
Depression
Submissiveness

Low and heavy

Sense of reality
Materialism
Narrow-mindedness
Arbitrary adherence to rules and forms
Sensual appetite (in pastose writings)
Hairsplitting

t-STROKES

In addition to the *i*-dots there is another accentuation of the upper zone — the high crossings of the *t-bars*. Graphologists of old saw in the high-dancing *i-dots* idealism, spiritual interests, and in the high *t-bars*, independence of thinking, willpower, domineering character, social ambitions.

Robert Heiss, professor of psychology and characterology at Freiburg's University, called the upper zone the zone of excitement in his book *Interpretation of Handwriting*. He further called all strokes which aim in this direction excitement strokes, which can represent either anger or joy. Here in this sample, where the *t*-strokes are downward-directed, we see deep-rooted anger and violence.

In spite of the calligraphic stylization, the downward slant of all the overlong *t*-bars in this inflated handwriting shows hostile tendencies.

High-place t-bars indicate

Ethics
Idealism
Tendencies to illusion
Enthusiasm
Social ambition
Excitability

Low-placed t-bars indicate

Pedantry (especially in a heavy writing with emphasis on lower zone)
Precision, thoroughness
Sense of reality
Narrow horizon
Power of observation

To the height-striving, knotted t-crossing

Striving for freedom
Despotic character

To the depth-striving, knotted t-crossing

Resignation
Obedience
Modesty, weakness

Deep penetration of lower zone

Lack of endurance
Fatigue

Upward aiming t-crossing

Contradiction
Aggression
Ambition
Tendency to nag
Quarrelsome

Downward aiming t-crossing

Negative criticism
Destructive tendencies
  (especially in high-pressure writing)
Obstinacy

A *tenacity hook* at the end of an extended *t*-stroke
shows persistence and tenacity, but also cruelty.

Variations of the t-strokes

't' hook on the final stroke = sensitive

't' stroke with crossing and hook on the final stroke = overcoming
  weakness

thickening 't' stroke = rising temper

very long 't' crossing = sarcastic

slanted upward = optimistic

t-Srokes

bent stroke to the right = trying to control

tapered downward to the right = domineering, irritation

large t-loop, t-stroke crosses half the t-stem = hypersensitivity

't' bar curved but strong = earthiness, brutality

if the 't' bar is curved and light = no sense of responsibility

final stroke goes leftward = withdrawal, introversion

club-like = cruelty, viciousness, physical violence

lance-like = sarcasm, sharp tongue, critical, aggressive

with a loop above the stem = persistence, mild eccentricities

Leftward tendencies in t-crossings = bound to the past

curly, ornamental = showmanship

long stroke above stem = visionary, enthusiastic

tall stem = pride

crossing to the left, not touching the stem= procrastination

short weak stroke above stem = laziness

slanted upstroke = social aspirations, ambition

slanted down = fighter, rebel, hostile

downward, almost vertical = dogmatic

not crossing stem = neurotic, arrogant, aggressive

incomplete downstroke above the stem = lives in unhappy fantasy

triangular = endurance, persistance

knotted with strong loop = persistent

upstroke = practical, showing initiative

low loop knotted = sensitive

high loop, knotted above the stem = eccentric

a triangular formed t-(together with a triangular lower *g*) = obstinate

hooked = tenacious

thick downward stroke = coarse, cruel

tapering stroke = quick tempered

't' bar straight = well-balanced self-confidence

't' bar wavy = gracious, humor

't' bar curved up softly = no resistance, strong imagination

't' bar curved downward = disciplined

't' bar short = repressed

't' bar long = impulsive

't' bar weak = timid

't' bar above the stem = blessing

't' bar heavy and straight = determined

't' bar omitted = forgetful, careless, (in a strong writing) = independent

't' bar too far left = inhibited, indecisive

't' bar in center = cooperative

't' bar far to the right = hasty temper, animated, hurrying

't' bar high above = dreamer with vivid imagination

't' bar just touching the stem = unrealistic

't' bar crossing in the middle = practical

't' bar crossing very low = fearful, guilty, underselling self

EVENNESS

We see it all the time. When a human being has reached an almost saint-like perfection, he writes small and humbly, without vanity, without self-admiration. Albert Schweitzer, the Alsatian philosopher, theologian, physician and musician, combined his talents and became a great humanitarian in French Equatorial Africa from 1913 on, where he worked for the poorest, establishing extensive medical facilities which received financial support from all over the world.

His even and simplified writing shows
Concentrated thinking ability
Love of detail
Introversion
Strength to carry responsibility, ethics
Tenacity to achieve the impossible (see Schweitzer's *t*-crossing)
Clarity and overview
Sharp discipline and self-control
Perfect organization (even distances between words and lines)
Inner modesty
Smallness of numbers (not materialistic)
Determination (small but triangular, energetic lower *g*-loop)
Persistence (extending final letters in Alsac*e*, Schweitze*r*, ergebene*r*)
Utmost diligence, economical way of using his time

UNEVENNESS

Unevenness in a handwriting appears as soon as the writer invents his own letter formations after leaving school and its trained writing forms. He can now create new, artistically influenced forms, can change the inner rhythm, the laws of arrangement. The individualistic varieties range from eccentric, extreme forms to new, dynamically created forms as this Picasso sample shows. (A)

(A)

The unevenness stems from the concentrated power of a genius. There is speed, dagger-like finals, inner drive, passion.

This is a man who is compulsively stimulated by forces he must obey. Every little stroke has the stamp of his art: the capital *Q* in *Que* shows the lightness, the charming playfulness. The shape of *Arte,* for instance, which looks in its simplicity like a living body, shows humor, the ease with which original forms are created.

(B)

How do we see the differences in the form niveau in these uneven writings? (B) is equally uneven, unquiet, has some daring swinging curves but cannot reach the high form niveau of Picasso's; the stroke picture is not eruptive and the forms are known.

212

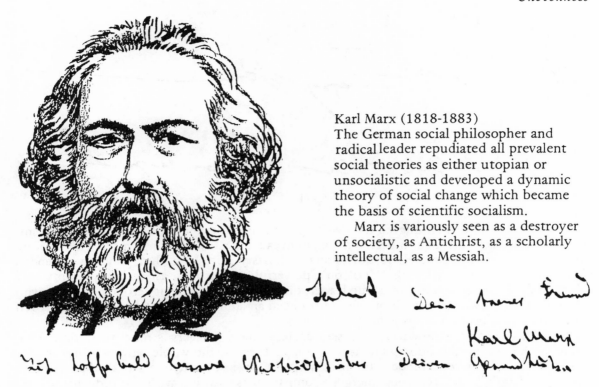

Karl Marx (1818-1883)
The German social philosopher and
radical leader repudiated all prevalent
social theories as either utopian or
unsocialistic and developed a dynamic
theory of social change which became
the basis of scientific socialism.

Marx is variously seen as a destroyer
of society, as Antichrist, as a scholarly
intellectual, as a Messiah.

His handwriting is almost illegible with its uneven, small middle zone with its continuous left trend, digging into the past. The unquiet handwriting with its wavering lines and the narrowness of the letters reveal a scientific mind, impatience and diligence — complete dedication to the task.

(A)

(A)   Napoleon's illegible handwriting is an extreme case because it belongs to a powerful personality, driven by enormous willpower, as the dagger-like strokes, the connected words, the straight lines prove. The unevenness inside the words shows ambivalence; but the whole chaos is organized by a compactness which shows elementary strength.

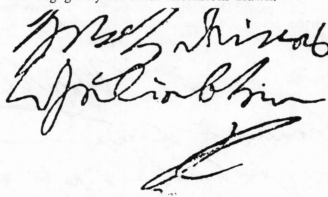

(B)

In comparison, here is an uneven handwriting with similar extensions, illegible letter forms. We can now easily distinguish between a high niveau and a lower form niveau. This uneven, unpredictable writing is merely restless, impatient, hasty, with long, thin, playfully-extended final strokes. Compared with Napoleon's powerful end-strokes, these imply empty verbosity, not the inner security of a true leader, one of the greatest conquerors in history, who promoted the growth of liberalism, who introduced an admirable code of laws and improved the economic condition of his people.

In Napoleon's handwriting one sees aggressiveness in every stroke, passionate emotions in the accent-like i-dots, and in the compactness of the whole writing an inner fire, ready to burn and to explode. In his sample (A), we see not one stroke that shows a moment of fatigue or decreasing energy. Compare these strokes with the ordinary writing of the sample (B) — how negligently are these extensions drawn.

The most famous, uneven handwriting of the genius is visible in the fluctuating, back-and-forth falling letter forms of Beethoven. We see in this 'wavering' a restless genius overpowered by the soundwaves coming to his inner ear. But also in this writing we discover the inner compactness, the periodic return of rhythmical forms, which seem to be guided by higher imagination; when we look at the first word on the second line we see curves of rare harmony and beauty.

Unevenness, yet rhythmical swinging, in the handwriting of a gifted dancer
with new, creative movements

214

FORMRHYTHM

Writing would lose its purpose if we all invented new, awkward forms which led to illegibility, like Napoleon's writing which is difficult to decipher. (It is said that he lost the battle of Waterloo because his desperate officers could not read his orders.) The variety of our writing forms embraces the legible, exactly constructed, as well as the individually-changed, disturbed form. If an adult still practices *school writing* he does not show an intellectual progression and the boring repetition of learned forms might develop into a kind of rigidity. If a form is united with a healthy, swinging movement and individualistically created, we speak of *form-firmness.* It may develop into varieties of forms with form-elasticity. Yet, in the moment when the form is being dissolved, we speak of form-disturbances.

The strong, legible form with a high form niveau belongs to a person with individuality, creativity and the desire to grow. He is simple, clear, ethical, persistent, and he has pride in and respect for tradition. In a low form niveau, legibility may belong to an infantile, immature person, dependent on rules, submissive, and one who avoids conflict at any price. If the form is stronger than the movement and dominates the script we have a person who tends to exaggerate his cultural background, loves formality and suppresses natural feeling and instincts.

The abstract painter Bernard Buffet

Individualistically-constructed writing forms reveal aestheticism, inner riches, and resistance to stereotyped, mechanical patterns.

The beautiful, charming actress Michèle Morgan

[signature]

Sarah Bernhardt

Form-mobility and form-variety reveal abundant interests, adaptability, seizing of opportunities, elasticity of the psyche and creativity.

how much I love you
ly seven lines, It wo
at least seven years
as that!

Love,
Lorne

When the inner movement is stronger than the form-feeling
we see the wild final strokes of an aggressive personality.

216

SPECIAL FORMS OF FORMRHYTHM

We find in handwritings individualistic rhythms which we do not see in typical formrhythm. We see odd singular forms — perhaps someone falls in love with his own creative letter forms and repeats them. Some letter forms arise from the unconscious and cannot be avoided. To these unwanted forms belong the series of directional pressures. We have *directional pressure from the past* which is seen in the to-the-left-bound downstrokes:

It means the writer suffered during his childhood from illness, poverty or psychic pressure in the parental home.

It results in   Disappointment
                  Discouragement
                  Easily influenced character
                  Self-protective attitudes to cope with anxiety

In *directional pressure from the future* the downstrokes are bent to the right and show: fighting one's fear of the future with stubbornness and self-esteem.

In the *double-bent lengths* we see
Heavy bodily and psychic crises
Resistance to natural instincts
(In this special case, leg-trouble has unconsciously formed the lower loops, reflecting the disease.)

Special forms of Formrhythm

The third directional pressure comes from above in caved-in t-crossings. They show that parental and school authorities have haunted the child.

[handwriting sample]

Strong differences in sizes of middle zone letters

Disturbances of self-confidence
Irritability

[handwriting sample]

Omission of downstrokes

Lack of roots
Lack of determination

[handwriting sample]

Supported and covered-up letter forms

Inhibition
Anxiety
Stilted behavior
Rigidity
Stiffness
Arrogance

[handwriting sample]

Swollen lower lengths

Physical and psychological deterioration
(67-year-old Swiss writer Conrad Ferdinand Meyer)

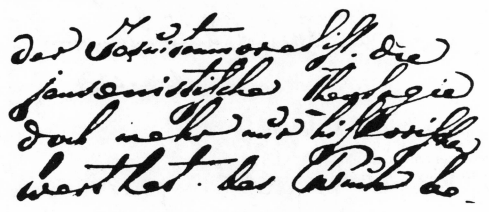

The downstrokes look like tree stumps. The strokes are broken, filled with ink and crowded at the end of each line. In the writer's last depression phase no self-control is possible.

Narrowness and crippled letter forms

Insecurity
Inhibition
Anxiety

Blotted, closed a and o vowels, d and g-heads

Insincerity
Inferiority
Secrecy

Printed letter forms

Literary interests
Escaping into printing (a cover up)
Hiding a weak character behind a façade of strength

Symbolic forms

Dollar Sign in the capital *S*

Sex symbol

Special forms of Formrhythm

Musical notes, quavers, violin and bass-keys in Mozart's writing

Omitting of important letters or letter parts

Weakness of concentration
Nervous irritability
Insincerity
Carelessness

Writing of mentally disturbed people

King Ludwig II of Bavaria (1845-1886) was the patron of Richard Wagner. In the year 1866, King Ludwig's insanity appeared and confined him to one of his fantastic châteaus on Lake Starnberg, where he committed suicide by drowning. Isolation is seen in the circular movement around his signature.

Friedrich Nietzsche (1844-1900) German philosopher, taught classic philology at Basel. His work had a poetical intensity that reflected the sensitivity of his mind and his devotion to music. In this chiselled, beautiful handwriting we see the young Nietzsche, before he became insane towards the end of his life.

Nietzsche's deteriorated mind is apparent from this enlarged, smeary, insecure, clumsy writing. What difference between the first sample (page 220) and this one. Tormented by pain, he created the 'superman': "The will of man must make the superman, who would be above good and evil."

Extreme letter formations

Powerful sensation-type, strong libido, earthiness, super-emotional actor

Displaced pressure shows displaced libido (energy seeks a variety of outlets).

Uncontrolled fluctuating slant

Ambivalence
Weakness in decision-making

Subconsciously crossing own letter formations means not liking to admit faults.

221

all the dangers, Shakespeare's

Letters look like numbers = good mind for financial matters

Yours sincerely

In a poorly developed handwriting

Impersonality
Modesty
Lack of talent and intellect
Banality
Being conventional
Simplicity

Ornamentation, empty talk, is visible in these exaggerated, conventional letter forms.

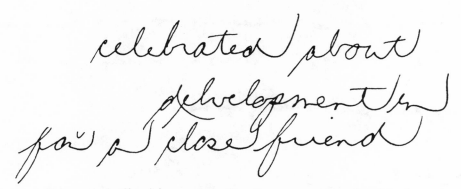

Stereotypically-rising endstrokes show a constant longing for
higher things in life without fighting for them, when the body of the writing
discloses a conventional, slow-moving person.

D-head formed like an ellipse

Expression of ambivalence

Sudden trembling strokes in a firmly constructed writing show the beginning of deterioration of body and mind which is called *ataxia* (Greek: lack of order) due to a breakdown in muscular coordination that manifests when voluntary muscular movements — like writing — are attempted.

Unnatural rigidity (more than regularity, bordering on compulsion, in a stilted, overexact handwriting)

223

[handwritten text]

Writing with an extra thick pen may indicate a desire to express strength, to make oneself noticed and to hide personality; or it may be the need to produce the heavy, saturated stroke picture of the sensation type.

THE STROKE

The stroke is the basic element of writing. If we were to use a metaphor and compare writing with a melody, the stroke would be the sound of that melody. No two people have the same 'stroke.' The stroke is the main vehicle of expression in the writing picture. If we see an ornamental writing with a flat stroke we know that the writer is superficial. We may detect a variety of character traits from the stroke - gliding, determined, rhythmical, soft, rigid, elastic, dynamic, caressing and many more - but there are three primary stroke structures: *the homogeneous stroke, the amorphous stroke, the granulated stroke,* which were defined by Rudolf Pophal, who also stated that the inner structure of a stroke does not change and that the stroke mirrors the depth of the personality and cannot be changed voluntarily.

The *homogeneous* stroke gives the writing a unified look.

Clear, pure, strong quality
Active, flexible, efficient
Willpower
Desire for success
Harmonious
Moderate temper
Faithful to oneself
Inner stability
Reliability
Inner purity
Conscientiousness

The *homogeneous* stroke looks like a firm-woven tissue with shades of light and dark.

Homogeneous stroke in the handwriting of a scientist

The Stroke

The *amorphous* stroke has a darker, muddy quality, as if it were executed with a painter's brush. The firmness has disappeared, the inner cohesion hurt. The stroke is characterized by

No vivacity
Psychic monotony
Lack of differentiation
Looseness
Burnt-out, washed-out look
No structure
Porosity
No clarity
Stained appearance
"Knitted" look

The *amorphous* stroke shows

A monotonous character
A character without differentiation
Boring person
No creativity
No inner firmness
Unreliability
Irritability

The amorphous stroke has no inner structure, much like the texture of a cake which has not been in the oven long enough. The main characteristic of this stroke is its complete lack of differentiation — it is monotonous and lifeless. The amorphous stroke often occurs in the writing of psychopaths and alcoholics.

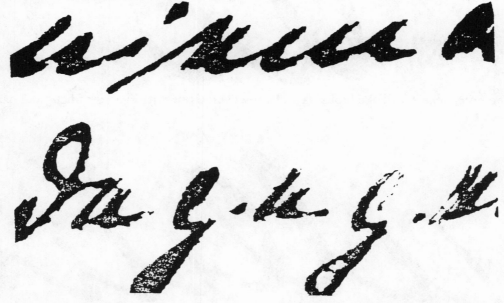

Enlarged under a microscope we see the irregular edges of the stroke like fringe, as if the pen had not the power to complete a healthy, strong curve or line.

226

The *granulated* stroke is indifferentiated, dissolved, and appears as particles, grains or granules. The inner continuity is interrupted and the stroke gets a more or less coarse-grained appearance. Drug-addicts and alcoholics create such ropelike strokes, with heavy disturbances at the edges.

The character of such a stroke writer:

No vitality
No creativity
Weakness
Nervousness
Inner instability
Unpredictability
Irritability

Granulated stroke of a psychopath
Note the rope-like texture of the granulated
stroke. We see the sudden interruptions,
the frayed edges, the insecurity
of the downstrokes.

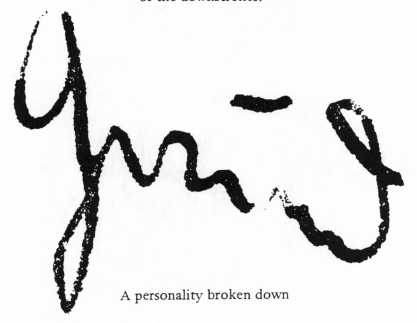

A personality broken down

STROKE VARIATIONS

This thin, flexible stroke is that of General Eisenhower. It is a mixture of varying tension, sharp and low pressure, and sharp and pastose strokes.

Napoleon's strong-pressured stroke with isolated sharp traits
and moments of smeary pastosity.

Change from Mussolini's youthful, insecure stroke — when he still lived in obscurity — to the dramatic, clublike stroke, demonstrating willpower.

228

The same insecure mediocrity
in Hitler's writing stroke before he
reached power

Smeary pastosity in the stroke
reveals Hitler's muddy morality

Smeary, brushed-on linear strokes
describe J. Paul Getty's organizational ability.

Ingrid Bergman's refined,
intelligently-chiselled stroke

Stroke disturbances at a young age are warning signs of trouble in the psycho-physio-logical make-up of the writer, stemming from deep in the motor-central-nervous system, producing all kinds of stroke irregularities. This trembling, chronic, irregular stroke shows signs of pathological origin.

Stroke disturbances in the handwriting of a 35-year-old nurse, who refuses to acknowledge the onset of deterioration of muscular coordination.

Dear Father St Charles Ill
I wish to request a mass offered
m or near October 26. For all the

Sudden changes of direction in the stroke deserve special attention. The smooth flow of the movement cannot be sustained, and certain harsh, obstinate, angular letter formations appear. The more energy the writer uses to hide his arhythmical, anti-gliding stroke, the more one sees the deep-rooted inability to control anxiety about possible physical illness.

Your next event is trip to India
not sure when, February

When we observe only a few trembling strokes surrounded by healthier ones we find more an episodic nervousness which can be caused by overwork or aging and which can cause sporadic interruption of the flow of the writing.

just a joke, but a goodone by
Capek

The softer, the more refined, gentle and fragile the stroke, the finer and more delicate are the physical and psychic impulses.

Your emotions are controlled
by reason
logical thinking

If the structure of the stroke is homogeneous (uniform in texture and quality), we see security, health, physical endurance, psychic energy and a strong *libido*.

One should not be misled by the degree of pastosity and pressure of this stroke. If one looks more carefully one discovers some breaks in the third stroke of the *m* in *my* (last line) the *r* in *writing* (third line). There is a deep-seated irregularity which may erupt at some point into real stroke disturbances.

I hope will be able to decipher the writing so she can help decode my personality

231

STROKE DIRECTION

above
mind and spirit

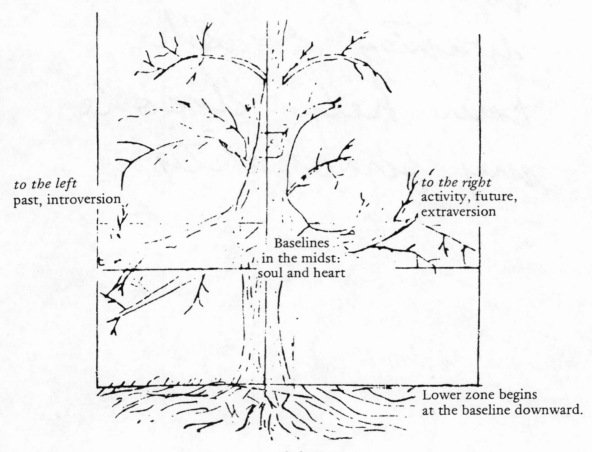

to the left
past, introversion

to the right
activity, future,
extraversion

Baselines
in the midst:
soul and heart

Lower zone begins
at the baseline downward.

below
Body, the materialistic region, instincts

In the chapter *Symbolism of Handwriting* we drew a cross to demonstrate how our writing stands in space, the writing paper. The cross symbolized the erect human being, arms outstretched. This symbolic tree with its branches striving upward, to the right, to the left, corresponds with letter-forms. The more we strive with our upper loops to the heights, the harder we have to fight gravity. The stronger the regions of materialism dominate, the deeper are the lower loops. They are anchored deeply in the earth like the roots of a tree.

Our writing develops in four directions: up, down, right and left, and as we learned

232

in the movement chapter *Depth of Writing*, into the third dimension, depth. Let us look now at our four directions: the stroke to the heights, the upward stroke, is a symbol of enthusiasm, excitement, striving ambition.

If the stroke toward the heights is insecure and weak the writer has a more passive nature. Reduced, crippled upper strokes show a low degree of spiritual expansion and activity. The writer lives a quiet life — no high voltage, no emotional excitement.

The downward stroke is the symbol of stability, firmness, sometimes tenacity, aggression and stubbornness (if a child does not get what he wants, he stamps his feet in anger and impatience).

The downstroke, symbol of anchoring and roots in the materialistic regions.

If the downward stroke is weak we see lack of determination and endurance. It belongs to a person who is easily impressed and influenced.

233

In our Western world the stroke to the right symbolizes forward movement expansion, extraversion. To the right always means activity, the embracing of mankind.

TEDDY KENNEDY

Opera singer Lily Pons

William Howard Taft (1857-1930)

A powerless stroke to the right symbolizes resignation. It can show a person's obsession with passive acceptance, for instance, masochism.

The more the stroke slants to the left, the greater the inner restriction, the more the tendency to withdraw, to detach oneself from society.

234

Pronounced leftward traits show love of the past, the desire to preserve things, to preserve sentimental ties and bonds with people from the past.

SIGNATURE

Centuries ago, writers employed seals to authenticate their communications. Such seals were generally recognized and as a result forgers were deterred. In the Middle Ages, each trade had its own emblem—a key, a hammer, a fish—usually painted on the wall of the residence. Even now there are in many small cities in Europe metal emblems hanging in front of the shops of the baker, the carpenter, the locksmith, the fishmonger, the barber with his large brass plate swaying in the wind. These emblems serve as "signatures."

In these days, the characteristics of the written signature and the composition of the underscoring express the character of the writer, who sometimes subconsciously exposes in his signature and its paraph just what he tries carefully to hide in his text writing. The signature remains therefore the most important part of the writing because it is done with great sincerity. It demonstrates the writer's social position, his own felt value, his self-image. The signature is *une carte de visite psychologique,* the psychological calling card. There are often differences between text-writing and signature; if there is artificial modesty in the text and exaggerated self-esteem in the signature the fundamental discrepancies and conflicts in the character of the writer are apparent.

sometimes its like this

In this sample the writer shows modesty in the text
and contradicts it in his signature, by using enlargement and flair.

Today the signature and its underscoring (paraph = a flourish made after a signature, originally as a safeguard against forgery) are modified. Yet they present the true, clear manifestation of the writer. One sees his pride, his disorder, his presumptuousness, his wickedness — in sum, one sees his psychological make-up. From the simplified underlining of the most impenetrable thicket of lines we are confronted with the writer's temperament, his hidden vices.

F.A. Mesmer (1734-1815), an Austrian physician who practiced hypnotism in connection with his theory of animal magnetism. It is no wonder that for the most part he preferred anonymity.

If the signature is illegible, the writer does not want to be recognized. It is mostly a sign of caution; if he sets a period after his signature, it is a sign of mistrust. One who has nothing to conceal writes with a legible open signature. Underscoring shows the need for a pedestal for a show-off personality. The *King-Signature* is the one without underlining; the name is important enough to stand alone.

In the signature we see attempts to impress the reader. The signature is usually free of school writing. It consists of the most expressive graphic gestures of the individual. One may have many signatures during a lifetime; as a child, as a student (when trying to find one's identity) and in maturity. The mature signature usually does not change until disease or old age when the composition of the simplified or amplified signature begins to alter.

In the following pages we will compare the signatures with text, to determine if the signature differs from the text-writing, for it is in the text that the true nature of the writer may be concealed.

If the letters of the signature are the same height as those of the text, and if there is no underscoring, it implies modesty and simplicity radiating from the personality of the writer.

Albert Einstein (1879-1955)

Unified personality, natural, adjusted, modest, content, genuine, wants to be understood; (formulas, text and signature equal in height, width, form; a harmonious togetherness).

Sven Hedin (1865-1952), Swedish explorer in Central Asia

If the signature is larger than text, more self-esteem and vanity are apparent. Personal interests are more important than worldly concerns.

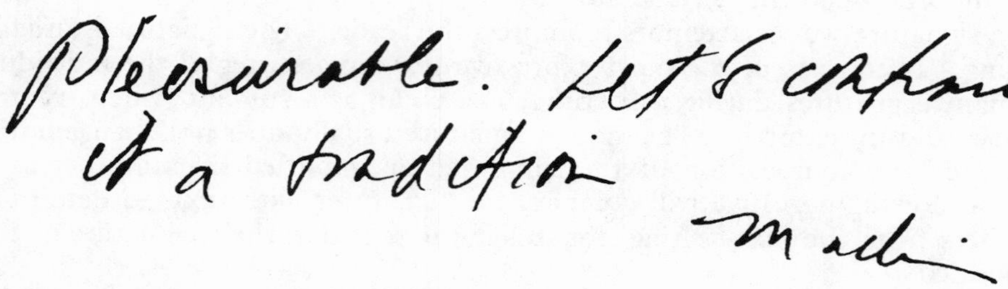

[handwritten signature]

If the signature is smaller than text we find insecurity, weak self-confidence, showing off, more modesty than there is in reality; more arrogance; "Look how humble I am."

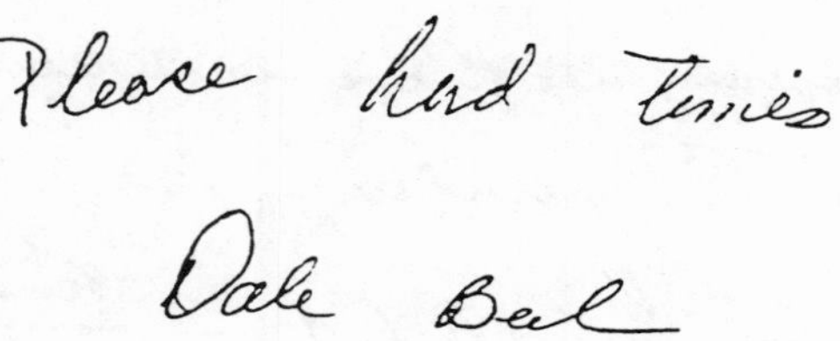

[handwritten signature: Dale Beil]

In this signature we see the second name *Beil* (the married name) smaller than the first name *Dale*. That means that at the time the writer was unmarried (Dale, symbol of youth) she had more illusions and dreams than she has now.

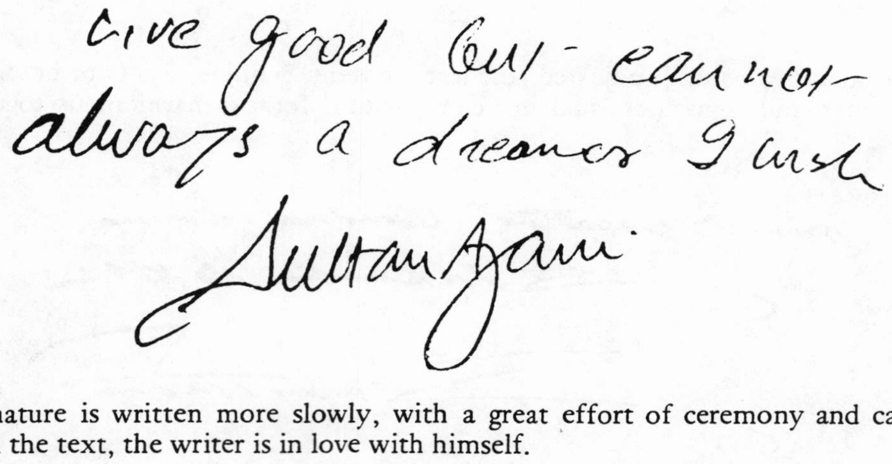

[handwritten signature]

If the signature is written more slowly, with a great effort of ceremony and carefulness, larger than the text, the writer is in love with himself.

He is a very hard working person

If the text is written slowly and the signature is scribbled in a hurry the writer regards his signature as a routine job.

hope I'll have the opportunity to visiting very often

Giuseppe Giovanni

If the text writing has a vertical slant and the signature tends more to the right, the writer is cool at the office and emotional at home.

like New York but we have visited

When the text has a right slant and the signature is vertical, the writer lives enthusiastically for work whereas his home life is cool and his social life artificial.

239

I lived in Bombay till

When the text is legible and the signature is illegible, the writer's private life is well-organized; in business he is secretive; no one may know exactly how he handles his affairs.

...ear to you there are divine things more beautiful than words can tell

Leaves of Grass – page 125

Walt Whitman

Holograph excerpt signed by Walt Whitman for *Leaves of Grass*

If the signature is larger than the text writing and has more pressure and pastosity, the writer is concerned how he is seen and regarded.

Text and signature of Louis Pasteur (1822-1895), French chemist and bacteriologist

If the signature is as vertical as the text, the writer expresses reserve and dignity.

The more new wrinkles a woman acquires the smoother she becomes."

O. Henry (1852-1910), American writer

If the signature is placed in the middle of the writing paper the writer thinks he is the center of interest.

If the signature is placed toward the left margin, the writer feels bonds to the past, has lost courage and tends to melancholia.

Yours sincerely,

If the signature is illegible the writer is self-protective, mistrusting, does not want to be recognized. He is deceitful, calculating.

241

Signature

Completely illegible signature
The writer avoids responsibility instinctively; he hates to be nailed down.

1908

1920

1925

1929

1937

1938

1943

1944

29. 4. 1945

The falling signature

As a 17-year-old, Adolf Hitler produced this typical falling which did not change even at the height of his career. It looks as if he is gliding downward, rushing to defeat and death. His life power was broken from the beginning.

Very sincerely yours,

Sincerely yours,

John F. Kennedy shows in his *rising signature*
a refined, intelligent, enthusiastic driving force.

The crossed-through signature

Lord Byron (1788-1824), English poet

If a signature is crossed through, the writer is disappointed with his achievements. We see in Byron's signature his stormy fight with pen against British society, his disappointment after fame, political exile, as well as physical chains (he was lame from birth).

Frank Lloyd Wright (1869-1959), American architect

Radical innovation as to both structure and aesthetics made Frank Lloyd Wright the pioneer of modern architecture in the United States and Europe. Should he have had reason to cross through his name?

Margaret A. Thatcher
Prime Minister of Great Britain

The powerful capital *M* in *Margaret* rolls out from the inside to the outside. This shows that she thinks before she speaks or acts.

The wide, so-called *protection*-stroke in the form of an umbrella as the t-crossing of *Thatcher*, symbolizes an inherent desire to govern, to lead, and to care for people. Her strong pressure shows her willpower, the creative curves, an inventive mind. With the long and strong underscoring-stroke she emphasizes need for power, authority; her nick-name, the "Iron Lady," is justified.

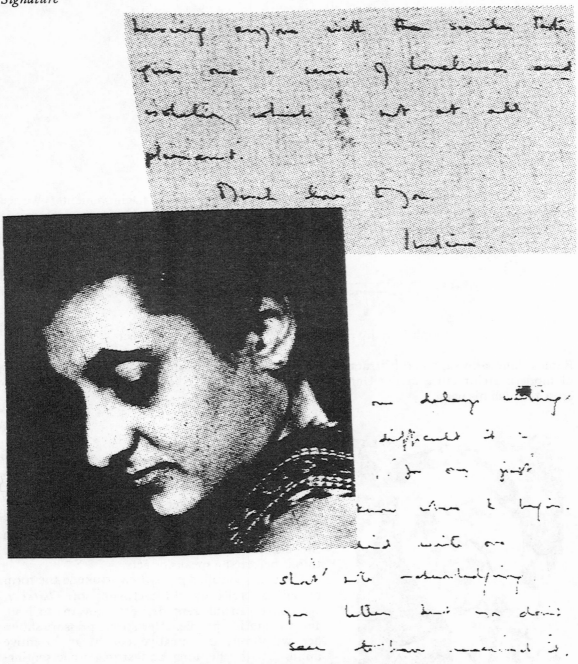

Indira Gandhi (1917-1984)

The intellectual, reason-dominated thread-like writing with the small middle zone, the wide distances between words and lines, show loneliness. The straight lines show self-control and willpower; the exactly set i-dots show conscientiousness, and the ascetic simplicity of the skeleton writing shows a pure thinking type. The daring, wide embracing capitals — last two words before *Indira* on the left side letter — show creativity and the ability to rule with an open mind, receptive to new thoughts and ideas.

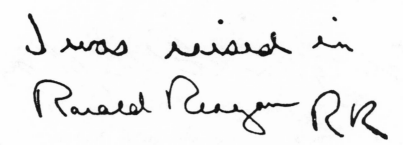

Ronald Reagan is a sensation type; he lives for the here and now. He acts best in a crisis. His colorful, pastose, vital stroke picture shows enjoyment of life. He is reason-dominated, pragmatic, has a strong will and determination. His fat, round, i-dots reveal a sense of humor. The simplicity of the letter forms shows an uncomplicated intellect.

Nancy Reagan unconsciously shows devotion to her husband by the use of his capital *R*; she lives for him. Her handwriting is stilted and meager, without lower loops (not materialistic). The juxtaposed letters show an analytical, clear intellect. Her self-discipline borders on asceticism. She has creative taste, is well-organized and warmhearted.

Shirley Temple as a child

The same slant, the same simplicity as an adult

It is rare that people use the same signature throughout their lives because the signature is modified according to the inner development of the character. Yet, there are some exceptions. Some do not change their signatures out of an unwillingness to leave childhood.

The change in signature

1) George Washington at the age of 17, a land surveyor

245

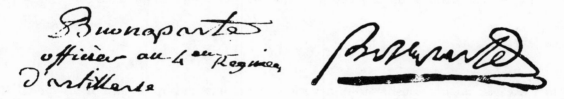

2)   3)

Both later signatures (2 and 3) stayed throughout his life. Note the playfully elaborated *t*-bar which balances the strong *g*-loop.

Dramatic changes in Napoleon's signature (1769-1821)

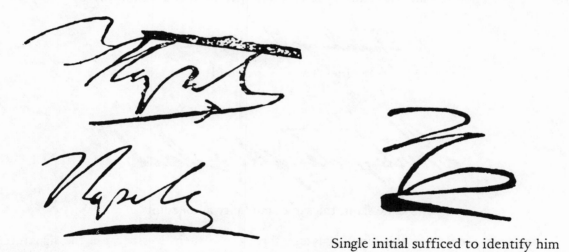

Napoleon Bonaparte signing the oath of allegiance as lieutenant of the artillery.

Single initial sufficed to identify him

Three signatures of Napoleon at the height of his power

Napoleon's deterioration and despair after his defeat at the Battle of the Nations at Leipzig when the war of Liberation began

246

The exploding strokes in Napoleon's signature
after the last battle of Leipzig, which sealed his fate

Despite the dramatic changes in Napoleon's signature, the *Gestalt,* the basic principles of his movements, graphic configurations, stay the same because they are directed from the brain.

The Rise and Fall of Three Powerful Men

Napoleon (1804), newly elected emporer

Napoleon (1809), the most
powerful man in Europe

Napoleon (1815), after Waterloo defeat

Adolf Hitler about to
become Führer (1932)

Adolf Hitler (1936), dictator
with enormous power

Adolf Hitler (1945) before his suicide

Sincerely,

Richard Nixon

Richard Nixon (1955)
an ambitious vice president
(Note the similarity between
the capital *N*'s of Nixon and
Napoléon)

Nixon (1973), a re-elected
president at the zenith of
popularity and success

Richard Nixon after Watergate, stripped of his power

These three terminal signatures seem to show the subconscious effort to conceal identity
by making the signature totally illegible.

Charles Dickens (1812-1870) wrote from experience
(his father's imprisonment for debts, and his sad youth).

Underscoring of a signature — one line or a whole ensemble of lines, as in Charles Dickens' — gives the signature an individualistic touch, because it is done independent of calligraphic teachings. The movement of the underscoring stroke is free and personal and more revealing than all preceding text-writing, for it does not follow any rules. It is the region where the unconscious reigns — fantasy, vanity, self-admiration. If the underscoring consists of two parallel lines, which imprison the name of the writer with one stroke above and one stroke below, we see caution, reserve, independence (as it is unconsciously reflected by Chopin).

Frédéric Chopin (1810-1849), Polish composer and pianist, framed his signature with parallel strokes above and below.

The circle or closed ring is a common symbol of anxiety, of the desire to enclose and shelter the self, to protect it from harm, as by a magic circle. Encirclement may therefore indicate withdrawal, caution, mistrust, self-protection.

Signature full of angles

Reinhard Heydrich, "Hangman of Europe," Nazi leader.

If the last letter of a signature is sharply pointed and massive, we see violence, need for power, and in the case of Reinhard Heydrich, brutality; note the dagger-like, ruthless downstrokes in his signature.

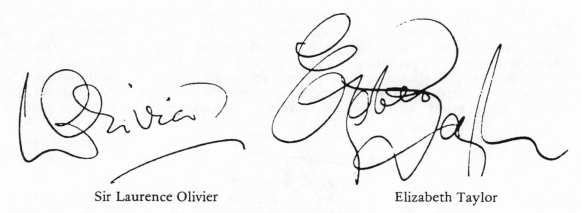

Sir Laurence Olivier   Elizabeth Taylor

Olivier's and Taylor's creative, efficiently drawn curves. There is not one straight line in their dancing, rhythmical writing. Their world is filled with aethereal elements of fantasy and emotions, on which they draw to recreate characters.

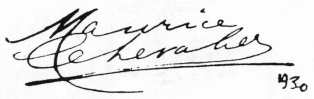

If someone creates a huge curve below his signature he admires himself enormously, as we see in Maurice Chevalier's signature. In his signature we see two underlining curves, the first coming from the capital *M* of *Maurice,* the second from the last letter *r* of *Chevalier.*

The simplified, legible signature shows natural honesty. The terminal hook at the *a* of *Greta* shows tenacity, and near-aggressiveness, toward society.

The disciplined, angular European handwriting of the first Prime Minister of Israel, Ben Gurion, breathes toughness and honesty. He demands from himself as much as from others.

EXTRAVERSION AND INTROVERSION

Psychologist Carl Jung categorized personality as either *Extraverted* or *Introverted*, depending on the individual's attitude toward the world. The extraverted type is sociable, likes to explore, and is in need of steady contact with his fellowman. The introverted type is less adaptable. He may be shy, self-centered or self-sufficient. He is often looked on as egotistic, which is not necessarily so — as egotists are found as well among extraverts.

To hate is never

Sample of typical *extravert writing*
The writer reaches to the right, to the future, to people,
upward into the intellectual spheres, downward to the materialistic regions.

If enrichment and effective stylization are added, we find persons who need external stimulation to function; they may be sensation-hungry, longing for new contacts and high self-presentation. They thrive in the limelight, in exaggerated activity, and may be excessively emotional.

The extremely large writing of a talented photographer

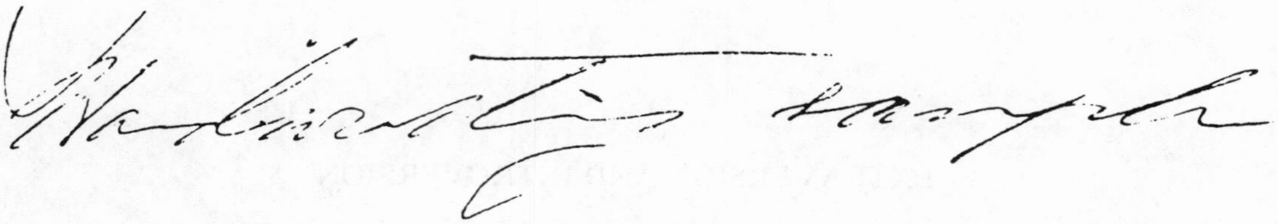

Extraversion with tendency to hysteria is seen in this exaggerated handwriting with its dissolved middle zone. The thread-like double curves are a sign of the over-adaptability of a hysterical person who lacks decision-making ability and character stability.

The graphological expression of extraversion

Speedy script
Right trend
Right slant
Large, angular garlands
Wide and deep garlands
Full ovals and forms
Wide left margin
Increasing left margin
Long upper and lower extensions
Rising lines
t-bars and i-dots long or placed forward
Large triangular lower loops

Janet Gaynor (1906-)

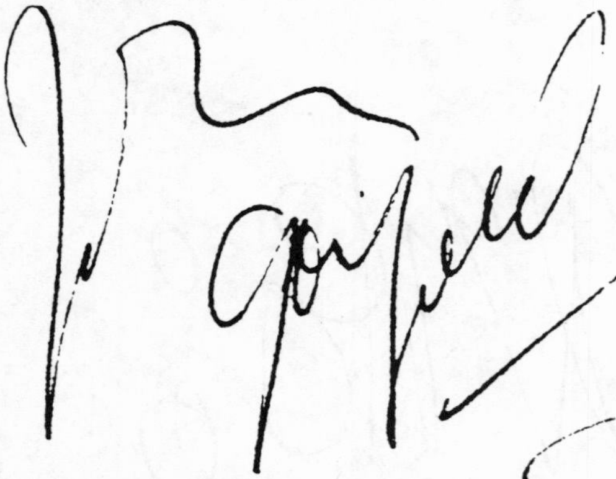

John Garfield (1913-1952)

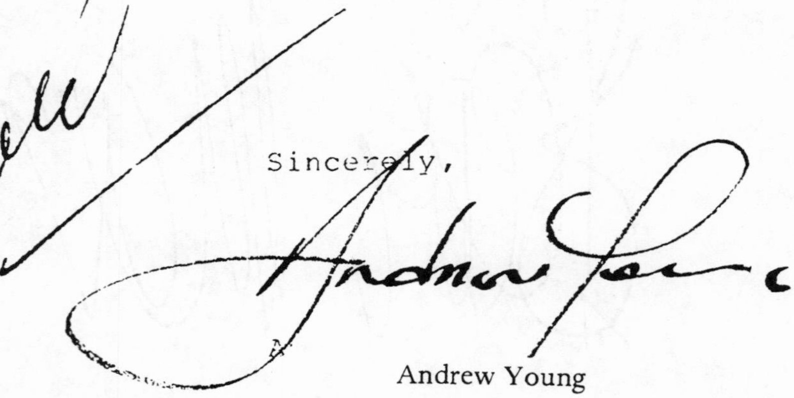

Sincerely,

Andrew Young

The handwriting of the introvert is smaller, more controlled, and the movement is more directed toward the center — so-called *centripetal.* The letters are unpretentiously formed and simplified.

The graphological expression of introversion

Small writing
Simplified writing
Meager
Small garlands
Often small angles
Narrow
Economical arrangement on the paper
Mostly vertical slant
Arcades show reserved attitude
Narrow margin
Large spaces between words and lines
Decreasing left margin (cautiousness)

Speedy-thinking introvert, strong self-discipline,
imagination, bonds to the past, to tradition, delicate sensitivity, easily irritated

Introversion with tendency to compulsion

The complicated, compulsive character is full of inhibition, tormented by scruples and anxieties. He turns his back to the world to escape, as if into a shell. Whereas hysteria is a psychiatric condition characterized by outward movement, as the exaggerated samples show, the compulsive person turns inward with his suffering and shows a rigid, narrow, often cramped handwriting.

The graphological expression of compulsive handwriting

Mechanized
Monotonous

The graphological expression of compulsive handwriting (continued)

The exaggeratedly small
Illegible, smeary, blotted
Very narrow
Rigid arcades
Rigid regularity
Breaks, welded strokes
Supported angles and arcades
Pedantically drawn horizontal lines

Compulsion and rigidity in puberty

The rigid, compulsive handwriting of the Nazi-Propaganda Minister Dr. Joseph Goebbels who forced himself to act against his better judgment—he forced himself to preach victory and died by his own hand in the end, taking his wife and six children with him. The signature of Goebbels is written like the German *Fuss* (clubfoot); people called him 'devil's advocate.'

PART THREE

PICTURE OF ARRANGEMENT

INTRODUCTION

Psychologists tell us that emotions and attitudes are expressed by our physical relationship to space. The ways in which we walk, sit, gesture all reflect, although sometimes subtly, the emotional state. In psychology this is referred to as body language. In handwriting, the parallel is arrangement—how a person distributes his script on paper. The space symbolizes how he perceives himself in relationship to society. Some writing stands pointed, shy and restrained; some writing is small; some writing leaps about the page without regard for aesthetic appearance. Each of these reflects the personal style. Shyness and fear cause some people to limit and restrain outgoing movements. Exuberance produces the grand gesture. Joy produces soft and easygoing behavior. Anger produces the hostile gesture. All of these find symbolic expression in our writing.

We create the space-picture in three different ways. First, we occupy the writing space with the size of our letters. Some letters expand upward, striving away from the middle zone in a *centrifugal* movement. Others concentrate on the middle zone in a *centripetal* movement. When they extend downward, away from the middle zone, or upward, away from the middle zone, we speak of large differences in lengths. When they are concentrated in the middle zone we speak of small differences in lengths.

Large differences in lengths (centrifugal)

Small differences in lengths (centripetal)

257

Introduction

The gaps created between the letter forms during the left-to-right movement determine the width of our writing. It may be narrow or wide. In the first way of "*occupying space*" we create:

the size of the handwriting
the differences in length
the width in the horizontal movement

The second way of *occupying space* deals with the *direction of the writing in space.* The *slant* determines the specific direction in which the writing moves in relation to the base line. In a right slant the tendency is to rush forward to the right; a vertical slant concentrates more on the up-and-down movement. Each of these directions (slant) represents an emotional or psychological tendency. Also relevant here is the direction of lines. We can, for example, identify a goal-oriented person by the way he writes even lines in an even slant. The more the lines and the slant fluctuate, the more confused is the writer. He does not know where to go, he has no aim. Determination and security are visible in straight lines.

The third way we *occupy space* is reflected by the *structure of the space picture.* This is created by the halts and resumption of movement. For a new beginning, just as the tiger in the jungle becomes momentarily motionless to get the scent of his prey before he rises and jumps, we have to interrupt our writing movement, to orient ourselves on the paper. We must observe the distance between words and lines. We must observe the left and right margin, which gives the script structure, even or uneven. When we write there is no bell, as on a typewriter, to warn us that we are approaching the end of a line. Many writers have so much to say and so little general overview that their terminal endings fall below the lines. These persons lack economic planning ability, lack of organization-ability and adaptability.

Hitler's uneconomical, over-the-edge-falling,
terminal letters symbolize overacting and verbosity.

While writing is actually done on the surface of the writing paper, a plane, there is also a *three-dimensional aspect. The first dimension* is the *horizontal one,* created by writing from left to right (width). In oriental writings like Arabic, Hebrew and others, the horizontal movement goes from right to left.

The *second dimension* is the vertical one, created by the up-and-down movement during the writing of the letters (the lengths).

The *third dimension* is created by the pressure of the pen on the paper—one can feel the pressure by lightly running the fingers across the back of the paper. We have seen this distinctly in the air bridge, where the pressure ceases when the pen flies through the air, forming an imaginary line.

In the writing process we divide the writing space into lines, the lines we divide into three zones: the middle zone with its small letters, the upper zone with its upper loops, and the lower zone with its lower loops. The picture of arrangement can vary considerably. In some writing the middle zone is dominant. In others there are crippled or expanding

258

loops. Some writers make overlong, penetrating lower loops, others create shrunken ones.

Word separation differs from one person to another as well. Some writers overcrowd the space by writing too narrowly. Others tear up the space by writing widely separated words.

Overcrowded space

Torn-up space

In analyzing handwriting, then, letter-length, letter-size, line- and letter-slant, and the amount of space between letters, words and lines, must all be considered. In total, these are the elements which constitute arrangement.

LARGE SIZE

In ancient times writing was focused in the middle zone. There were no upper or lower loops.

Latin Capitals on the shaft
of the *Trajan* column in Rome

SAEPTIMAPOSTDEC
ETPRENSOSDOMIT
INTEREALONGUM

The so-called Uncial writing
(uncial = Latin) a twelfth part
of an inch; a large, rounded letter
used in Greek and Latin manuscripts between 300 and 900 A.D.

The middle zone remains the core of modern writing. It is measured by the size of the small letters a, e, i, o, u, etc. Over 3mm is regarded as a large, and below 3mm a small handwriting.

Publications and magazines.

A middle zone overexaggerated in height is usually created by a person who is very much occupied with his own Ego and who demands room for the expression of his 'precious' personality and who knows how to get it. In French they say: "Ôte-toi que je m'y mette," ("Move on, I'm taking over.") Such a taking over is a short step from arrogance and pretentiousness.

This extravagant, large writing has both centrifugal movements, fleeing from the center into heights, and centripetal movements. Look at the proportionally small *m* in *am*. In this writing we see vitality, the desire for freedom and independence, and an optimistic concept of life wherein courage, joy and zest reside. This powerful writer, a fashion designer, can use her dreams, her illusions, her visions for her work. And her fantasies about imminent success may be justified. There is flamboyance combined with aggressiveness.

Broadway star and dancer Anne Miller is accustomed to the sweeping body movements which are reflected in her writing. She is demanding, powerful, efficient in her stage work and able to fulfill all the demands made of her.

The daughter of President Ronald Reagan proves, with her wide-stretching upper loops and deep-penetrating lower loops, that she is willing to make it on her own. Her love of the unlimited, extraordinary things in life is apparent.

Large Size

Fluctuating large size shows insecurity, sensitivity, a flexible mind.

politics were

The sudden, irregular, larger and smaller letters in the middle zone reveal disturbances in self-esteem; if word-endings get smaller, we see diplomacy and psychic insight. When the final letters are larger than the preceding, we see naiveté and outspokenness.

Gaily lightly

Enlarged upper zone letters imply exaggerated self-esteem; in this sample with a low form niveau we see boldness, impudence, and a kind of pomposity. When the lower loops strongly penetrate the lower regions we see a person who is deeply anchored in tradition and earthly things and who has strong roots.

upon whether a solid (eg: magnesium hydroxide) or a liquid is used. showed how it's possible

When the middle zone letters are so high that they reach into the upper zone, the writer is very self-conscious and tries to meddle in others' affairs. When the final letters in the middle zone penetrate the lower regions and fall below the base line, we see a person who is materialistic.

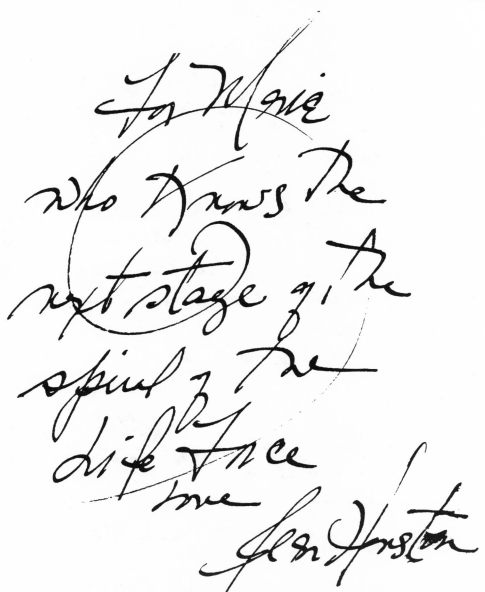

For Marie
who knows the
next stage of the
spiral of the
life Force
love
Jean Houston

In an extremely high form niveau the upward and downward expanding strokes reveal a desire for spiritual growth and at the same time the desire to penetrate the subconscious, the material realms.

SMALL SIZE

Small writing is the result of a centripetal movement; it starts from the periphery and aims toward the center, toward the Ego.

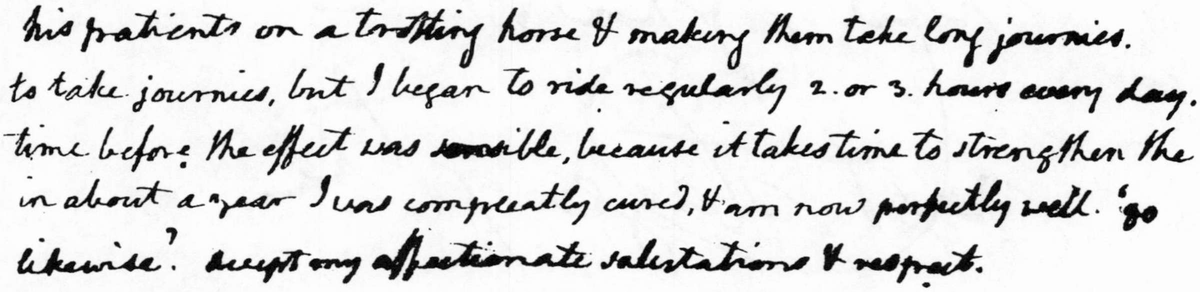

[handwritten text, reproduction of Jefferson's letter:]

> his patients on a trotting horse & making them take long journies.
> to take journies, but I began to ride regularly 2. or 3. hours every day.
> time before the effect was sensible, because it takes time to strengthen the
> in about a year I was compleatly cured, & am now perfectly well. 'go
> likewise'. accept my affectionate salutations & respect.

How humble is this legible writing of Jefferson. It shows a sense of reality, soberness, un-pretentiousness and impartiality. The more someone knows, the more he concentrates on the simpler, essential things in life.

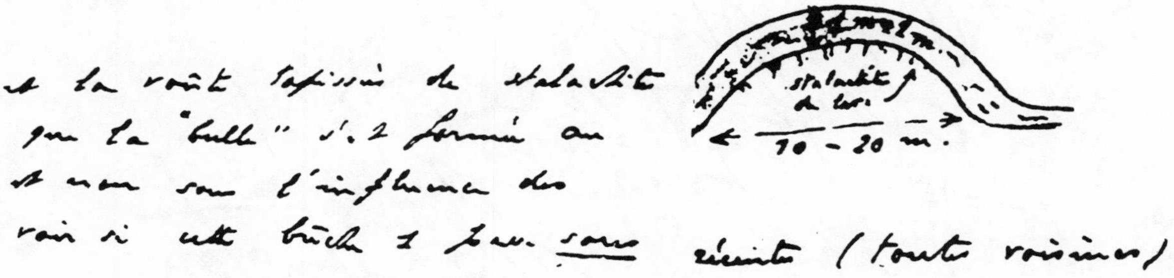

[handwritten text with a small sketch/diagram, partly in French]

Pierre Teilhard de Chardin (1881-1955), French philosopher, Jesuit, anthropologist, also writes small. In a high form niveau we find such scientific types as Schweitzer, Roentgen, Einstein—the intellect dominates, thought is penetrating.

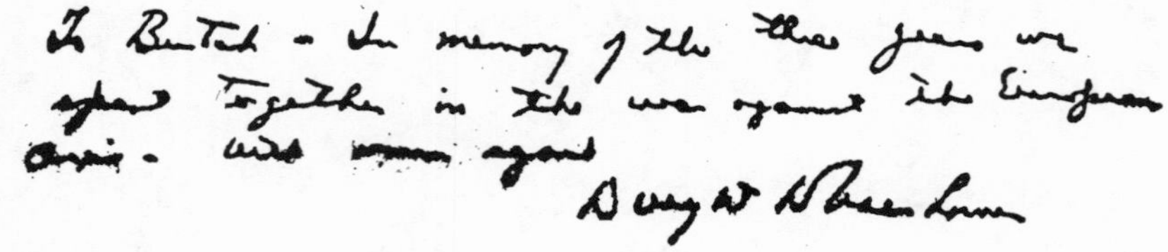

[handwritten signature of Dwight Eisenhower]

In Dwight Eisenhower's extremely small writing we see a concern for detail, bordering on pedantry.

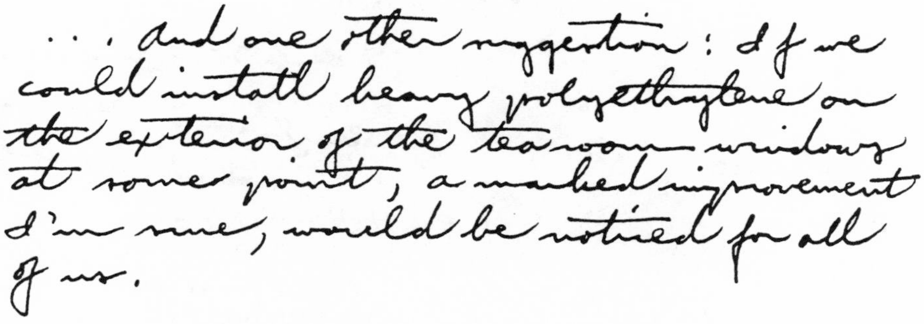

[handwritten sample]

> ... and one other suggestion: If we could install heavy polyethylene on the exterior of the tea room windows at some point, a marked improvement I'm sure, would be noticed for all of us.

In a small writing with mediocre form niveau we see the characteristics of the small writer's delight in detail work, adaptability, preference for a small circle of friends, inherent submissiveness and narrow-mindedness. He is anxious and feels vulnerable, as in the sample above where the small middle zone shows inhibition.

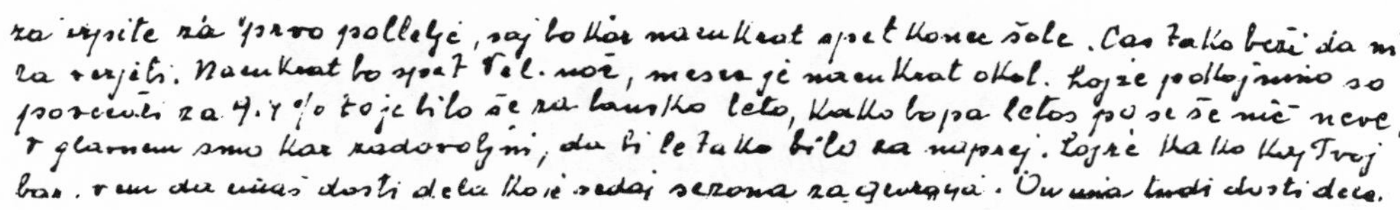

[handwritten sample]

A microscopic, small writing demands much of the reader's attention. The detail work is done beautifully in this sample, but what kind of person hides behind such unusually refined smallness? Is it not a hermit, who feels suppressed and retreats into solitude, who is without social initiative, who is surrounded by books and who probably enjoys research?

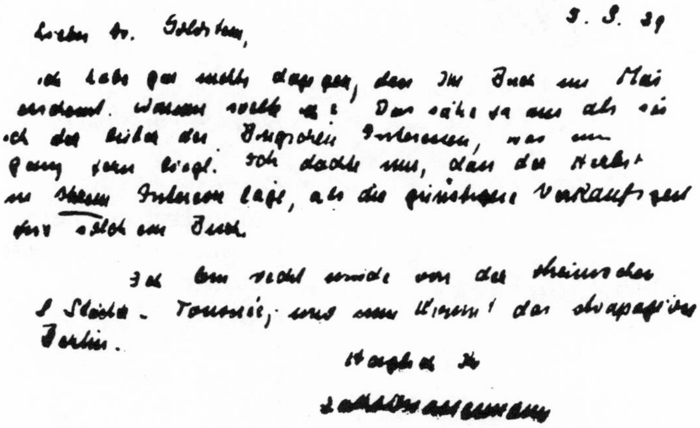

[handwritten sample]

Jacob Wassermann's writing. He was born in Germany, a famous Jewish author (1873-1933). He based many of his novels and short stories, such as *Kaspar Hauser,* on historical persons and events. As in his novels, Wassermann concentrates in his handwriting on the most minute detail; every letter is clearly executed. Still, one can see that the upper zone is higher than the lower zone. Despite the overall size of the tiny writing, the *relative* height reveals an intellectual at work.

265

Small Size

Table for Smallness

It was real nice

Low Form Niveau

No vitality
Measured self-control
Submissiveness
Pedantry
Pettiness
Dogmatism
No fantasy
Indecision
No self-confidence
Greed

High Form Niveau

Striving for overview
Concentration
Detail-loving
Intellectuality
Criticism
Family-oriented
Patience
Ability to sacrifice
Precision

Table for Large Size

Low Form Niveau

Naiveté
Impostor
Megalomaniac
Acting without thinking
Uncritical optimism
Egomaniac
Excessive vanity
Show-off
No tact
Narcissism
Likes to speculate
Childlike optimism

High Form Niveau

Dignity
Enthusiasm for heroism
Honor, aristocratic ideas
Courage
Activity
Demand for authority
Convincing mind
Imagination, fantasy
Desire for greatness
Pathos of emotion
Passion
Pride, generosity
Leader qualities
Need for "space"
Striving for independence

266

WIDTH

Horizontal expansion in writing is called *width*. The handwriting is regarded as wide when the distance between the small letters *m* and *n*, etc., is wider and longer than the downstroke is long.

Width is a centrifugal movement, striving away from the center (the Ego) to the 'you.' It shows besides goal-orientation, ambition, eagerness, impulsiveness, desire for freedom and broad-mindedness, and if it happens to be in a low form niveau, superficiality and careless-ness:

(1) Width in a lower form niveau

(2) Width in a high form niveau

As we see in these samples, the movement is loose, forward-striving; in the first it implies receptivity to new things, freedom, artistic talent and generosity of an aristocratic nature (high form niveau). In sample number two we see creativity, myriad interests, scientific curiosity and an over-eagerness to know everything and to dominate everything. The writer is without prejudice, industrious, likes to live in large rooms, needs independence, likes to socialize, needs elbow room, and chatters a lot—a real extravert.

267

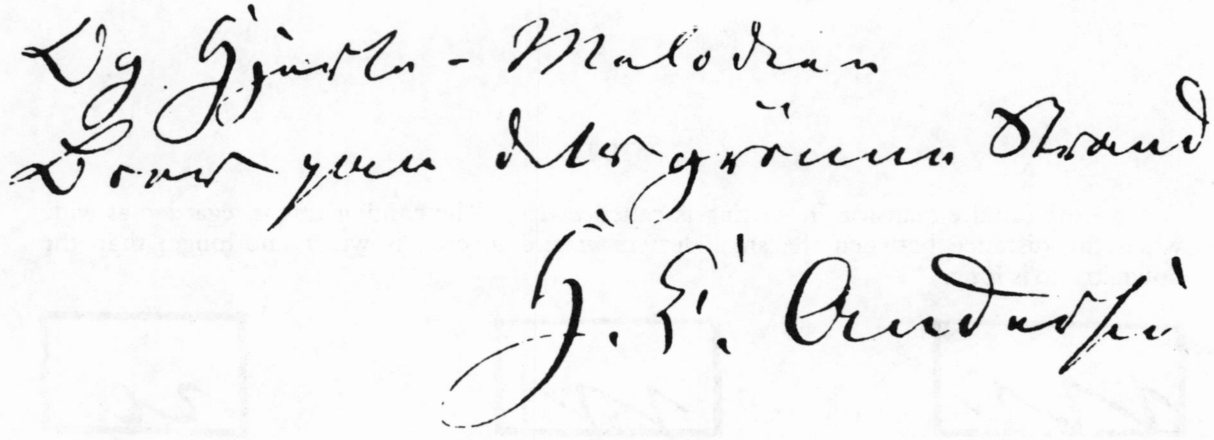

[handwritten signature of Hans Christian Andersen]

Hans Christian Andersen (1805-1875) spins his fairy tales with wide-swinging garlands.

Secondary Width

If the expansion in the middle zone is not created by broader letter forms but by large spaces between the individual letters we call it *secondary width*.

Secondary width   *[handwritten: no noon]*   secondary width

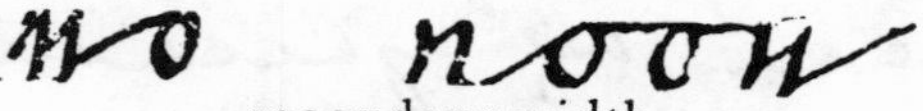

Secondary width shows a writer who is eager to be correct and who wishes to give the impression of generosity, broadmindedness and laissez faire, laissez aller (room for everyone, do as you please).

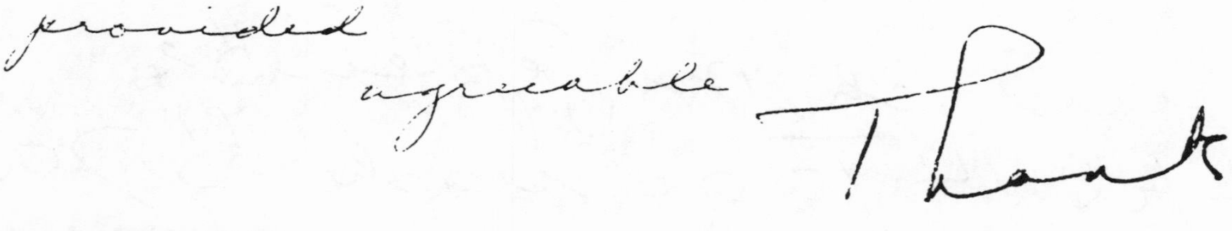

[handwritten: provided   agreeable   Thank]

Special forms of Width

1) Width and regularity = activity, desire to conquer the world
2) Width and regularity and angles = strong-willed, goal orientation
3) Width and irregularity and looseness = no inhibitions, no self-control

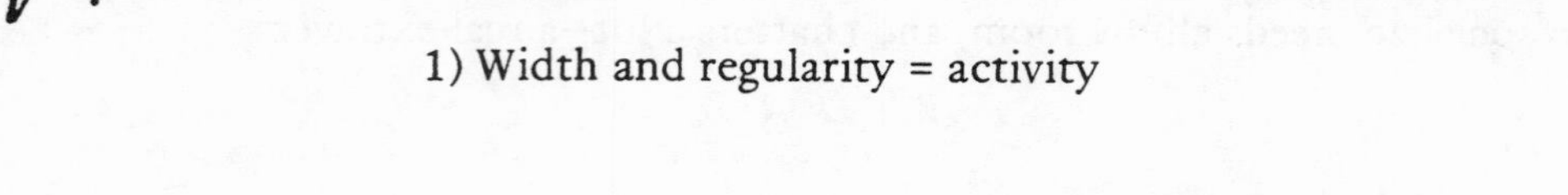

[handwritten: Honorable Sir!—]

1) Width and regularity = activity

268

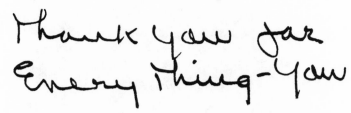

2) Width and regularity and angles = strong will and goal-orientation

3) Width and irregularity and looseness = no inhibitions, no self-control

269

NARROWNESS

In contrast to the forward, to-the-right, to-the- "you" movement of the wide script, the narrow script appears reserved, restricted, tamed. In width we find an open-hearted character who will fight for his independence and freedom. In narrowness we see cautiousness and the desire for seclusion. Narrowness can arise out of a strong inner tension. In a normal handwriting, narrowness shows a movement with the "brakes" on, an inner self-control, but it can also mean fearfulness and narrow-mindedness. The guiding image of a generally narrow-writing person is usually discretion, fear, lack of courage or cautiousness. Such a writer has no desire to explore or to take risks. He moves with small steps. There is lack of spontaneity, too much reserve and hesitation. It takes him a long time to make a decision.

as you know, I love him. But I hope that he will heal. If he does not, pleasure to know him

In this sample we see the reserved cautious movement of someone who does not expect much of life. He has a moderate, self-controlled character. He needs to submit to authority, may have an inferiority complex, and may have little self-confidence. In his work he is meticulous, almost pedantic, and he is in love with details.

at same time as an excellent teacher of musical form, of counterpoint, of orchestration a.s.o. In any Institute for musical education his activity will prove of a rare value for his pupils.
New York, 26th March 1939

Bruno Walter

In this high form niveau writing of the famous conductor Bruno Walter we see the positive qualities of a narrow writer—a personal ethic, need for honor and self-respect, conscientiousness, a striving for clarity and order. We see critical ability in the sharp endings of the angular middle zone—a personality with great determination and energy.

vienna,   *interesting composer*   *recommend*

Narrowness and regularity plus angles and vertical slant = self-control

feelings change Mrs. , my children midnight

Narrowness combined with irregularity and rigidity = restriction

abstract expressionist style.

Narrowness and evenness = security, self-confidence

I was born in Miami.
I go to a boarding in New Jersey
I live in Sarasota, Florida.
Dear Lieta,

Exaggerated narrowness, where the letters seem to be glued together,
means immaturity, the need to lean on someone, dependency.

could end in my dreaming.

When in a normal wide writing the word endings decrease and become more narrow it
means the writer becomes more economical, more cautious about his own person, as if to
compensate for earlier generosity.

Special Forms

Secondary narrowness = narrow letter forms, wide connections

Ethical tendencies
Striving for clarity and order   *factory*
Danger of formalistic thinking
Lives according to principles
Accent on appearance

271

Narrowness

Narrowness arranged and formed

Concentration
Tension
Intellectual limitations
Inner strength

Narrowness empty and dry, without life

Tendancy to pedantry
Limited views

Change of Narrowness and Width

Flexible mind
Insecurity about goals
Insecurity in relationships

Tables for Width and Narrowness

Width

Initiative is strong, dynamic
Vivacity
Openness, looseness
Mobility, naturalness
No inhibitions
Loves to be comfortable

Width (continued)

Difficulty in concentrating
Eagerness, ambition
Demanding authority
Love of action
Verbosity
Extraversion

Narrowness

[handwritten note: I love you. You are a very kind and caring man. Maybe the next year will bring us less anxiety and a nice paced life.]

No initiative
No spontaneity
Tension
Timidity
Embarrassment
Anxiety
Inhibition
Narrow-mindedness
Mistrust
Reserve
Control
Self-discipline
Concentration
Tenacity
Persistence
Scientific thinking ability
Caution
Calculation
Taciturnity
Introversion

SLANT

All letter forms develop from the baseline up, move in different directions—to the right, to the left—or they stand vertically (against gravity). In spontaneous, upright-striving we see the will to be independent, courageous and 'upright.' Whereas an animal moves horizontally over the ground, the human being moves vertically on the earth, and (like plants and trees) raises his head to the sun.

Our writing slant expresses our relationship to the environment and it changes often according to mood. In an official address one usually writes with a vertical slant whereas a passionate love letter tends to be written with a right slant. If a writer never changes his slant we see an element of stability which we may then use in evaluating his character.

When we look at a right slant, we observe that the upstroke determines the direction whereas the downstroke becomes a contra weight. The upstroke leads, the downstroke receives, symbolizing openness to the world. The more the right slant tends to tilt over to the right, the stronger is the upstroke accentuated and the downstroke more passive. All unconscious expectations are symbolized by the right slant, a yielding to the *you*, to society, altruism and strong emotions. Some writers glide easily over the paper with wide relaxed movements to the right, showing abundance of feeling. The right slant means the heart rules the head. Goethe believed: "Feeling is everything," as symbolized by his to-the-right flowing letter forms:

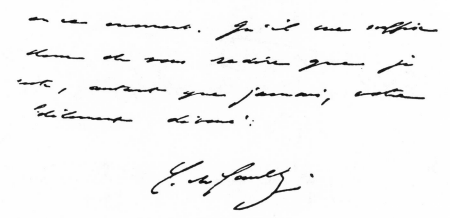

Charles de Gaulle

In General de Gaulle's dynamic, speedy right slant we see impulsive moments, sudden bursts of excitement, used so effectively in his speeches. It shows devotion to goals, the ability to sacrifice even life for France, and a predominance of power.

The more the right slant increases, the more susceptible is the writer to influences of all kinds. He gives in to instinctual urges, is submissive; he needs to lean on someone for warmth and comfort. He is easily excited, easily irritated, has little control or inhibitions. He loves people, is easily seduced, lacks critical abilities and may tend to hysteria.

When the right slant is counterbalanced by vertical endings, which stand up against the emotional current like a dam against an overflowing river, we see a passionate person with self-discipline.

Slant

Right Slant in a High Form Niveau

Wilhelm Furtwängler (1886-1954) German conductor and composer, shows in his handwriting enthusiasm, devotion to art and music. The last letter arises vertically in his signature—he stems the tide of overflowing emotion shown in the right slant.

Right Slant in a Low Form Niveau

Need for sensations, absence of reserve, absence of moderation

Table for Right Slant, High Form Niveau	*Table for Right Slant, Low Form Niveau*
Connected with the world	Easily influenced
Dependent on society	Yielding out of weakness
Likes entertainment	Not independent
Extraverted	Tendency to give in quickly
Diversity of interests	Not able to be alone
Readiness to oblige	Lack of reserve
Altruistic	Always on the go
Sympathetic	Thoughtlessness
Courteous	Immoderate
Kind	Easily seduced
Informal	Impulsive
Strong instincts	Hasty
Impressionable	Easily irritated
Passionate	Sentimental
Can be jealous	Curious
Emotional	Need for sensations
Strongly motivated	Self-pitying
	Obsessive
	Unstable

276

Right Slant in a Low Form Niveau

VERTICAL SLANT

The first writing signs (about 5000 years ago), the Sumerian, Egyptian, Chinese 'characters,' were formed vertically, symbolizing the human body which moves upright, with self-esteem and intellect, into the world. The vertical-writing person has the same attitude—a conscious ruling of mind and will power and a cautiously practiced distance from people. In a vertical script, the letters stand upright; they don't care about their 'neighbor'-letters, especially in a so-called juxtaposed handwriting, where almost every letter stands isolated.

mind coming anytime after 7-30 tomorrow as he is later reaching home.

The person who writes with a vertical slant judges objectively and coolly because his reason dominates. He even regards personal experiences with a certain criticism and cautiousness. His mind is conscious and clear, in contrast to the right-slant-writer who will be often over-whelmed by passionate impulses and enthusiasm.

We see in the above sample of a vertical slant the virtues and faults of the writer. His upright position mirrors an upright noble character, straight-lined nature, a fidelity to the self, objectivity and reserve. The writer isolates his letters just as he isolates himself from his surroundings, with some arrogance and pride. This is sometimes done out of inner coolness, sometimes out of inner shyness, or sometimes because the writer thinks himself better than others and overestimates the power of his mind. Nobody can influence him, nobody can lure him from his path of duty, his responsibilities. Objective judgment accompanies him all his life. The reproach one makes of the strict, vertical writer is lack of feeling, because his passion is suppressed by the power of reason, which rules him.

Oh, when I was in love with you.

Then I was clean and brave.

Table for Vertical Slant

Upright
Need for freedom
Overcoming earthiness of the senses
Spontaneous activity
Self-confident
Intellectual interests
Reason-dominated
Reflective
Reasonable
Contemplative
Love of solitude
Reserve
Seriousness
Moderate
Cool
Indifferent
Egotistic tendencies
Self-control
Self-discipline
Wise
Objective
Calculation
Introversion
Endurance
Willpower
Faithful to personal ethics
Self-sacrifice

Ezra Pound (1885-1972), American poet, lived mostly abroad in Italy and Spain. During the war he broadcasted anti-American propaganda from Italy; he was declared insane after the war and placed in a prison hospital. In 1949 he was awarded the Bollingen prize for *Pisan Cantos,* which anticipated and pioneered many trends in modern literature. His influence on modern lyric poetry was strong. The proud upright handwriting shows critical judgment, emphasized in the sharp pointed end-strokes.

[handwriting sample]

In right slant writing the heart rules; in the vertical slant, reason rules; and in the left slant we see overcontrol, fear. The left-slant writer creates an unnatural distance between himself and his neighbor. It may stem from anxiety, fear of the "you," an attachment he wants to avoid. He does not like to make commitments. The left slant represents a shielding, defensive gesture, a negative attitude; the writer feels he must ward off imagined dangers. Over-strict, to-the-left-tending writing symbolizes an unapproachable person.

[handwriting sample]

In this strong, left-slant writing we see striving for independence and the attempt to be different, a rejection of authority, opposition and stubbornness. Also we detect a bit of arrogance, a blasé attitude, a lack of adaptability. There is strong activity behind this left slant construction. Self-conquest and self-restraint are necessary to create such affectation and the forced attitude of opposition to one's fellowmen.

[handwriting signature]

In this left slant signature, one sees forced self-discipline. Out of insecurity the writer suppresses every natural feeling, keeps his distance, is reserved, and tries not to be involved in other people's problems.

Special Forms

Middle zone vertical or left slant, upper loops right slant

[handwriting samples: "wonderful" and "love"]

Struggle between feeling and reason
Suppressed desire to yield to others
The Ego (middle zone) dominates

Middle zone right-slanted, upper lengths vertical to left-slanted

home.

Strong contrast between motivations

Right slant increases

started tending

Explosion of temperament, lack of self-control, lack of caution, impatience

Increased vertical word endings

What else can I say? Life love make me very happy

Self-control, reserve, mistrust, suppression of feeling

Irregular fluctuations of slant (middle zone left, right, vertical)

to exist with God on this earth liberty, as free men unshackled the chains of tyranny.

Inner conflicts, chronic uncertainty, unreliability, unpredictability

first visited in 1551 Co dormin has grown into the world's most asked for change.

Table of Left Slant

what you will
you were very
Glen's personality.

Reserved
Unapproachable
Cautious
Shy
Escape from reality
Mistrust
Vigorous suppression of feeling
Inner insecurity
Vulnerability
Introversion
Egocentricity
Inhibitions
Self-conquest
Self-denial
Obstinacy
Extravagance
Not genuine, a phony
Vanity
Affectation
Pretentiousness
Subjective judgment

and two shades of eye shadow.
was a pink color and one was
My name is Cheryl

It is only natural that many teenagers use the left slant. They seek to be different. No school system in the world teaches left slant. To show opposition to rules and authorities they use a slant which symbolizes rebellion, revolution, anti-ness.

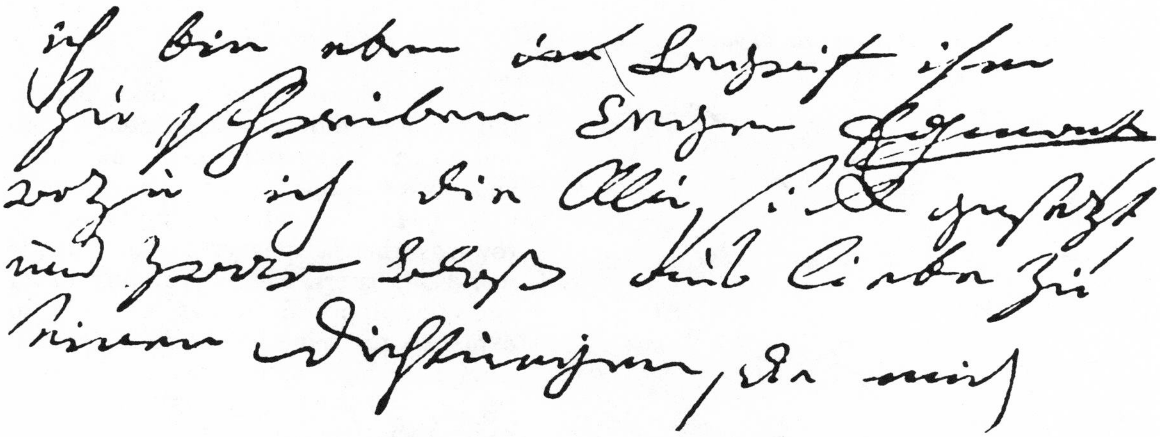

FLUCTUATING SLANT

[handwritten Beethoven script in German]

The fluctuating writing of Beethoven's script symbolizes genius torn by emotion, pain and suffering. He was deaf and could "listen" to his musical creations only in imagination—with his "inner ear." Rhythmical waves determine his writing picture; it looks like a colorful carpet, intensively woven out of fantasy, held together by will power (the straight lines and the precisely dotted i's). He is conscientiously devoted to his God-given talent. The chaotic lines are the mirror of the inner struggle of a creative giant thrown to the heights and to the depths while trying to find a form for expressing his inner visions.

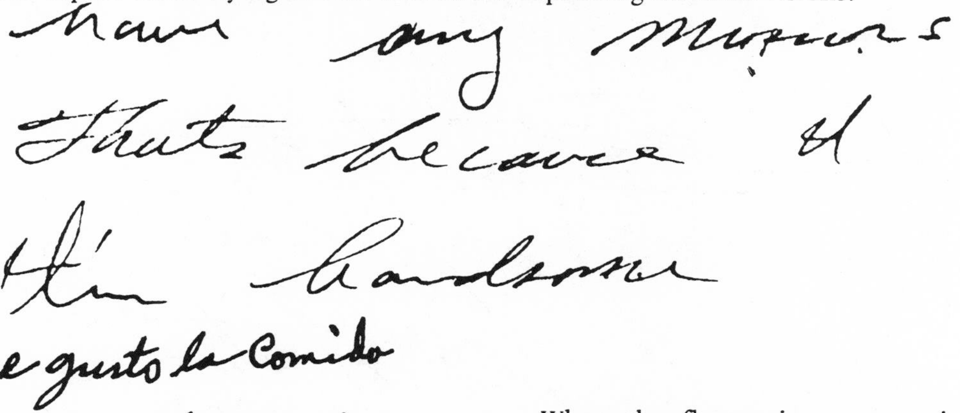

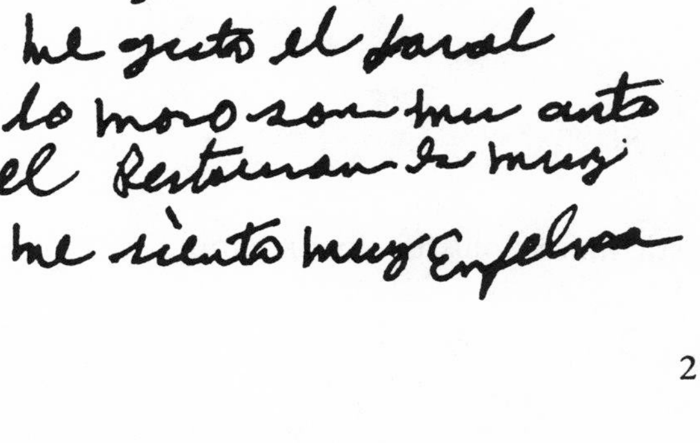

[handwritten script samples]

When the fluctuations appear in a low form niveau script we find insecurity, a vacillation between emotions and reason which makes the writer unpredictable and moody.

283

GREAT DIFFERENCES IN LENGTHS

Whereas the true size of a writing is measured in the middle zone, the expansion into height and depth creates a discrepancy with the absolute size of the middle zone and reveals a *decentralization of the psyche*.

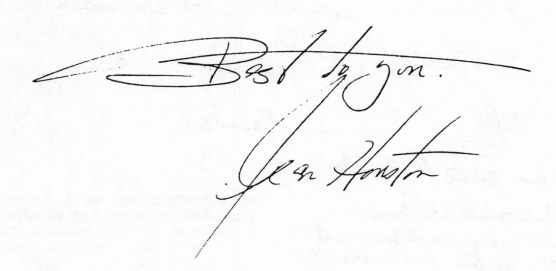

In this sample we see such a discrepancy: the crippled middle zone—center of soul and heart— is smaller than the upper and lower loops which are extended away from the center, the middle zone, towards the periphery, to the outside world. Writers with expanding lower and upper loops are restless, they try to explore, to experience their 'space.' They have high aspirations; they want to rise beyond their limitations; they seek to broaden their horizons.

When the middle zone remains small and undeveloped, as in the above sample, there is insecurity, lability, lack of self-esteem and self-confidence. These writers escape from themselves—a kind of decentralization of the psyche.

In a high form niveau, where the middle zone is small but firm, there is no danger of losing sense of self. There is only a development of new interests.

There are no spiritual and materialistic limitations for this free mind.

284

From the relatively small middle zone of Jacqueline Kennedy's writing grow long, beautifully-shaped curves to the heights, symbolizing intellectual yearning; and into the depths, representing materialistic interests.

The charming, unconventional, lissome curves of Marilyn Monroe.

From Marilyn Monroe's extremely long upper and lower loops we see her striving to be someone important. She was ambitious and longed for self-development. There is a rather healthy middle zone here; her expanding into the heights was not due to delusions and escapist tendencies but to a true progressive striving toward higher goals. There is an abundance of playful fantasy, as the swinging curves demonstrate. This also mirrors the danger of self-admiration, a kind of child-like narcissism, romantic dreams, restlessness, youthful impatience, love of excitement, adventure. The overlong capital *L* in *Love* shows the discrepancy between her dreams and the ability to give. She did not recognize the limitations of her character; there was an obstacle between planning and the fruition of those plans. She always wanted more, in complete dedication to her profession. But the over-large differences in lengths show distractability, extraversion and tensions which hindered quiet contentment. She was longing to stretch her intellectual capacities too much, trying to live in circles which were too demanding for her inherent limitations. The fluctuation between intellectual and materialistic goals was disturbing to her.

Table for Large Differences in Lengths

Escapism
Longing for growth
Never satisfied
Eccentricity
Inner tension
Progressive nature
Ambition
Competitiveness
Richness of contrast
Entrepreneur type
Versatility
Dissatisfaction
Non-uniformity
Tendency to accentuate differences
Unbalanced self-confidence
Sensitivity
Desire to broaden horizons
Many interests
Little restraint
Ambivalent nature
Discordant, conflicting natures

The samples to the right are chosen because of the small middle zone in comparison with high upper and lower loops. Note the discrepancy.

love my children

When all zones are large we speak of a *large* handwriting (size is measured in the middle zone); the character is balanced.

287

SMALL DIFFERENCES IN LENGTHS

To understand small differences in lengths let us once more concentrate on the importance of the middle zone, where the small letters reside: *It is the center of the psyche.* It houses the feeling capacity, relationship with the past, contemplation, effects of heritage. It mirrors the relation to the 'you,' need for love, altruism, generosity, empathy, unselfishness, compassion.
It is the center of the Ego and houses

Possessiveness
Egotism
Business acumen
Manipulation of others and environment
Indifference, calculation, envy, jealousy
Self-assurance
Irresponsibility
Activity, goal-orientation
Consistency, obstinacy
Verbosity, lack of inhibitions, dependency
Giving in easily, unembarrassed
Expansive ego; hates to be alone
Increased need for space
Aggressiveness
Readiness to attack
Wickedness

All these negative and positive qualities are offered in the middle zone. When we have a writing which is concentrated in the middle zone, on psyche and Ego, without longing to escape to the heights and to the depths with upper and lower lengths (to weaken, to dilute the power of the middle zone), we have a more penetrating view of the writer's character. It may be perfect, good and harmonious; or it may be vicious and boring, according to the form niveau of the writer.

Mahatma Gandhi (1869-1948)
Gandhi's strong but ambivalent middle zone
shows he relies on flexible, inner power.

Joseph Stalin (1879-1953)
Stalin's pastose writing bears some similarity to
Gandhi's in the dark, ink-filled stroke picture.

Both leaders rely on strong personalities. It is the quality of their letter formations in the middle zone which shows clarity (Gandhi) or muddiness (Stalin).

When the middle zone is accentuated and the upper and lower lengths reduced, we speak of centripetal movement, executed from the Ego. *Absolute size* of the writing is measured in the middle zone. *Relative size* includes the upper and lower lengths of the writing.

The more unified the heights of the small letters in the middle zone the more we see consistency, balance, harmony and loyalty in a character. The writer almost *rests in himself.* Between the Ego and the environment exists a constant, harmonious relationship. Pure feeling is more important to him than intellectual and materialistic interests. Such writers seem to us wise, humorous persons who can rise smilingly above daily troubles. Yet, if the upper and lower zones are non-existent or crippled, we must assume lack of intellectual excitement and tension. The writer without upper and lower lengths is utterly engaged with himself; he must have peace and quiet from which to draw strength.

In a conventional lower form niveau writing, small differences in lengths show a person who prefers to live like a snail (in the house) and who lacks lively connections with the world.

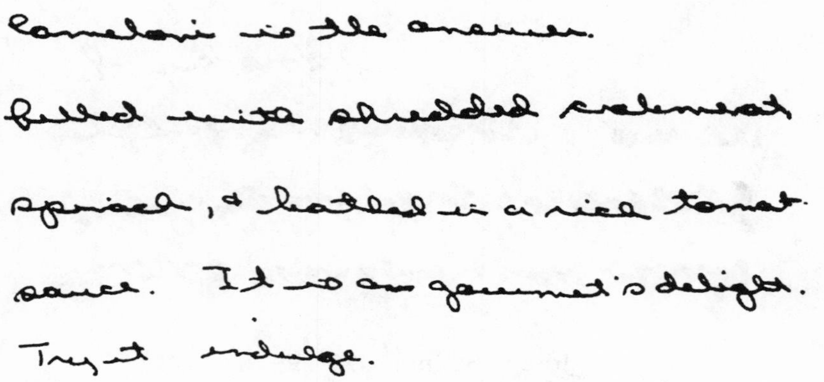
… is the answer.
filled with shredded crabmeat
spinach, & bathed in a rich tomato
sauce. It is a gourmet's delight.
Try it indulge.

Her household gives her happiness and satisfaction. Nothing else is required.

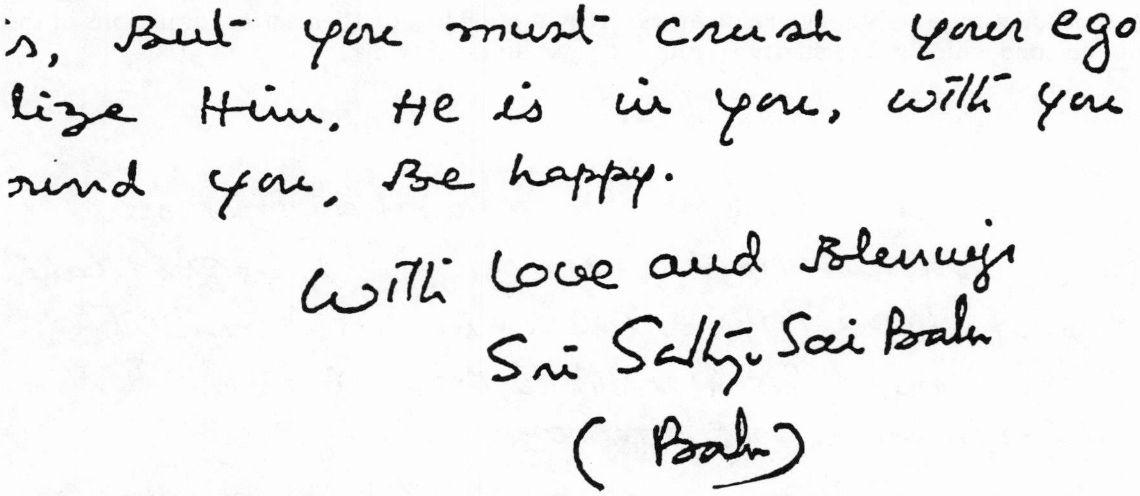
s, But you must crush your ego
lize Him. He is in you, with you
mind you. Be happy.
With Love and Blessings
Sri Sathya Sai Baba
(Baba)

Here is a wise man who preaches all the virtues of the small-difference-in-lengths writer. We see a harmonious, even middle zone, which shows inner strength. He is true to himself, consistent, self-content, self-aware and self-secure. He likes to stay in a consistent, balanced state. With steady, constant efficiency he fulfills his mission. His personality is uniform. His inner power is greater than his desire to move into other fields of activity. He is quiet, relaxed, calm, composed, and his strength is within. He is not materialistic; he is a feeling type and his heart rules.

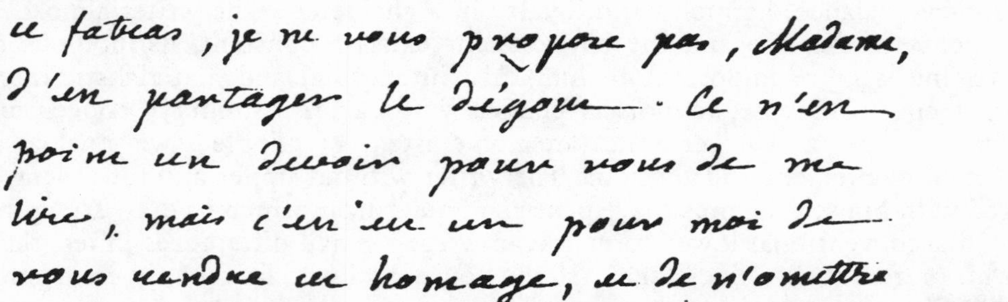
ce fateau, je ne vous propose pas, Madame,
d'en partager le dégoût. Ce n'est
point un devoir pour vous de me
lire, mais c'en est un pour moi de
vous rendre cet hommage, et de n'omettre

Jean Jacques Rousseau (1712-1778), French philosopher, author, politician, theorist has a modest, refined, chiselled script, without upper or lower lengths. It indicates an intellectually-driven mentality.

Table for Small Differences in Lengths

Concentration on the self
Self-restraint
Reserve
Moderation
Conservatism
Tendency to equalize differences
Tendency to decrease contrasts
Harmony of the heart and soul
Content, happy
Self-esteem
Self-sufficiency
Self-contentment, self-satisfaction
Indifference, narrow-mindedness
Adaptability

Albert Schweitzer's humanitarianism and altruism are reflected here.

Theodor Herzl (1860-1904), born in Hungary, was the founder of Zionism. His unpretentious, small writing, with its crippled lower lengths and the irregular upper lengths (look at the word *Brief,* 4th line) shows indifference to personal advancement. He lived only for an ideal—the Jewish State.

ACCENTUATION OF UPPER LENGTHS

According to the symbolism of space, the upper lengths show striving beyond the conventional into the spheres of enthusiasm and illusions, and sometimes further into speculation and dreams. If the upper lengths are much longer than the lower, we speak of a stronger stimulation, impulse, mobility and desire for freedom. If the upper lengths are drawn fully, with inflated upper loops, we have illusions and utopianism, visionary schemes for achieving perfection.

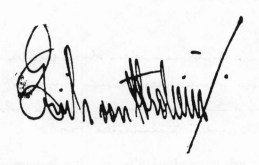

Erich von Stroheim's enormous upper loops show a striving for wisdom and education, and ethically-based pride; the meagerness reflects theoretical, abstract thinking ability. He is prejudiced, skeptical, has a strong sense of honor.

He has the highest ambitions, as the narrowness of his script demonstrates; he has a tendency to fanaticism. He is arrogant, has a compulsion for recognition, and is self-adoring. He lives in an aura of unrealistic desires, illusions and dreams; extravagance is easily enflamed; the needle-like middle zone shows irritability. The unusually high-shooting upper lengths in *Erich* show the need to dominate, stemming from ambition. He loves to take risks and has an urgent desire to rise above the average. The inflated *E*-capital of *Erich* shows illusions, a visionary nature, and a tendency toward speculation. To bolster a meager writing with such inflated E-capital curves shows self-deception.

The father image is the symbol of authority, and the relationship of the child to the father mirrors the relationship to authority, discipline and the law. A negative father connection creates an undisciplined, disobedient adult who opposes authority. Sometimes the daughter who has contradicted her father all her life develops in her father's image and as a grown-up prefers a male profession. She may also demonstrate masculine traits in her sexual activities.

Illustrations of formations in the upper zone

1) 1) *The lyrical,* left-bound *d*: Contemplative, reflective

2) 2) *The to-the-left,* bent-in capital *D*: negative father image

3) 3) *The pointed capital I:* Aggressive from the father image

4)    4) *The lasso form of the capital S:* A rejection of the father

5)   5) The same happens with the capital T

Ambivalence toward the father

6)   6) *Urgent desire to dominate:* Audacious, impudent attitude

7)   7) *So-called protection stroke:* A desire to dominate

8)   8) *Rejection of authority*: due to negative father image

9)   9) *Opposition*: daring, own will

10)   10) *Arcadic transformation in the upper zone:* artistic self-presentation

11)   11) *The so-called religious curve:* The need to recognize a higher power

Table for Accentuation of the Upper Lengths

Psychic, intellectual activity
Need for freedom
Superiority
Intellectual mobility
Lightheartedness
Carelessness
Lack of restraint
Devotion to ideals and ideas
Abstract-thinking ability
Consciousness, alertness
Ambition
True and exaggerated idealism
Enthusiasm
Striving for the light, the Divine
Ecstasy, exaltation, eccentricity
Tendency toward transcendental, spiritual
Mysticism
Distraction

Special Forms of Upper Lengths

Inside a word shooting upper lengths = ambition to be a leader (1)

(1)

Regulated upper lengths = ethical tendencies (2)

fy that they

(2)

Accentuation on upper lengths in a pastose writing = intellectualization of instincts
Accentuation in a low form niveau = self-deceptive enthusiasm (3)

Succeed

(3)

Enlarged middle zone letters are so high that they have the same size as upper lengths = pushy (4)

wonderful mu birth dau Todau

(4)

Middle zone letters penetrate the lower zone = violence (5)
Materialistic, practical interests; excitability, inflated upper loops = verbosity, boasting, illusions (6)

any

(5)

I think I love you

(6)

  To-the-right, bent-in upper lengths show active energy and determination to overcome fate in a strong handwriting, whereas in a weak handwriting they show a lack of courage, melancholia, and fear of the future.

To-the-left, bent-in upper loops often appear in puberty, reflecting disturbance during the psycho-physical growth process, and can later become directional pressure from the past, showing suffering during childhood.

Arcadic transformation of bows and angles = acting talent, artistic ability

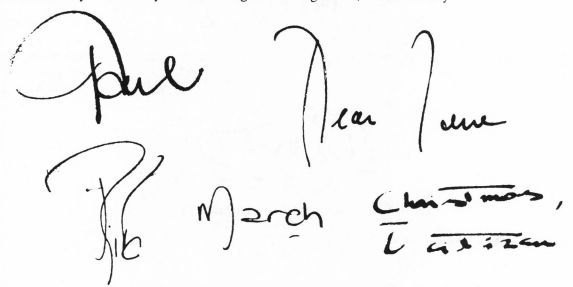

Too-high, swinging t-crossings = desire for freedom from the father/authority, idealism and independence.

Upper lengths move down into the lower zone = materialism

Middle zone letters (mostly finals) escape into the upper zone (lettre suspendue) = escaping from reality into illusions and dreams.

295

to analyze

When upper and lower zones are shortened and the middle zone becomes predominant, the interests are personal, not social.

Unfortunately the holiday home

When upper and lower lengths are equally accentuated, theoretical and practical abilities are equally developed.

Sir Laurence Olivier's signature

Natural balance in capitals

Sense of superiority
Nobility of heart, mind, soul
Dignity
Tolerance
Self-confidence
Stability

Square Forms of capitals

Arrogance
Presumptuousness
Servile with the boss, but
    impudent with subordinates

Low and small forms in the upper zone

Anxiety, hesitation
Lack of intellectual versatility
Introversion
Concentration

China. The atmosphere for four years

296

Uneven Fluctuations of Upper Lengths

Lack of psychic balance and harmony
Irritability
Fluctuating self-confidence
Frustrated ambition

To-the-right-bent upper loops signify in a strong handwriting the energy to overcome resistance and penetrate the higher spiritual regions, as in this beautiful, curved signature.

To-the-left-bent loops in the upper zone mean a longing for the past, resignation, discouragement.

To the category of accentuation of upper lengths belong the high set *i*-dots, the *t*-crossings, the final strokes into the height, the size of the capitals, and the poetic quality of the lyrical "*d*" as we see it in this sample of Oscar Wilde's handwriting.

In politics the balance of power is more readily achieved when leader and subjects are equally strong and rarely achieved when a despotic leader rules over obedient masses. The same is observed in handwriting. The capital—the leader of the following letters—becomes a despot and isolated when it is drawn overlarge, representing enormous ambition and the desire to dominate.

Joseph Stalin

Accentuation of Upper Lengths

In the isolation of capitals we see

Belief in one's infallibility
Self-demonstration
Megalomania
Need for respect and influence
Tyrannical domination
Presumption
Intolerance
Unwillingness to communicate

298

ACCENTUATION OF LOWER LENGTHS

Generations of graphologists have stressed that the upper and lower lengths show only the direction of intellectual and materialistic activity. In high upper lengths we see more the theoretical, intellectual interests, idealism and illusions, whereas the lower lengths mirror the practical, technical earth-bound interests, the commercial instincts, and a sense of reality. The material elements are definitely connected with depth. Our food grows on and under the earth. Coal, minerals, oil, precious stones come from within the earth. Some see depth as having less value than height—the individual who seeks material things tends to be generally less respected than a person with high-striving ideals. One who is materialistic will be rewarded with money and riches, like the oil king Getty, whereas one who strives toward intellectual, scientific discoveries may get the Nobel prize, glory, and world-wide recognition of a higher value. This concept has prevailed for thousands of years and must play a role in handwriting evaluation as well.

Let us concentrate now on the lower lengths:

Rudolf Augstein, head of German magazine "Der Spiegel"

This is the handwriting of one of the most intellectual personalities in West Germany. It shows us penetrating lower lengths, the seat of materialism, biological instincts and subconsciousness. In the handwriting of such an intellectual personality the sharp, meager lower loops symbolize abstract thinking ability. This person is anchored deeply in the soil, which gives stability, consistency and thoroughness. It is not very often that an intellectual worker shows such strong roots. They reflect in their sharpness the strong empire of criticism that "Der Spiegel" has become.

The lower lengths are the roots of the writing and provide insight into the solidity, immobility or steadfastness of the writer. The person who emphasizes his lower loops tends to be thorough, concrete, conservative and likes facts. It is as if the intellect orders the writer to anchor deeply in the ground, to balance his whole being so he will not succumb to illusions and dreams. He sees things soberly and abstractly. Here lies the basis of our existence, the sphere of sexuality, libido, the purely practical and materialistic interests, the joy of body functions like dancing, gymnastics. In the lower zone lies Freud's Id, the impersonal animalistic nature of man, curious, exploring, observing.

The more emphasis there is on the lower zone, the more active is interest in the instinctual pleasures of life like drinking, eating, earning money, sex, love, nature, all the things an Arab proverb condemns so harshly: "The only thing that makes a man is his mind. The rest you can find in a pig, a horse or a donkey."

The more pastosity in the lower accentuation of the lengths, the greater the tendency to enjoy life to the fullest.

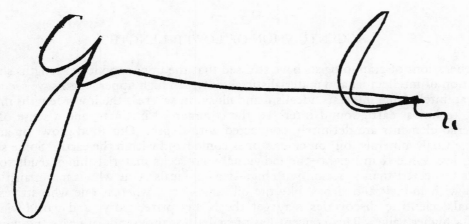

Signature with deep-rooted lower loops and rising phallus-symbol shows the writer's one-sided interests.

Healthy, fulfilled sex-life and anchoring in the earth.

In this heavy handwriting with its long, full lower loops, we see self-preservation and a phlegmatic way of life, with a sense of reality and facts, dependency on instincts, vanity and sensuality, practical intellect, deep-rooted bonds with family, home, friends and ancestors, and love of nature.

say enough want. ? Love, ! Money what is it I really or both ,

When the lower loops are crippled there is lack of vital connections, weak instincts, no roots, no anchoring, lack of solidity, excitability. Indolence and laziness due to physical and psychological weakness often appear.

sending it — and even more for teaching!! You really opened my eyes — and I've been drawing + working on the art every day. I

Despite the strong pressure and the healthy appearance of this writing there are disturbances in the lower lengths. All usually closed and swinging lower loops are open and look like crossed swords, pointed and aggressive, which means that the sex approach is also aggressive and hostile or the sexual impulse is denied.

Would you analyze my handwriting also?

handwriting analysis

Triangular lower loops symbolize the "tyrant in the kitchen." Such women can have the most tender handwriting but the triangular lower lengths mean sexual frustration and a domineering streak.

301

Summary

Special Forms of Upper Lengths

Increased upper lengths within a word = ambition
Decreased upper lengths within a word = pride, patronizing attitude
Accentuation on upper lengths and regularity = ethical principles
Accentuation on upper lengths and rigidity = egotistical tendencies
Upper lengths emphasized in a pastose writing = sublimated biological instincts
Emphasis on upper lengths in a weak, irregular writing = self-deception (hiding a weak personality behind a glorious façade)
Partly enlarged middle zone letters which penetrate the upper regions = tendency to mix in others' affairs.
Upper or middle zone letters penetrating the lower zone = practical, materialistic interests, sometimes with violence and irritability
Inflated upper loops = tendency to illusion, imagination, poetic style

Special Forms of Lower Lengths

Irregularities in development of lower loops = depression and fatigue
Accentuation on lower loops with high-flying i-dots or increasing word endings = people who would like to overcome their materialism
Ornamentation of the lower loops = ambition to show 'refined' behavior
Triangular lower loops = frustrated sex life and unhappy domestic situation; tyranny
Upper and lower loops showing equal accentuation = intellectual and materialistic interests are balanced; theory and practice are united
In a speedy, well-organized writing = organization

Joan Collins creates harmony between upper and lower lengths.

Accentuation of the Upper Lengths

Intellectual interests
Spiritual and psychic flexibility
Ambition
Idealism
Tendency to mysticism
Ability to think abstractly
Intellectual activity and mobility

Accentuation of the Lower Lengths

Psycho-physical activity
Firm anchoring in the ground
Passivity, lack of resistance, giving in to instincts
Materialism
Striving for self-preservation
Egotism
Practical and technical interests
Concrete, reasonable thinking
Pedantry, thoroughness
Powers of observation
Sexuality
Sensuality
Vanity
Love of athletics
Love of exercise
Love of traveling, love of nature

No accentuation of Lower Lengths

Lack of vital security
Weak biological urges
No tradition
No roots
Not "solid"
Not steady
Not trustworthy
Impracticality
Lack of physical activity

LOWER LOOPS AS A KEY TO SEXUAL BEHAVIOR

Graphologists use the lower loops in handwriting as the main source of information about the love life and sex life of the writer.

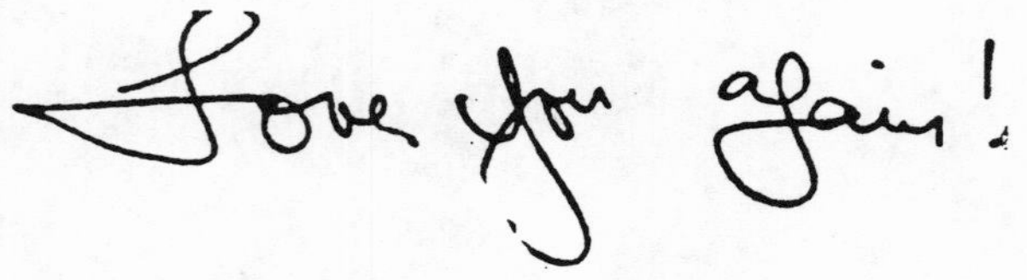

[handwritten: Love you again!]

Here we see the handwriting of a passionate woman who pretends to love her husband, but when we look at the triangular formation of the lower loop of the capital *L* in *Love*, and the suffocated *y*-loop which show sexual frustration (closed above the baseline means that she has an infinite appetite and will never be satisfied) and the clumsy, fat *g*-loop in *again*, we know that all her exclamations of love are more possessive than an expression of the feelings of a woman in love. Someone who has such a powerful, triangular lower loop (*again*) is not able to feel deeply. All her solemn declarations of love will be disproved in times of crisis. An examination of the lower loops, together with the overall impression - the pastosity, the demanding fullness of the curves, the vertical, reasonable slant, the sharp final strokes in the writing—will reveal a person who uses tyrant-like, possessive strength to dominate her family.

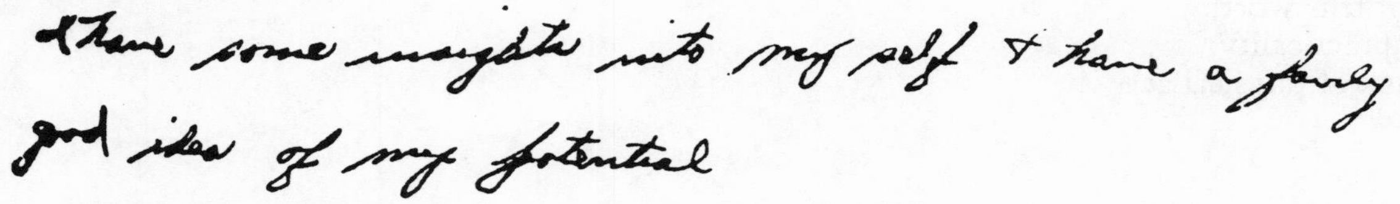

[handwritten: I have some insights into my self & have a fairly good idea of my potential]

This weak, small, fluctuating, insecure handwriting belongs to a male masochist and transvestite. He is dependent on moods; the lower crippled lengths show a lack of vitality; "born to suffer," he yields to his partners.

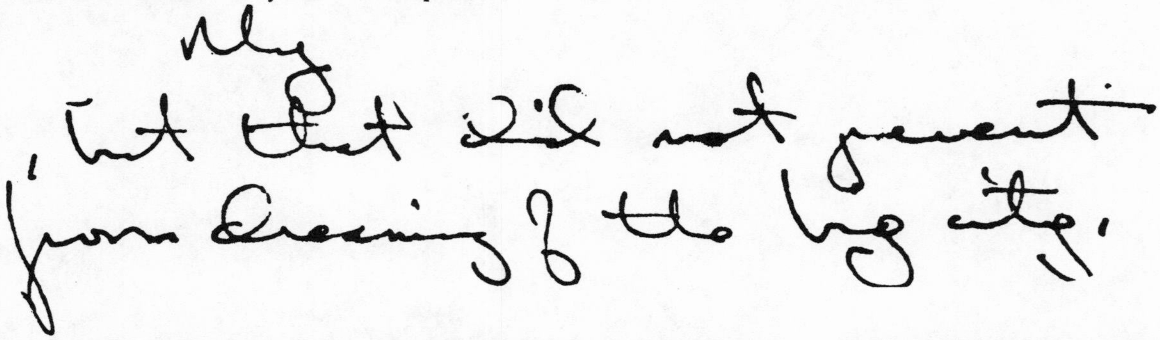

[handwritten: but that will not prevent from dreaming of the big city.]

The grasping lower loops with their final hooks in this artistic *persona writing* show the unsatisfied sex life of a more aggressive homosexual. The blotted vowels show practiced secrecy.

If the writer has a natural and healthy sex life, the lower loop of the *g* has a full, smoothly swinging oval form.

regards   *analysis*

If the writer closes the *g*-loop above the base line, his instinctual needs are suppressed.

originally Cooper first Onglet living

If he closes his *g*-loop below the base line, his sex desire is not fulfilled; he feels restricted and restrained.

Stanley   writing   everything

If the writer uses ornamental bows and curves to embellish his lower loops he will enact his sexual fantasies.

say   Buckley   originally

If the lower loop stroke is triangular-like, the natural sex desire is suppressed and the persons become nagging, dominating, and often, domestic tyrants.

filmmaking   looking

Crippled, weak lower loops reveal a disturbed sex life.

my   holiday

When the downstroke is done aggressively, even furnished with a hook, we see a writer who is denying sexual urges.

305

When the lower loops turn immediately to the right we see altruism and sublimated sex desire; the energy has been redirected to more spiritual and intellectual goals.

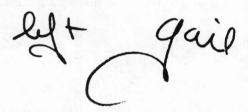

The arcadic "claws," to-the-left-bent, appear in the lower loops. They reflect a need for financial security. They often rise out of anger, frustration and bad temper.

Oscar Wilde's lower loops, turning to the other-side-of-the-normal lower loop's movement, speak to an avoidance of attachment to women.

To-the-left-swinging, wide lower loops show a lasting attachment to the mother which can later appear as homosexual tendencies.

Here a physical disability (crippled legs) rules out a healthy sex life.

When the lower loops are wide open we see deep sexual disturbances.

When the loops make an unusual turn, the sex life is not normal.

306

When the lower loops are exaggerated in their expansion, the writer himself will never be satisfied and will look continually for new adventures.

When the lower loops are drawn like narrow channels we find a puritan with a double standard of morality.

When the lower loops are pointed we can expect prudishness and irritability from the writer.

With this crippled, merely suggested lower loop we see disturbance during puberty and change of life.

When the lower loops are strong and filled with pastosity and the lower loop-crossing does not reach the base line we see an unsatisfactory sex life.

In this sample of fearfully to-the-right, bent-in lower loops we have both an unsatisfying sex life and fear of the future. (In the to-the-right, bent-in loops we see directional pressure from the future.)

307

On this unforgettable day

you are adding to the

many pleasures you

gave me by wanting

my handwriting.

If one is examining the sex life of a woman one should also look at her lover's writing. This male writer shows tenderness with the smooth gliding of his pen over the surface of the writing paper. The imaginative, open lower curves show a tasteful, aesthetic way of treating a woman, and only one goal—to give her the pleasure she desires. He is not resigned in his sex life, nor is he brutal or overpowering. He has a charming, convincing way of showing his affection for a woman, his enthusiasm for her femininity, and a natural understanding of the female longing to be loved.

GREAT DISTANCES BETWEEN WORDS

[handwritten]

Dear Chester and Bill —
I do not understand
why the problem of Nixen
is not yet fully settled
and why this bad publicity
seems to continue.

Here, Howard Hughes fills the page, with wide gaps between the words, according to an unconsciously demonstrated need for room and space and distance from other people. His script shows an inner desire for isolation, reserve, and in this case also the need for clarity, overview and organization. Nietzsche called this inner distance *wanted but not given;* in other words, one cannot influence the desire for solitude; it is unconscious.

The famous graphologist Roda Wieser speaks of *Ego-islands,* when the I-pronoun is isolated as we see in the Hughes' sample. When the distance between words is larger than the distance between lines, as in this sample, it shows a character who is outwardly courageous and inwardly often insecure and full of inhibitions which he tries to hide behind elegant manners; but the social life is superficial. The writer remains a stranger.

[handwritten]

Lieber Jawlensky!
Lieber Blauer Bruder!

The extreme distances between words written by a painter during the Hitler era when he was condemned to give up modern art. It is another proof that the distance between words happens from the unconscious, whereas the distance between lines represents a keeping of that distance, which the writer consciously controls.

309

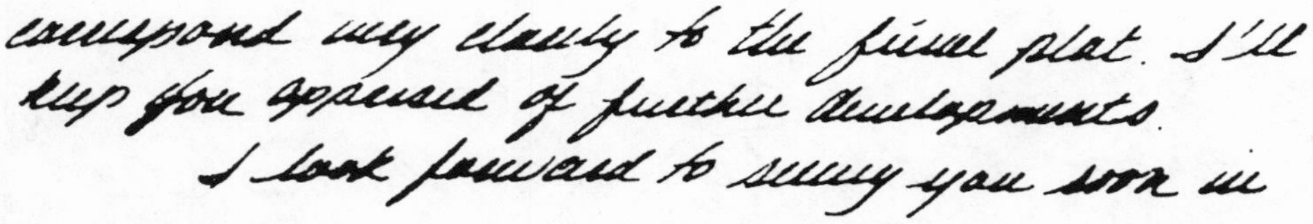

[handwritten text in cursive]

Here the narrow spaces between words would ordinarily mean natural ability to socialize, but the straightness of the lines shows a forced rigidity which contradicts the joy of contact-seeking and gives the writer an artificially good behavior. He is in fact insecure.

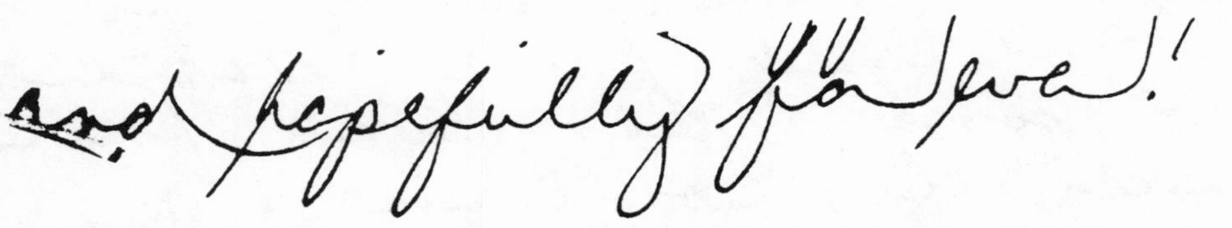

[handwritten text: "and hopefully for Eva!"]

When words are almost connected we see a short-sighted, over-industrious person who cannot be alone, lives in a thicket of restlessness and who may be neurotic.

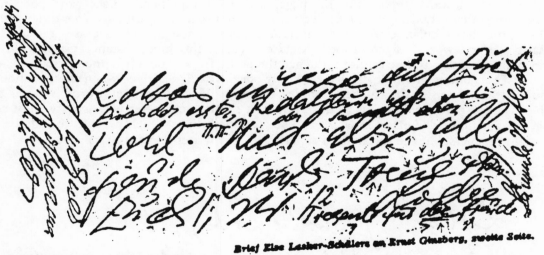

Brief Else Lasker-Schülers an Ernst Ginsberg, zweite Seite.

Else Lasker-Schüler (1869-1945), expressionistic lyricist, shows in her crowded, imaginary, creative writing how the thoughts pour out of her and fill the page. Every free space on the paper eventually will be filled with these large, strange letter formations. Her sense of individuality is not limited and here we have no too-narrow, too-crowded, too-thicket-like arrangement. It is interesting to note that there are no entanglements between lines; we may admire the genius that explodes in wild space-using, but she would never interfere with others' lines, as entangled writing people do. Her conscience controls her social life.

DISTANCES BETWEEN LINES

Distances between lines determine the structure of the script, reveal the writer's ability to organize, to plan, how he adapts himself to society. If the lines are widely distanced and not entangled, the writer respects other peoples' ways of living and protects his own lifestyle.

The organized, clear handwriting of Carl Gustav Jung

PROF. DR· FREUD

WIEN, IX., BERGGASSE 19

Narrow distances between lines means a stronger depth of penetration—sometimes creativity or the tendency to exceed the bounds of possibility. This is the case with Freud's entangled

Distance between Lines

lines, where all conventional laws are disregarded. He was too near his subject, which led to conflicts with colleagues who did not share his views. The prejudices of a hostile world forced Freud to live completely in his own ideas. He 'fenced' himself in, as the symbolism of self-entanglement in the writing shows.

Great distances between words	*Small distances between words*
Introversion, reserve	Extraversion, longing for the *you*
Self-preservation	Wants to conquer the world
Cautiousness	Love of parties
Shyness, inner isolation	Spontaneity
Lack of spontaneity	No tact
Contemplation	Verbosity
Likes to dream	Restlessness
Mistrusting	Cannot be alone
Inhibition	Escaping from self
Psychological disturbances	Lack of inhibition

Increased expansion (horizontal)	*Decreased expansion (horizontal)*
Need for room and space	Modesty
Expansion of the Ego	Being economical
Arrogance, vanity	Greed
Aristocratic lifestyle	Reserve
No inhibition	Self-control
	Inhibition

Special Forms

Large distances between words and width = no talent for diplomacy, compromise

Large distances between lines and width = playing at social reserve, but natural at home and with friends

Large distances between words and lines and wide margins = independent, hard to please

Word and line distances are wide = self-controlled but lonely; no contact with people

Word and line distances narrow = Verbosity, curiosity

Word distances narrow, lines wide = Able to make contact but inner distance from society remains

Narrow distance between words and clear firm lines = inner insecurity but outwardly correct, superior attitude (pretense)

Word distances narrow, line distance narrow = longing for contact but unable to forsake isolation because of inhibition

Entanglement of lines = lack of intellectual clarity; in strong dynamic handwriting, disregard for others' right to live; recklessness and carelessness

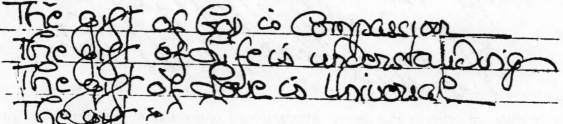

Small distances between words, narrow distances between lines leads to entanglement.

DIRECTION OF LINES

The way we move along on the paper—with rising lines, falling lines, horizontal or wavering lines—describes our basic emotional lives, which reach to the depths of our personality. The impulsive movement in different directions on the paper mirrors the writer's momentary moods. When he writes on prescribed lines he shows an inner guiding image which requires security and correctness. The given lines help him to fulfill his desire, albeit the support is artificial.

These straight lines show

Steadiness
Goal-orientation
Love of detail work
Stability of moods and emotions
Persistence, endurance
Emphasis on convention, sometimes dull and boring

Rising lines belong to the restless entrepreneur, with eagerness, optimism, excitement, *élan vital*, ambition, high self-esteem.

Falling Lines show

Not persistent
Melancholia
Weakness in decision-making
Pessimistic moods
Worries, resignation
Depression
Easily tired, lazy
Fading strength

present ... in almost ... the center of 80 acres of
where my son came to build his dream house,
son came to build his dream house when

Concave lines
Early difficulties will be mastered; eventually fatigue will be overcome; spontaneous spells of discontent will be overcome; early mistrust will change to confidence.

The left hand of
the ...

Convex lines
Starting out with strong enthusiasm and eagerness, changing to disappointment; cannot follow through; growing weak all too soon.

Nobel Prize-winning author Thomas Mann (1875-1955) was born into a patrician family (*Buddenbrooks*).

Roof-tile lines
Every word falls down and every following word tries to begin at the same height as the preceding; one sees the always new beginning, the attempts to regain psychic balance through self-control. Thomas Mann reveals in his roof-tile lines a constant struggle with an inferiority complex and downhearted moods.

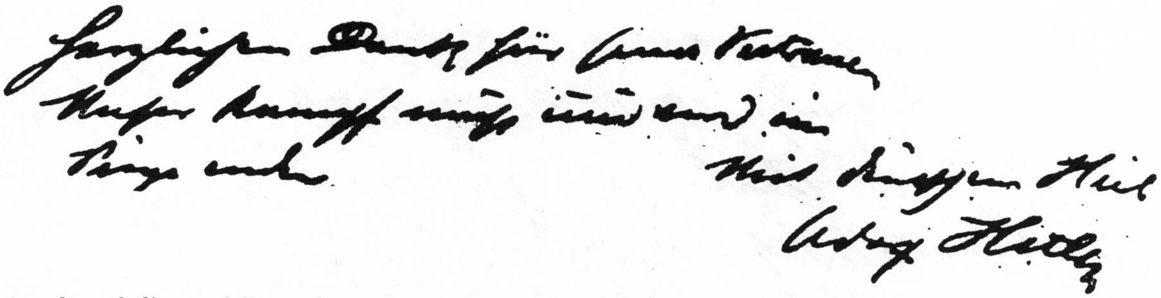

[handwritten German text, Adolf Hitler signature]

Ends of lines falling down shows lack of planning, self-deception; overcompensation for inferiority complex leads to aggressiveness, excessive verbosity, extreme eagerness, as seen in Adolf Hitler's lines.

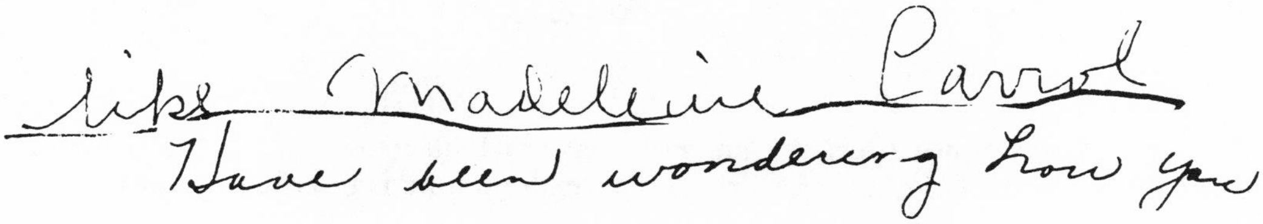

[handwritten text: "likes Madeleine Carrol" / "I have been wondering how you"]

Wavering lines
Changes of mood, indecision, lability of feeling, insecurity, sensibility.

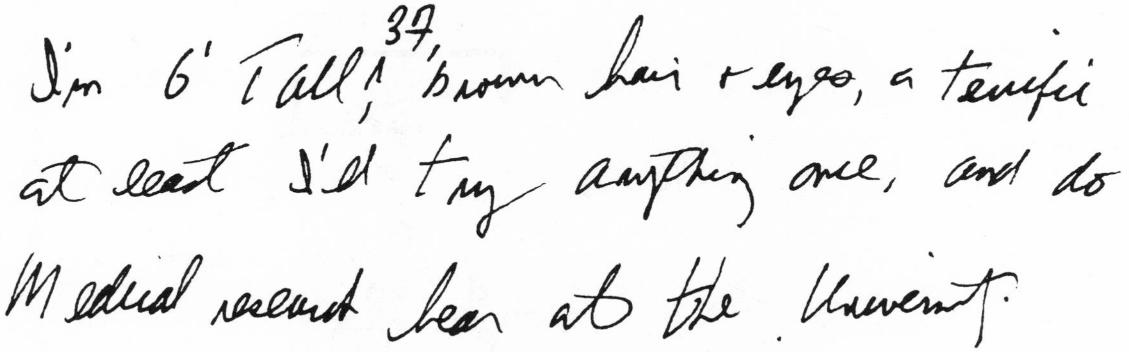

[handwritten text: "I'm 6' Tall, 37, brown hair + eyes, a terrific at least I'd try anything once, and do Medical research here at the University"]

Fluctuating lines
A restless, up-and-down dancing, like a boxer who warms up for a fight; unpredictable.

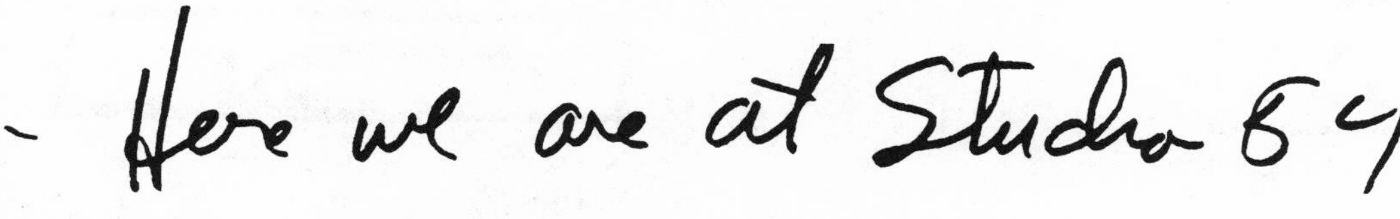

[handwritten text: "— Here we are at Studio 54"]

Irregular writing on prescribed lines
Independent, trusting only one's own judgment, against law and order, fighting conventional behavior, lack of adaptability, stubbornness, undisciplined.

to be world policeman
Certainly express my views
Thank you for your
Offer of support it
your encouragement .

Jimmy

Jimmy Carter's convex lines speak to an enthusiasm which grows quickly but fades even more quickly. He suffers from an inferiority complex which he is not able to master.

Tables for direction of lines

Rising lines

Vivacity
Increased activity
Eagerness
Courage
Ambition
Optimism
Euphoria
Need for social contact
Lightheartedness

Falling lines

Depression
Shyness
Hesitation
Moodiness born of weakness
Resignation
Lack of courage
Melancholia
Easily tired, lazy
Not persistent

Roof-tile lines

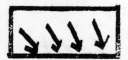

Suppressed eagerness
Controlled ambition
Trying to conquer weakness
Fighting a lack of courage
Trying to conquer moodiness

Falling lines at the end only

No sense of organization
Verbosity without end (Hitler)

Convex lines

Short-lived enthusiasm
Not persistent
Too many promises, nothing kept
Easily tired
Unrealistic planning

Concave lines

Initial difficulties overcome
Theoretical pessimism
Practical optimism
Increased efficiency
    (writing structure regulated)

Straight lines

Strong persistence
Goal-oriented
Firm, uncompromising
Relentless
Fanatic
Consistent

Fluctuating lines

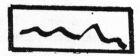

Moody
Lack of decision-making ability
Bound to the moment
Physical and psychic weakness
Adaptability at any price
Excitability

Wavering lines

Wavering emotions

Adolf Hitler falls into an abyss at the end of every line, which graphologists interpret as a subconscious foreknowledge of downfall and eventual suicide.

THE MARGINS

The writing paper is like the world with its limitations and the problems which must be dealt with. The margin is the frame which helps to bring out the beauty of the writing. Wide margins provide a better frame for the writing; they show organization, overview, reserve, critical perception and artistic taste, and generosity which goes almost to waste when there is a lot of empty space around the writing.

Small writing, produced when all space is filled, displays a readiness to give, to fill the room, to be near people, surrendering and yielding. In a low form niveau, small or non-existent margins belong to people without culture.

Harry Truman's exactly measured margins show a sense of order, organization, pedantry and economy. (He was so conscientious he never took a stamp from the government for his private letters.)

Irregular left and right margins

Disorder
Carelessness
Indifference to social relationships, insecurity
Negligence, inattention
Nonchalance

Broad margins on both sides of Thomas Jefferson's letter show cultivated lifestyle, aestheticism, individualism and reserve.

318

Small margins at both sides:

> My dear Mrs Olga,
> The topic of my lecture will be : (the
> desert, and their mentality). It is a very original, at
> lecture; I am speaking according experience. the lad
> dressed in my arab clothes; the fact is that I shal

Without individualistic personal style
Not broadminded
Economical, greedy, stingy

No margin at either side

> Love all, trust a few,
> Do wrong to none: be able

means no possibility of adapting to changes in life. The writer must use all available space with pushing and talkativeness; content is more important than form; he takes advantage of others.

The wider upper margin,

> 474. Apt 5.
> Central Park West
> New York City.
> the 17th March 1929.

the distance between the upper letters and the actual start of the letter, shows respect for superiors, servility, submissiveness, devotion, and a conservative education when the handwriting is cultivated.

The Margins

No margin at all,

I love God and nature. My ... is to extol his virtues upon

together with a low form niveau-writing, shows a person without orientation, wildly grasping at everything he can take without understanding for his fellowman. He is greedy. Only a false appearance counts. He pretends to have no fear but the handwriting belies this. (Sample of an escaped prisoner)

No upper margin

Dear Paul,

I am happy that you were

When someone begins a letter just near the upper edge of the paper, he tends to: want to be noticed, have no respect and little education, and he tends to push forward without knowing reserve.

It is too co New York so m

From large writing, small margins we deduce natural activity, security and need for room and space, without much regard for others.

> warn you about it.
>
> Obviously, the statio's not mine but it was the most decent paper I could find — no pauenaiya ka na (also with my writing!)
>
> Well, how are all of you? I do hope you are enjoying and forgetting what you left behind. I also hope you are all well and healthy (?!!!). All of us are still okay.

In a very small writing with very narrow margins (or none at all) we see a person with a modest lifestyle who is extremely economical and pedantic.

LEFT MARGIN

The placement of the left margin is important because at the outset the writer tries to make his best impression. Every kind of left margin —broad, narrow, even, decreasing, increasing— is a symbol. If we see a writing with an even left margin we know the person tries to be correct and is disciplined, according to the given aesthetic and moral elements of his form niveau. Wide left margins are usually preferred by people who like to practice generosity, even to the point of being wasteful. A narrow left margin is that of a cautious, economical writer. Let us explore the left margin:

An even left margin

Eagerness to be correct
Strong self-discipline
Always wants to make a good impression
Orderly
Will not deliberately hurt anyone
Is reliable, has sense of duty and responsibility

When the left margin is narrow

The writer is economical, cautious, punctual, conventional, orderly, and needs security.

I'm canadien citizen
I love girls
I love dancing
I'm from Burundi
I born in Burundi
I'm very Nervous

Oh! What a life
Said the queen &
"Three months next
nine months pain

Wide left margin in a large writing reflects good culture, aristocratic lifestyle, broadminded-ness, good manners, aestheticism, generosity, aloofness, and, as in this wide writing, wasteful-ness.

Decreasing left margin:

When the width of the left margin decreases we see caution; increasing, self-control, mistrust, doubtfulness, fear of losing one's reserve, inhibitions. Economical attitudes increase as the margin-width narrows.

Widening left margin

Impulsiveness
Vivacity
Activity
Impatience
Goal-orientation
No self-control

Left Margin in steps

even
left
margin

even
left
margin
(indented)

Konrad Adenauer (1876-1967)
(A)

(B)

When a person blocks two lines or three lines together regularly, as in the sample above, and then turns two lines together into another "step," we see a disciplined person who has to change his lifestyle for diplomatic reasons. The inner order remains but the forced giving-in attitude is done with inherent regularity. (A)

Irregularity of the left margin

When the left margin is irregular it means the words begin at random, without a plan; it shows a person who is not punctual, and who is indifferent, sloppy. (B)

Left Margin

The so-called concave left margin

Four score and seven years ago
Our fathers brought forth on this continent
a new nation conceived in liberty and
dedicated to the proposition that all men
are created equal. We are now gathered
on a battle field of that nation

Early graphologists interpreted the left margin as a symbol of the degree of greed or wastefulness. W. Preyer wrote in 1911 in *Psychology of Writing:* "If the left margin grows larger in the middle of the writing and gets smaller at the end of the writing we see a person who tries very hard to become economical but his enthusiasm and his inner generosity breaks through and after a while his conscience warns him to save (money) instead of wasting (it) and he returns to his former, somehow restricted left margin."

The so-called convex left margin

P.S. Word is that Pgh. went amazingly
well: standing ovation at the ball park,
six minutes on TV news, mob scenes
at the Ethnic Fair walk-through. Most
encouraging.

is created when a writer wants initially to be generous but gradually an economical, greedy attitude overwhelms him and the left margin gets smaller and smaller with each line, in convex form. His inborn stinginess takes over because during his writing he forgets the form and concentrates more on the content of the letter. The true stingy nature eventually breaks through.

RIGHT MARGIN

At the end of a writing line the pen stops voluntarily. This stop occurs according to the need of the writer - whether he likes to communicate with distance or with overwhelming verbosity. If the writing movement is strong and active, the halts of the pen will be inconsistent. When the writer is in the mood to continue his flowing thoughts it will be difficult to stop immediately; the right margin will be overstepped and the words will be squeezed in. If the writing movement is more passive and restrained, it is easier to construct an even, more exact right margin.

The treatment of the right margin reveals both the writer's ability to tame his own impulses and his readiness to communicate. The writer can put the brake on his own writing movement out of free will or out of a need for security. A *wide right margin* shows the writer's love of freedom, self-control, form-feeling, and cautious distance from society. In a weak writing it shows inhibition, need for security and a lack of self-confidence.

> .) was born in Nevada, raised in Los Angeles. I'm thirty-three years old and about to marry this man next to me.

A wide right margin shows a strong sense of responsibility and a strong will when the writing is regulated and the right margin is regulated. Quick reactions to difficult situations, excellent feeling for form and space, security in decision-making are revealed.

> the prent
> engrossed. But
> the bits of
> mental typefaces?
>
> believe that strength
> remainder — they try
> wend.

Right margin wide and irregular

Reserve
Cautiousness
Anxiety
Fear of the future
Fear of reality
Hesitation
Striving for self-protection
Liking for travel
Restlessness
Difficulties in organizing
Shyness

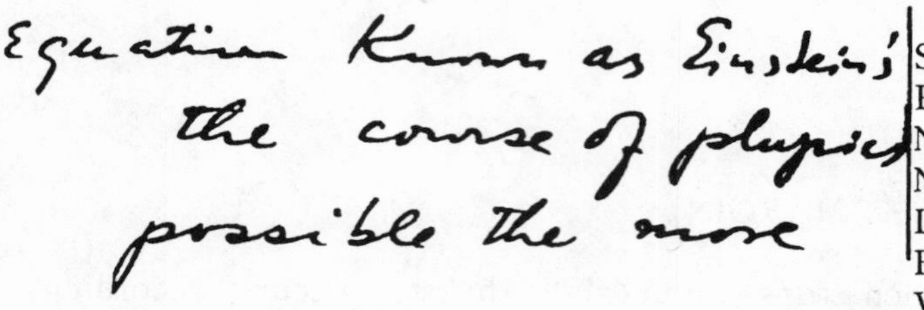

Equation Known as Einstein's
the course of physics
possible the more

Spontaneity
Readiness to communicate, activity
No distancing from society
Need for talking
Longing for knowledge
Economical attitude
Varied interests

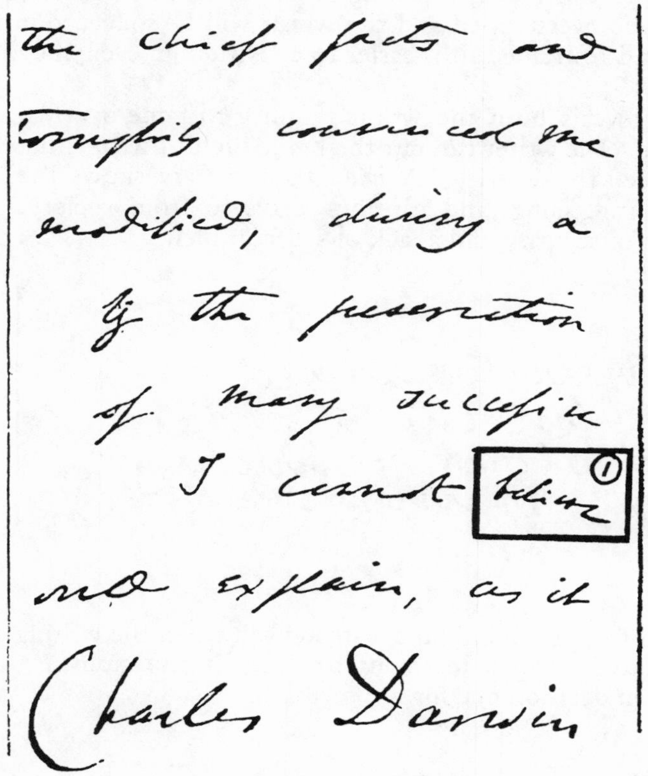

the chief facts and
fully convinced me
modified, during a
by the presentation
of many successive
I cannot believe ①
and explain, as it

Charles Darwin

Right margin cramped; lines and words are bent down

Exhorbitant demand on self
Overworked
Over-strained
Not enough organization of work
Exhausted by using too much willpower
  and doing too much leads gradually
  to discontent.
Some words are cramped because of
lack of space (*believe*) (1). The
writer does not separate what belongs
together; he needs the whole concept
of the thought on the line.

English naturalist Charles Darwin (1809-1882),
who developed the concept of evolution.

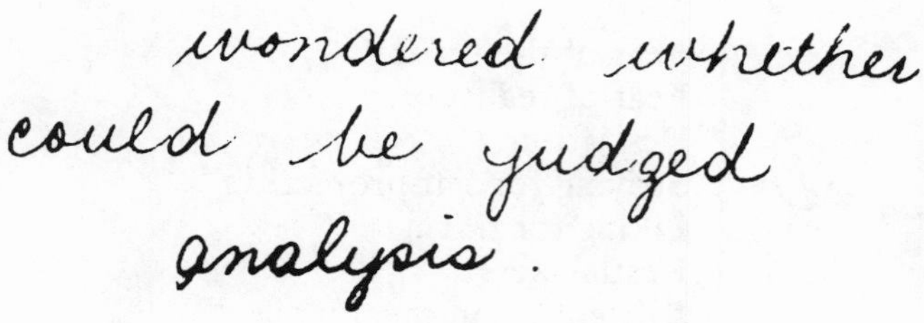

wondered whether
could be judged
analysis.

Increasing width of the right margin

Doubts own courage
Lost inhibitions return
Good intentions to communicate
Breakdown due to increasing anxieties

York from
in Brooklyn.
aspiration
preparing food

New York has been
persevering because

Decreasing right margin means forgetting former shyness and efforts to contact, becoming talkative, yielding, in spite of usual strict behavior.

Right margin wide and even

I PROMISE NOT TO Break
your Mat. Black Fountain pen.

Desire for independence
Organization ability
Aestheticism

My Name is Pete Holden

I Live in Unionville Ct

J. am Jirzy eight year old

married American Male 1234567890

Right Margin

Right margin wide and uneven

Reserve, fear of the future, fear of reality, hesitation, caution

Irregular right margin but rhythmical

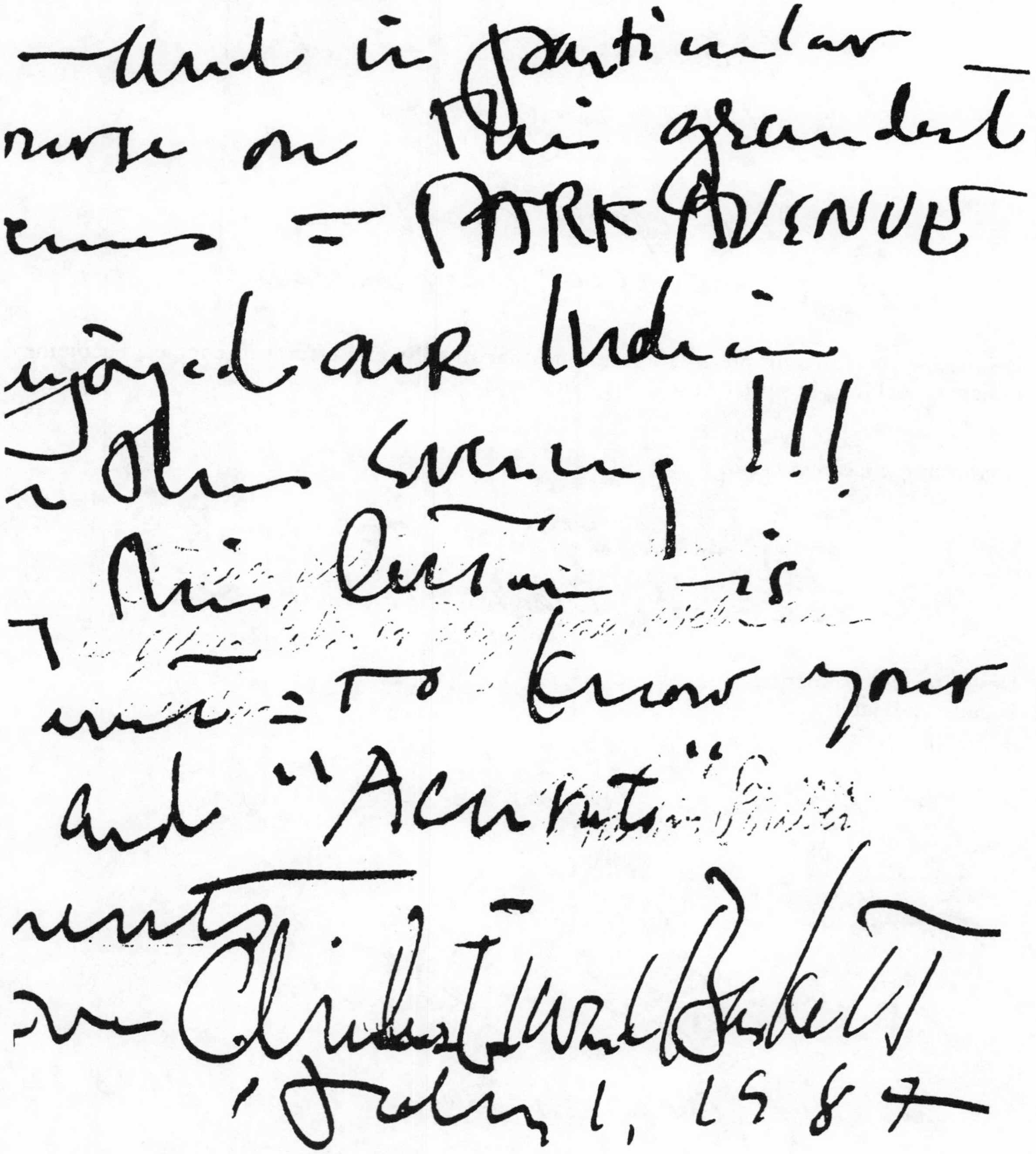

[handwritten text]

Loves people and life, bursting with energy and ideas

THE ADDRESS

All graphologists know how important the addressing of the envelope can be for diagnosis in a handwriting analysis. Very often we see a discrepancy between the text content and the envelope writing. This has a psychological basis. The graphological laws about right and left accentuation on envelopes are the following:

The too much to-the-left-drawn address means: cautiousness, prudence, hesitation, anxiety and inhibition. *The too much to-the-right-placed address means:* carelessness, spontaneity, consideration. Early graphologists also spoke of the so-called step address, going slowly from the top to bottom of the envelope, which symbolizes a careful hesitant nature, mistrustful and suspicious.

Placement to the left side
Consideration, reserve, caution, timidity, anxiety, inhibition

Placement to the right side
Spontaneity, vivacity, carelessness, no consideration, not aloof. communication talent

Placement in the upper area
Need for freedom and independence, pride, presumptuousness, no respect, pushy

Placement on the lower edge
Modesty, submissiveness, respect

Placement in the center
Firmness, stability, concentration, self-importance, cordiality, warmth, subjectivity

Spread across the whole envelope
Variability, longing for the unlimited, openness, relaxation

Stepping down
Taking no chances, cautious, suspicious, mistrusting

The Address

Placement in the extreme upper right
Intellectual extraversion

Placement in the extreme lower right
Show-off attitude

Placement in the extreme lower left
English fashion

THE STRUCTURE

To create a clear writing structure we need separation of words, lines, sentences, paragraphs. Not only the margins which frame the written word but also the distribution of space within a text comprise the structure of a script. The structure of a script shows the writer's ability to distinguish important thoughts from unimportant ones, his striving for clarity and overview, organization, distance from people, form feeling — high or low form niveau — restriction, rigidity, favoring bureaucracy and pedantry, and many more elements derived from an examination of structure.

If the general structure of a script is positive and not disturbed, we see a well-balanced, well-integrated personality. If the general writing structure is very narrow one discovers behind it an anxious and defensive person.

Dear Madame Marcus,

I was so pleased to see you last Thursday, but I did not mind you looked so well as usual, I hope you are feeling better now.

In this sample we see a *mechanical structure*, very regulated. It shows an analytical intellect, a need for clear expression, danger of formal thinking and falling into rigidity. The wide gaps between words are called *sand-banks* and demonstrate how large the distance between the Ego and the 'you' can be, and how (progressively) loneliness may develop.

Claude Monet's (1840-1926) writing structure is distinguished by the distances between the letters being as great as the distances between words. This shows social contact difficulties and sensibility.

331

I know of no place where you could find a reproduction of any of my scrawls. I'm better to and do fact that few people can now read anything which I write —

Sincerely yours

Eleanor Roosevelt

In Eleanor Roosevelt's (1884-1962) well-structured script we see a brilliant sense of organization, systematic, methodical acting, need for intellectual, ethical, theoretical order, dogmatic principles, and superior self-presentation.

neighborhood —

We are Americans —

my husbands hero is

Thomas Jefferson

In a wide structure we see generosity, a broad outlook on the world, ability for long-term planning, openness to all new impressions, high form niveau, aristrocratic form feeling and lifestyle, demand for room and space.

This charming construction of drawing and letter formations shows the arbitrary use of space in a very unusual, artistic way by the "enfant terrible" of the French poets, Jean Cocteau (1869-1963).

Salvador Dali (1904-), Spanish surrealist painter
From a sketch-book: aphorisms, thoughts, new ideas, together with drawings give an impression of a working artist and his well-structured world.

The rising, optimistic lines, the even left margin, the simplicity of this concentrated writing, the security of the drawing-strokes make this script an artistically-structured picture of a diligent person.

[Handwritten manuscript in cursive script — Jesse Jackson's script]

Jesse Jackson's script

This crowded, vivacious script has, despite the absence of margins, an excellent structure. There are no entanglements. The distances between the lines is just right, the even margin speaks of eagerness to be correct and the speedy combining writing shows speedy reactions. The legibility of the words shows clarity of mind and the scribbles at the edges (allowed on a work sheet), show Jesse Jackson's bursting verbosity and passion. The straight lines show will power and the ability to organize and to convince with inherent enthusiasm due to youthful élan.

*a very special year for me ;
it I am not certain whether
good or bad, but most of
my life I believe are going
toe .*

This full use of space with entanglement of lines is the product of a person who lives by her own rules. It is a space-using, presumptuous way of spreading out without consideration for others. (This is especially true when the form niveau is not very high.)

*I am very skept
about what you
say. I have done
palm Reading on my*

This is the disorderly structure of a person who cannot plan his life, has no overview, no rationality — a sloppy Bohemian nature without true artistic talent. He tends to pushy insistence and a child-like confusion and carelessness. How careless is the structure of the letter formations, the many inside corrections, the primitive form of the I-pronoun (looking like an embryo), the wide irregular gaps and wavering lines. There is no inner or outer structure.

I like felt tipped pens. Four score and seven years ago. Our path on this continent a new nation conceived in liberty and dedicated to that all men are created equal.

Leonard,
231 E.
Avy.
28845

When the writing is surrounded by a lot of empty space we see a person who is anxious about the future and has trouble finding his way. The script looks isolated, afraid and cramped.

Je serai encore ici jusque vers le 10 Septembre, je serai enchanté de recevoir votre volume ici, je vous en remercie d'avance.
Je compte quitter la rue de Rivoli en octobre pour aller au 28 place Dauphine, nous allons donc être voisin, j'espère que nous aurons le grand plaisir de vous voir quelquefois, ces occa=sions sont vraiment trop rares.
Amicalement votre
C. Pissarro.

Camille Pissarro (1830-1903) French impressionist painter. In contrast to the above sample we see here the intelligent and confident use of space by an artist. In the excellent structure of his script we see systematic work, overview, a sense of harmony with the universe.

The eyes are the windows to the soul.

Dean Edward Stitz, M.D.

Elegantly combined thought processes are energetically held together by a justified self-confidence seen in this harmoniously structured writing.

Can you have lunch with me? I really need your help.

Charles

In this excellently structured, overconnected writing one sees the powerful, speedy, yet well organized thinking ability of the world's best-known autograph dealer Charles Hamilton.

APPENDIX

WHAT WE SHOULD KNOW BEFORE WE BEGIN TO ANALYZE A HANDWRITING

We have now covered the graphological elements which comprise the analytical tools, however, there are several other factors which should be considered and these are: Which hand does the writer use? The gender of the writer, the age of the writer, and if possible his occupation. If the writer is left-handed, for example, the element of slant takes on new meaning.

It is also important to know the nationality of the writer, because every country has its own graphic style, as taught in its schools. American schoolchildren learn the Palmer method, Israeli schoolchildren write from right to left without vowels, children in Haiti learn to write the French method (mostly vertical and small letter forms), children in Jamaica learn the British method (soft and curved and connected). In Indian writing we see the ornamental, voluptuous form of their alphabet. German letter forms are more economical and sharp. It is useful to ask the nationality before we begin to analyze a handwriting because writing in English will incorporate traits of the writer's homeland script.

NATIONALITY

The drawing of Chinese characters is mirrored in the English writing, which is full of ornamentation, extended letter formations and swinging curves.

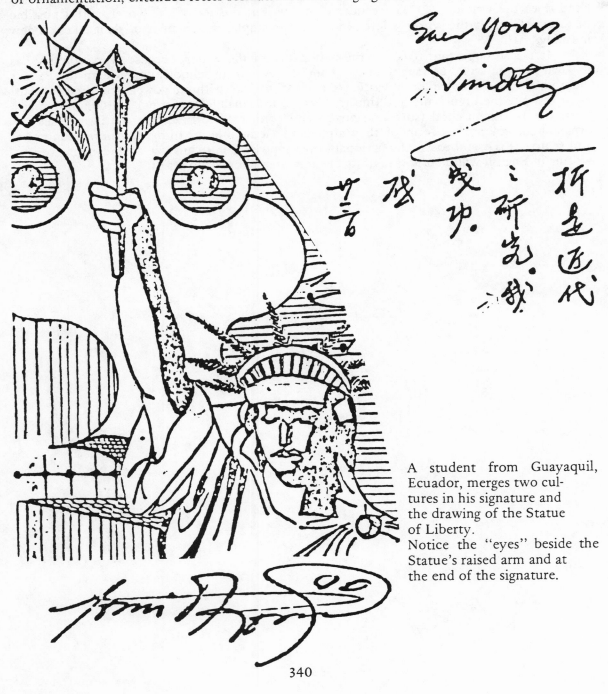

A student from Guayaquil, Ecuador, merges two cultures in his signature and the drawing of the Statue of Liberty.
Notice the "eyes" beside the Statue's raised arm and at the end of the signature.

The round formations of Indian letters are repeated in the English words. A handwriting of a young voluptuous Indian girl whose body curves are mirrored in the soft curves of her script.

Marie

Course in

writing Anaylsis

interesting .

Lekha Pandit .

Bombay

India

लेखर मेरी

यूसर कोर्स इन हैंड राइटिंग

अंगाकुसीस इज वै बेरी

इंटरेस्टिंग

लेख पंडित

इंडीया

बॉम्बे .

The strict British education is visible in the simplified letter formations of a student from Trinidad.

I was born in Trinidad in the Town of Port-of-Spain

is a republic under heavy British influence and education

French education shows in the angular European letter formations of the student born in Haiti.

J'etais née en Haiti. et j'a-

résude à New York, depuis

1 ans

The flowery Spanish writing, learned on the Island of the Sun, Santo Domingo. The two cultures of French Haiti and Spanish Dominican Republic are mirrored in the handwritings. Mulattoes have dominated Haiti and cling to the French cultural tradition; their religion is predominantly Roman Catholic. This explains the rigidity in the schoolwriting of the young student from Haiti. The Dominican Republic is more oriented to the West and encourages immigration of European refugees to enlarge the white population. The handwriting of the DR student shows more liberty and free swinging than that of the Haitian one.

years old. Juan Estévez.

The handwriting of an Iranian student in New York City. Notice the similarity of the lower loops, in *fascinating* and *truly*, to the Iranian letter formations.

fascinating با تشيم احترامات تأكيدی

me a lot. مارا بيرناد

IRAN «Tehran»

yours truly

The handwriting of an Indian student; the movement and formation of the Indian letters are seen in the English version.

am born in Indiaa + parcially

हिन्दी *Hamdhou Sijh Bist*

HINDHI ਹਰਿ ਰਾਏ ਖਾਲਸੇ

AGE

We should ask the age of the writer before we analyze his handwriting because there are youthful writings of old persons, and young people who are mature may have a fully grown-up writing, as we see in the case of this 17-year-old girl, a contestant for the Miss America crown.

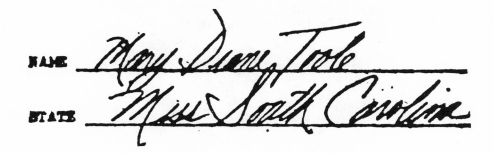

Note the youthful rhythm and vivacity in the handwriting of a 90-year-old woman.

The handwriting of J.P. Morgan, here in a complaint directed to a teacher while he was still in school. The energetic *t*-bars, the even, straight lines show willpower, reflect his goal-oriented need for security; the simplified original letter formations and the strength of the signature describe a young man with high intelligence who knows what he wants.

How youthful and emotional was the handwriting of the 80-year-old General de Gaulle. His comma-like-*i*-dots reveal his vivacity, the right slant his devotion to his ideal, and the straight lines his consistency and fidelity in striving toward goals.

PROFESSION

It is always useful to know the profession of the writer. A politician writes differently than a schoolteacher. A stage personality has more flair and glamor showing off. A theoretician does not need the limelight and gives us simplified expressions from his scientific intellect. The great conductors, who lead hundreds of musicians with light gestures, have to be powerful personalities. Toscanini symbolizes the magic of his conducting in his swinging *t*-stroke. Great painters like Picasso develop their own styles of writing according to their fantasy.

Proud self-representation of a politician

Modest, conventional writing of a schoolteacher

Eruptive passion of Picasso

Toscanini's signature mirrors the swinging of his baton.

345

$$\frac{\partial u}{\partial V} = \frac{konst}{\sqrt{T^5}}$$

Utmost simplicity in Einstein's writing

PLEASE WRITE YOUR NAME AND STATE BELOW:

NAME

STATE Washington

This bombastic use of space was created by a 19-year-old singer.
who thinks the world is waiting for her to conquer it.

The artistic self-demonstration of a well-known movie director, Veit Harlan

346

GENDER

In psychology, according to Philipp Lersch, there is a school of thought which ascribes subconscious, unexpressed characteristics to each gender:

The positive qualities of a man

Organization
Enthusiasm
Fantasy
Determination
Abstract thinking
Initiative
Dignity
Objectivity

The negative qualities of a man

Restlessness
Emphasis on principles
Feeling of superiority
Arrogance
Impatience
Aggression
Desire to dominate
Easily irritated

The positive qualities of a woman

Harmony
Warmth
Security of instincts
Intuition
Fidelity
Strength to endure suffering
Passivity

The negative qualities of a woman

Lack of principles
Preponderance of instinct
Subjective thinking
Lack of activity/drive
Talkativeness
Vanity
Possessiveness

Every individual is a blend of masculine and feminine traits. Jung called the female soul *Anima,* the source of wisdom and tolerance in the male. He called the male soul *Animus,* the source of spiritual and intellectual strength in the female.

Dominance of *Anima* in a male handwriting: exaggerated right slant, to-the-left-swinging lower loops, softly curved letter formations.

347

The strong, active writing of a successful businesswoman with "male" qualities

The harmonious balance of male and female qualities (*Animus/Anima*) in an artistic hand-writing: soft-swinging, rhythmical curves together with energetic, sharp strokes, such as the triangular form of the *g*-stroke, kicked to the left of the final *g* in *Eingang*, first line.

LEFT-HANDEDNESS

Before analyzing a handwriting one should know whether the writer is right-handed or left-handed. Most of us are right-handed. We use the right hand as the master hand and the left hand as support. The dominant strength is then on the right side of the body and is controlled by the left hemisphere of the brain.

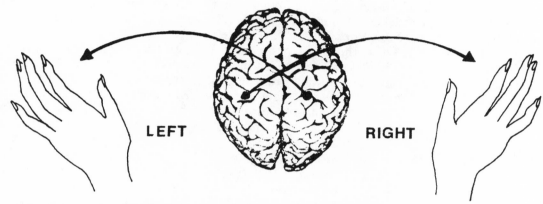

As we see in this drawing, the human brain resembles the halves of a walnut, two similar-appearing, convoluted, rounded halves, connected at the center—the left hemisphere and the right hemisphere. The human nervous system is connected to the brain in a cross-over fashion. The left hemisphere controls the right side of the body and the right hemisphere controls the left side. If one suffers a stroke or accidental brain damage to the left half of the brain, the right side of the body will be most seriously affected, and vice versa.

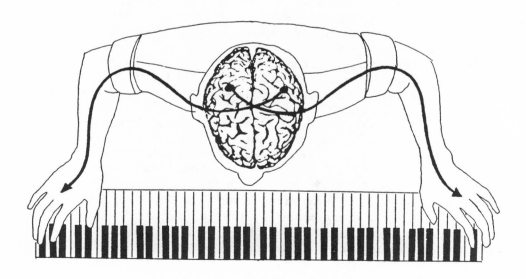

Left-handedness

When a pianist's left hand touches the keyboard, it is obeying motor impulses originating in the right side of the brain. When a child draws some X's and circles them and signs his name, first with one hand and then with the other one can see from the degree of control which hand he prefers. Right-handers consistently draw their circles counter-clockwise; left-handers tend to draw them clockwise. The left-handed pupil has to adjust to the mechanical skill of school-writing, which is designed for the majority, the right-handed students.

We often see the left-handed pupil reversing the direction of the horizontal strokes which the right-handed youngster easily makes from left to right. As soon as the left-handed pupil leaves school he usually returns to his former left-handedness and writes again with the left hand.

Some left-handers have later difficulties, like former vice-president Nelson Rockefeller. All his life he suffered from a tendency to read backward, from right to left, a difficulty that may have had its origin in his father's unrelenting efforts to change young Nelson from a left-hander to a right-hander. "Around the family dinner table," reported the writer of Nelson's obituary in *The New York Times*, "the elder Mr. Rockefeller would put a rubber band around his son's left wrist, tie a long string on it and jerk the string whenever Nelson started to eat with his left hand, the one he naturally favored." The result: "The boy achieved a rather awkward ambidextrous compromise." Dyslexia, reading disability, was also a result. Rockefeller was unable to see the difference between words like "pot" and "top," or letters like "d" and "b," which are mirror images. And because our language is written and read from left to right, and a left-handed child's natural tendency is to scan a page from right to left, he will be easily confused.

King George, father of the present Queen Elizabeth, was also a natural left-hander who was compelled by a rigorous governess to write with his right hand. This created a condition known in psychology as a "misplaced sinister." It affected the king's speech so much that it became necessary to edit out the pauses in his broadcast tapes in order to produce coherent messages. His stammer developed between his seventh and eighth year.

Benjamin Franklin, statesman, author, philosopher, inventor, a man of incredible diverse genius, wrote what is perhaps the most encouraging letter the sinistral could ever hope to read. It was a serious attempt to recommend ambidexterity to the teaching profession. He called it: "A petition to those who have the Superintendency of education," and he spoke as though he were the personification of the left hand: "From my infancy I have been led to consider my sister (the right hand) as a being of a more educated rank. I was suffered to grow up without the least instruction. She had masters to teach her writing, drawing, music and other accomplishments. Nothing was spared in her education. But if by chance I touched a pencil, pen, or a needle I was bitterly rebuked, and more than once I have been beaten for being awkward, and wanting a graceful manner. . .Condescend, sirs, to make my parents sensible of the injustice of an exclusive tenderness, and of the necessity of distributing their care and affection among all their children equally. I am with profound respect, Sirs, Your obedient servant, The Left Hand."

The left hand, slightly weaker due to genetic, anatomical, environmental and emotional factors, has been an object of persecution throughout the centuries. Even today a certain African tribe adopts the following procedure: If a child should seem to be naturally left-handed the natives force the child's left hand into a hole, pour boiling water into it and ram the earth down around the child's hand. By these means the left hand becomes so scalded that the child is bound to use the right hand forever.

The Nuers of Sudan, on the border of Ethiopia, force their youngsters to put the left arm out of action for months and even years by pressing metal rings into the flesh of the left arm from the wrist upwards. The rings are placed so tightly that sores and great pain result, thus rendering the left arm useless.

In Sierra Leone, between Guinea and Liberia on the Atlantic, the left hand is not used for eating. The right hand serves the upper part of the body and the left hand the lower part of the body. Men engaged in sex play may touch the woman's genitals only with the left hand. As much as possible, women must avoid using the left hand when preparing food, and food must only be carried to the mouth by the right hand (no doubt for reasons of hygiene).

On the North American continent, native Indian tribes strapped their babies to a cradle board which was carried on the mother's back. The right arm was free, but the left arm remained immobilized. When the use of the traditional cradle board was abandoned, left-handedness among North American Indians increased dramatically.

In antiquity, left-handedness and ambidexterity are mentioned mostly in connection with the use of weapons. Homer writes in the *Iliad*: "The divine Achilles lifted his spear and Asteropeo, who was ambidextrous, hurled both his lances." Plato writes of the Scythians, the ancient Persians, that they used their bows with right and left hands.

Cesare Lombroso (1836-1909), an Italian physician and criminologist, emphasized the difference between normal and pathological laterality. The reason that more left-handed people had been found among stammerers, epileptics and mentally afflicted was due to the forced re-education of the right hand instead of tolerance of inherent left-handedness. (Even today, in interviews with prisoners, we hear about cruel beating of the left hand by parents and teachers, thus explaining a crippling and damaging influence during childhood.)

Nowadays, however, most of us think differently. If there are natural left-handed people who do not go against their natures and give in to "artificial" right-handedness, regarding it as a serious and unjustifiable interference, they are accepted as normal, efficient members of society, even if they do comprise the minority. Bryng Bryngelson, who studied left-handers for 35 years at the University of Minnesota, said that as a group they are more highly imaginative, creative and sensitive than right-handers.

We see this especially in the handwriting of the left-handed artists: Albrecht Dürer with his tender, sensitive left-handed curves:

Michelangelo, with the strong masculine stroke he needed for sculpting, wresting from a solid marble block the robust, powerful shapes which are so characteristic of his art.

One deduces that Leonardo da Vinci never drew with his right hand because his strokes of pen and brush slope down from left to right. He used mirror-writing to keep secret his thoughts about nature and God lest the Inquisition, the general tribunal established in the 13th century for the punishment of heresy, find him out.

The left hemisphere houses reason, logic, speech and thought. The right brain or right hemisphere is the seat of the artistic side, giving rise to music, color, drawing, dreams. Picasso's left-handedness is seen also in these dynamic, brush-like strokes.

In his painting Swiss-born Paul Klee (1879-1940) combines abstract writing with geometric lines.

Auguste Rodin (1840-1917)—
the sculptor's extraordinarily
connected writing symbolizes a
striving toward the future.

Standard style of writing
left-handed: if the lines of writing
are to be straight, the paper
has to be at an angle.

In hooked left-handed writing,
the wrist is bent, the paper is straight,
letters do not slope backwards
and wet ink does not smudge.

LEFT   RIGHT

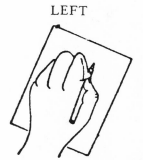

Non-inverted writer

353

LEFT

RIGHT

Left hander, inverted

Right-hander, inverted

In 1971 Jerre Lewis described evidence that those left-handers who adopt the hook-style (inverted left hand) have language functions primarily in the left hemisphere while those who write with the left hand pushing across the page have language localized mainly in the right hemisphere, which lodges the arts.

I am happy to present my natural left hook in which you are about to analyze and whatever you discover about my erratic ways and a few of my shortcomings.

The writing of a talented young artist with the *hooked* left hand.
Both hemispheres working equally promises intelligence and art.

SAMPLES OF HANDWRITING ANALYSES

6/21/82

①

② Richard Johnson, Carpozi , Lachman,

③   I read some of the articles you
④ wrote about me. I liked the stuff about
⑤ Jodie but the rest was rather critical.
⑥   I'm just a regular guy. Don't turn
⑦ me into a monster.
⑧   Here's a clue for you all. Jodie will fall.
⑨ I've got a great poem
⑩ for you if you want it.
⑪   You asked for it.
⑫   Say hi to Les Stenson for me.

⑬ St. Elizabeths Hospital
⑭ 2700 Marten Luther King Ave
⑮ Wo trents D.C. 20032

John Hinckley Jr.

356

The restless, ambivalent, back-and-forward staggering of Hinckley's writing shows inner insecurity, his being torn between uncontrollable forces. There are aggressive moments here, as the pointed, club-like endstroke of the *2* in *82* (right corner above) and the pointed, dagger-like *t*-crossings in *articles* (2), *don't turn* (5), show. These all differ in degrees of intensity, often wild and child-like, curved like a scimitar as in *about* (3). The over-exaggerated high-stretching *I* (2) overpowers all other capitals and symbolizes Hinckley's enormous self-esteem and self-demonstration, repeated in the capitals of his signature *John Hinckley Jr.,* and in the capitals in the names *Elizabeth, Johnson, Carpozi, Lachman.* These reveal a longing for greatness, ambition. Yet, he is not able to maintain this high Ego-image. The *I*'s of lines 4 and 6 are reduced to half-size. Only from time to time do the long-shooting upper lengths occur [the *l* in *fall* (2)]. But in the end, the last high-stretching *l* loses its energy and the moment it touches the imaginary base line the whole energy is lost—note the pale downstroke when it "lands." This is the core of Hinckley's being: Immense aspirations without the physical or psychic power to fulfill them. This conflict makes him angry and aggressive and gives the whole writing its unsteady stroke picture—in one moment wild, heavy, juicy, pastose, blotted strokes which make the writing smeary and unclean, and the next moment almost clear-cut letter formations, as we see in the address *Elizabeth Hospital,* the simplicity of *Washington D.C.,* and the forcefully drawn numbers *6/27/82* and *20032.*

His is a sensual nature, as the full, round swinging *y* and *g*-loops in *guy* (6) and *Washington* (15) show. Not all *g*'s and *y*'s have the power to lead the instinctive urges to the baseline. These stay half-closed, below the baseline, and symbolize psychic and physical frustration. He tries to sublimate his longing by leaving the ground of reality and escaping into dreams and illusions. In almost every word we see suspended letters, as in *Jodie* (5) and *I've* (6). Only the word *poem* (9) falls below the line in despair. He may fear that his creative ability is not strong enough to ensure immortality.

He has no real connection to the *you*, as the incomplete construction of most of his *you*'s show. Most are done with a blotted vowel , a symbol of secrecy and inability to love, to open himself to the other. His *y*'s in *you* are not written normally with two stems, also a sign of a crippled connection to the *you*. Half way there, he starts to hesitate to contact the other, yet the narrow distances between the words show a need for people. Further, all the downstrokes end sharply on the baseline; there is no outgoing, friendly curve to meet the other person half-way. If he penetrates with long downstrokes the lower regions as in *of* (3), the *f*, (*stuff* (4), *if* (10)), we see a heavy sex denial, an angry indiscriminate aggressiveness. Particularly when the downstroke as in *if* (10) is furnished with a hook, we see fear of human contact. The reduced energy in the downstroke shows a lack of natural power. That is the clue to his weakness. He wants more than he

357

can give. His sensual longing (as we see in the pastose, smeary stroke picture with its round, full lower loops), has no value if he finds no one to turn to. He has no outlet for his sexual desires, as the smeary blotted vowels *e,g,a* in *regular* (6) and *great poem* (9) reveal. He cannot put his sensuality into poems alone or into dreams and illusions. Further, all *g*'s and *y*'s are bent-in to the left—the so-called directional pressure from the past—which means he suffered as a child, and a sense of regression accompanies him all his life. This in turn has become a restless, fluctuating insecurity, inferiority (weak downstrokes), which he tries to overcome with occasional aggressiveness, as the wild-swinging pointed *t*-crossings in *Don't turn* (6), *about* (4) demonstrate.

His logical thinking ability is in excellent order. I see no sign of insanity. There are even creative letter formations, the artistic construction of *King Ave* (14). Also, the well-formed capitals *S, J,* and the curved *g*'s and *y*'s show longing for beauty.

The counterstrokes in some words, *you, turn, regular* and *poem* are nothing unusual for a young man who fights society. We see in the sharply drawn, high signature the enormous degree of his self-admiration. Such fluctuation in writing is also characteristic of young, spoiled boys. Only the sudden fading of energy sheds some light on the insecure, weak moments, which may derive from physical and mental interruption of inner rhythm. We see a discrepancy between an extraordinary desire for greatness (high stretching into the intellectual spheres) and the sad reality that his inherited talents are too small for his high aims. In spite of his willpower (straight lines with no entanglements), his eagerness to be correct, (even left margin), mostly accurate i-dots (reliability and gift for detail work) he has seen all his efforts wasted. Sporadically, we see a word fall into the abyss of despair, and the *you* of the 8th line, but quickly he then leaves the baseline and escapes into illusions and dreams. This appears in most of the words.

Hinckley is a young man with high aspirations, some creative thoughts (*King Ave*), clear concepts of financial affairs (excellent letter formations (*D.C.*), and good sense of organization, as the straight, simplified letters of the address show.

As long as he is able to present such a well-organized script with legible letter formations one should not speak of insanity. One may however question his sense of morality when one sees the dirty, smeary middle zone and the abrupt endings of his finals, which reveal a tendency to sever relationships abruptly. Yet the clarity of the rather intelligent shaping of the script points to a person who knows what he wants.

358

Overall Impression - well-organized, legible, self-confident, sharp

First Impression of Movement - determined

First Impression of Form - often incomplete, simplified, demanding

First Impression of Arrangement - well arranged

Inner Rhythm - partly disturbed, cautious, secretive

Degree of Individuality - knows what he wants

Degree of Form Stability - consistent

Symmetry of Distribution - constantly well distributed

Writing Pressure - irregular pressure, especially in the downstrokes

Pen Pressure - according to mood—partly stronger, partly weaker

Type of Stroke - sharp

Formation of Stroke - curved and linear

Tension of Stroke - irregular

Writing Speed - alive, average speed

Connectedness - connected

Disconnectedness - no disconnectedness

Connective Form - angles, firm garlands, some arcades

Size of Script - irregular middle zone, mostly average-high

Width - average

Directional Trend - left-bound loops (left trend), sharp extended strokes (line 3), like number 2, combining *oh* in *Johnson, th* in *the*—future-oriented

Enrichment - simplification of the capitals

Initial Accentuation - enlarged capitals and signature (self-confidence)

Terminal Accentuation - *sharp cut-off endings* (almost all finals)
> *counterstrokes* you (3), turn (6), Monster (7), rather (5)
> *arcadic finals* Martin (14), I'm (6), regular (6)
> *half completed u-forms* of you (10,11), half n's, r's
> *thinned, final downstrokes* looking like needles: St. (13), about (4), stuff (4), but (5), rest (5), just (6), Don't (6), fall (8), got (9),

great (9), *if* (10), wan*t it* (10), i*t* (11), *t* in *Luther* (14)
suspended finals—me (7), *want* (10), *Jodie, the rest* (5), jus*t* (6),
Don't (6), *you* (10, 11), *Martin* (14)

Slant - slight fluctuation between right to vertical to left

Writing Zones - irregular middle zone, high upper zone, mostly deep penetrating lower
lengths

Differences in Length - large (restless)

Fullness - meager, due to sharp middle zone

Distance between Words - small

Distance between Lines - sufficient

Direction of Lines - slightly up and down

Left Margin - even left margin

Right Margin - sufficient

i-Dots - most accurately dotted i's, some changing in thickness, *if* (10), some running forward, *Hinckley* (15)

Overall Structure - well-structured in spite of the heavy fluctuations, no entanglement of
lines, good overview

Added Observations:
Directional pressure from the past: To-the-left-bent downstroke *j* in *just* (6), the *g*
in Washington, regular (6), *y* in *guy* and *you* (8), (10), (11)
Irregular I-pronoun, very large in (3) with strong mother image, smaller in (4) with
larger father image, normal Ego image in (6) and (9)
Inventive forms as in *King Ave* (14)
Inside a word, fluctuations and falling finals - as in *guy* (6), *you* (8), *poem* (9), *into* (7)

I'm going to pray for you, Rosina, that you find alot of friends in this world and that you find someone to love, who can be with you and share his life with you.

Goodbye, Rosina, and thank you for caring. Take care.

Yours Truly
David B.
(Sam)

In this pastose school writing the murderous David Berkowitz shows no control system. The plump, clumsy, primitive script with bursts of irregular pressure reveals explosive and uncontrollable instincts. The writing rolls slowly along with its thick, smeary, blotted strokes, sometimes even so thick that one can deduce changes in blood circulation and sudden compulsions.

This simple school writing shows no special intellect and the slowly wavering slant, from vertical to right, back to vertical and to the left, shows a kind of comfortable laziness. The first impression is that it seems to have been written by a simple-minded person who could not harm anyone. But looking closer we discover in these fortified, muddy strokes the result of highly-charged outbreaks. The outwardly well-organized script with its even left margin shows eagerness to be correct and to work conscientiously, with occasional procrastination, as the to-the-left-set i-dots disclose.

Sensuality is mirrored in the fat strokes of *you, Goodbye, thank, Yours truly,* and *Sam.* The thick, muddy lower loop of *y* in *you* shows an abnormally primitive sex-drive which sometimes results in frustration (when the lower loops do not reach the base line as in the *y* of *Goodbye* and the *y* in *truly*). He is self-protective and cautious, as the final arcades of *h* and *n* in *with* and *can* show. The cut-off endings in *someone* and *love* show the tendency to sever relationships abruptly. The suspended finals (*with you*) show his escaping from reality into illusions and dreams. The lower loop of the *y* of *you* is smeary and reveals excessive sensuality. The *g* in *caring* reveals partly unfulfilled sexual urges.

Where is Berkowitz, the murderer? There are some clues. The capital *G* in *Goodbye* shows directional pressure from above—this means that all his life he had to submit to perceived authoritarian influences—teachers, parents, employers, commanding officers He felt worthless and small. The wide gaps between words show how lonely he feels. He tried to have revenge. We see it in the counterstrokes of the *r* in *for,* the last stem of the *n* in *Rosina* and the last stems of the *u* in *you,* which symbolize hate and rebellious thoughts. He killed out of hate for society, driven solely by primitive instincts and frustrated sensuality (the victims were loving couples). The sudden swelling of the lower loops which appear so colorful and fat in the otherwise normally written script show changes in blood pressure, fits of sexual arousal which became a compulsion to murder those who were happier than he. This happens in the old part of the brain, which is not controlled by the new brain, and we see it in the stroke pictures of other murderers. (Look at the ax-like crossing of the words of the 16-year-old Ernst Waldow, who killed his parents. We see battering strokes, brutally drawn.) Irregularity in pressure is always a sign of sudden emotional outbreak, a disturbance in hypothalamic behavior. It occurs also in the script of Lee Oswald with its smeary, blotted letter-formations, which show yielding to instincts without the controlling force of reason of the neo-cortex brain (as we learned from Pophal).

362

Vicious 16-year-old murderer Ernst Waldow,
whose hammering blows appear in the thick, smeary downstroke—
a primitive, violent limbic brain.

Brutal killer who murdered for money, revealed by the enrolled numbers, the primitive
forms of the figures, and the merciless, harsh stroke.

Lee Harvey Oswald

Blotted, smeary stroke picture (instinctual urges)
Primitive letter formations
Harsh severing of relationships, *or* (second line)
Blotted vowels (secrecy and anxiety)
Incomplete vowels *a = o* in *Thank, Harvey*
Lower loops swinging to the left too much, a regressive sign of leaning on someone's shoulder; detachment from the mother; did not succeed in psycho-sexual development.
Lower loops do not lead to the base line (frustration).
We need only study the sudden smeary, blotted, pastose-appearing, enlarged letter formations of all "David Berkowitz's" to become alarmed about compulsiveness, abnormal behavior changes, and potentially dangerous mood swings.

363

Handwriting Analysis of David Berkowitz

Overall Impression - primitive, directional pressure from above (fears authority), ambivalent fluctuations in slant and pressure

First Impression of Movement - slow, cautious

First Impression of Form - school writing (calculated)

First Impression of Arrangement - well arranged

Inner Rhythm - slow-creeping along

Degree of Individuality - emotionally disturbed

Degree of Form Stability - outward stability

Symmetry of Distribution - mechanically distributed

Writing Pressure - soft

Pen Pressure - soft

Type of Stroke - pastose, smeary, blotted

Formation of Stroke - curved

Tension of Stroke - relaxed

Writing Speed - slow

Connectedness - connected

Disconnectedness - none

Connective Form - drooping garlands, covered vowels, arcades

Size of Script - irregular in size

Width - average mixed with secondary width

Directional Trend - left-bound loops (left trend)

Enrichment - rich, full letters

Initial Accentuation - some initial letters enlarged as *s* in *someone* (4)

Terminal Accentuation - *cut-off terminals*: for (1, 8), that (2), lot (2), in (3), that (3), someone (4), love (4) = ending relationships abruptly
suspended finals: with (6), Rosina (7), you (6)
counterstrokes: for (8, 1), you (2, 6)
sharp, fortified finals: take care (8), someone, share (5), Goodbye (7) = energetic determination
Arcadic finals: can (5), with (6) = calculation

Slant - slightly wavering from vertical to the right and back

Writing Zones - irregular middle zone in width, size, slant

Differences in Length - average

Fullness - full

Distance between Words - irregular

Distance between Lines - large (lonely)

Direction of Lines - straight

Left Margin - even (eager to be correct)

Right Margin - sufficient

i-Dots - mostly accurate, to-the-left, *with* (5,6), *friends* (3), procrastination

Overall Structure - mechanically and slowly done to hide inner disturbances (uncontrollable emotions seen in the stroke picture)

HANDWRITING ANALYSIS OF WILLIAM SHAKESPEARE

In his book, *In Search of Shakespeare* (Harcourt, Brace & Jovanovich), Charles Hamilton says: "It is amazing that no professional handwriting expert has ever before made an examination of the Shakespeare documents to be able to deliver a handwriting analysis," and he suggested that I do the analysis.

Trusting his meticulous research and knowledge of paleography I felt secure, especially when I studied his comparison of the identical words between the lines of Shakespeare's *last will* (A), in Shakespeare's *Application for a Coat of Arms* (B) in 1599 and in the writings from the years 1592-1596, in the so-called *Northumberland Manuscripts*.

I decided to choose the flamboyant pages of the *Application for a Coat of Arms* for my analysis — Shakespeare was 35 years old then, in 1599, — at the height of his fame. He was director of the Globe Theater under the protection of Queen Elizabeth I. He wrote the plays that he directed, composed the drum and trumpet music, and designed the props and costumes for each of his plays in which he took small parts, mainly to supervise his actors during each performance.

This kaleidoscope of talents and activities is mirrored in his incredibly speedy, vivacious script. Wildly crossed-out lines and a fluctuating slant on surprisingly straight lines show discipline victorious over his bursting temperament.

The so-called *lyrical d's* throw their heads to the left, revealing bonds to the past, to the sources of fantasy, dreams, creativity, and childhood memories. The simplified capitals are swinging to the right, to-the-left-open to all new influences, shooting beautiful curves into the air with efficient artistry or landing below the words, underscoring them with utmost self-admiration. The pastosity of this fat, juicy stroke picture shows a lust for living, a sensuous appetite for all pleasures the world has to offer. But the strict frame of the script and even left margin show how inner development will progress — to an ethical, moral, probably even rigid character in old age.

Hamilton states that the small scribbles between the lines in the last will (see arrow) convinced him that the whole three pages of the will were written by the poet in the year 1616 when he suffered from shaking palsy, a progressive muscular weakness and tremor which impaired the voluntary writing movements. Yet, the whole script has the same known qualities of the writer, — the pressure, the slant, the to-the-right-swinging lower loops, the to-the-left turned d-heads, the small gaps between words and lines, overlong lower lengths. The ataxia of the signature is probably due to its having been written a month or two later when Shakespeare was nearer to death.

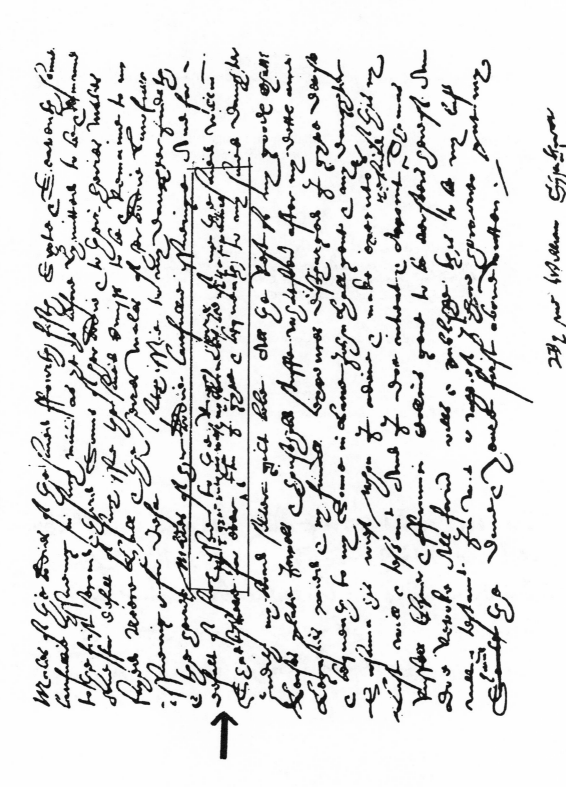

By me William Shakspeare

Shakespeare's Last Will and Testament

(A)

Handwriting Analysis of William Shakespeare

Comparison between the added interline words with the authentic signature:
Both are identical.

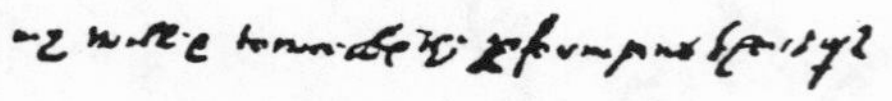

1)

2)

First line (1) is taken from the
interline 8 and 9.

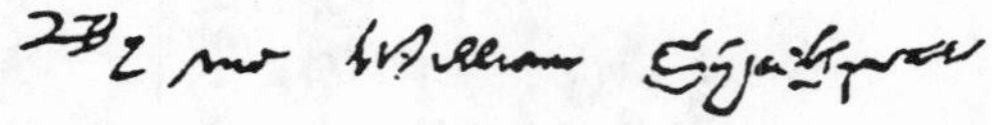

Shakespeare's signature
by me William Shakespeare

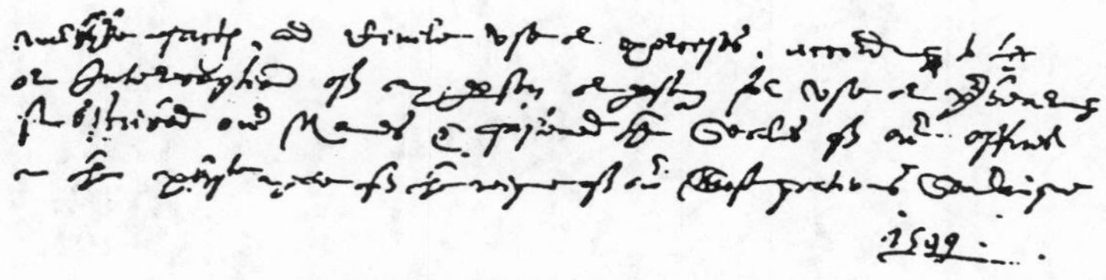

End of draft of Coat of Arms

The capital *D* in Shakespeare's writing

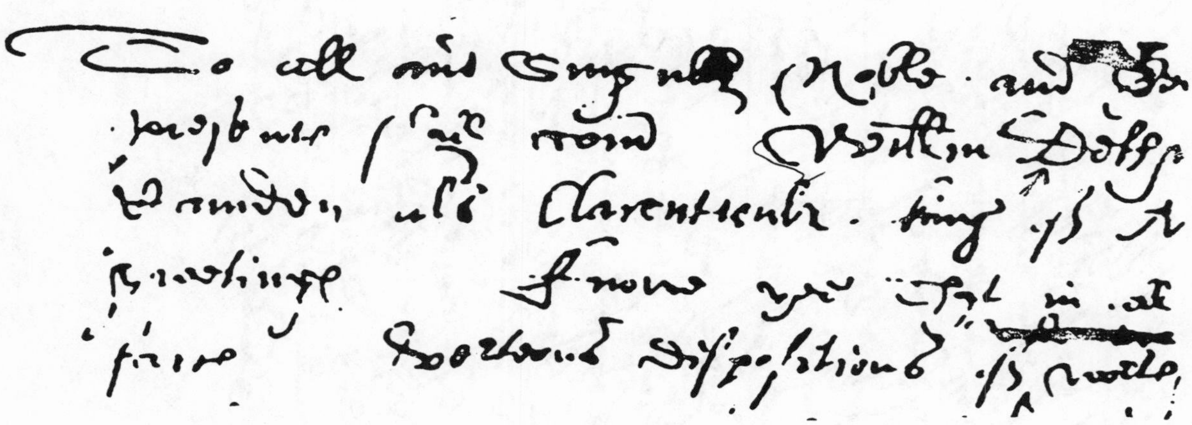

Draft of Coat of Arms

					Writing of last will
					Samples of writing of the Northumberland Manuscript (1592-1596)
					Authentic last will
					Authentic Northumberland Manuscript
					Authentic last will
					Authentic Northumberland Manuscript
					Authentic last will
					Authentic Northumberland Manuscript

The comparison of authentic writing-samples — last will, application-draft for the Coat of Arms, and the Northumberland manuscript — proves that all three writings are identical and written by William Shakespeare.

(B)

On October 20, 1599, Shakespeare worked on a draft of an application for a coat of arms in the name of his father, John Shakespeare, as required by the College of Heraldry. The handwriting on this draft is that of William Shakespeare. He also drew the sketch of the falcon on the weapon.

This Coat of Arms script looks as if a hurricane has blown through its middle zone, crushing it into pieces only stopping for a moment when it approaches the name of his father *John Shakespeare* in the upper and lower line of this sample (B).

Suddenly we see the obedient son respectfully standing before his authoritative father, and the handwriting gets at once orderly, regulated (in the even middle zone with each letter distinguished), and legible for the first time in the whole running script. The next words — after this reverence for family — are again shortened, cut-off, dancing in all directions with happy rhythmical movements. The rarely set *i*-dots become accent-like commas; the partly connected, partly disconnected flight of the letters show his artistic combination of logic and intuition. Only the left even margin and the even distance between the straight lines guarantee a perfect sense of organization in the midst of surrounding chaos. He needs freedom to create. He is his own master, who makes his own rules in spelling, punctuation and abbreviation in the most fantastic way. He omits vowels (as in the Hebrew alphabet), and simplifies words (as in the modern New York advertising *Nite* for *Night*).

Like a wild river he storms forward with this unpredictable spelling, the inconsistencies; he cannot think within narrow boundaries. He is lucky to live in the Elizabethan era, where only Latin was taught in schools and spelling was regulated and precise. English was regarded mainly as a spoken language and any spelling was acceptable as long as one could understand the meaning. Shakespeare took advantage of this freedom. When it came to capitals he left the decision, large or small, to his ever-changing moods. When his capricious mind wanted to play he invented two *l*'s for one, two *m*'s for one and the vowel *i* would be sometimes replaced by a *y*. His fiery, passionate writing style showed preference for the writing style of the *secretary hand* over the *running hand*, used in the Elizabethan era, but spelling remained unpredictable in both.

So it happened that this great poet, who created immortal verses as well as dramas, gave headaches to his contemporaries by his illegible handwriting and no doubt remained a mystery to most of them. They probably only guessed at the beauty of his free-swinging inner rhythm, expressing creative genius in the impatient, passionate speed.

It is due to patient and dedicated researchers like Hamilton that we are able to compare the key words from the application with key words from the poet's last will, and thus, identify this script as Shakespeare's. In the poet's last will we see the sad destiny of a fiery mind chained by the progressive disease, shaking palsy which caused the voluntary finger movements to no longer function and contributed to his death at the age of 52.

Secretary and court hands from the 1891 edition of Thomas Wright's *Court Hand Restored*

Secretary and court hands from the 1891 edition of Thomas Wright's *Court Hand Restored*

Running-hand Alphabet

of the

XVᵗʰ & XVIᵗʰ CENTURIES:

Designed to facilitate the decyphering of old manuscript Letters, &c.

Secretary, or running, hand from Thomas Astle's
The Origin and Progress of Handwriting (1784)

DOCUMENT EXAMINATION

DOCUMENT EXAMINATION OF JOSEF MENGELE'S RESUME
(1937/1938), AS COMPARED WITH SAMPLES, FOUND IN A BRAZILIAN HOUSE, SHORTLY AFTER HIS ALLEGED DEATH.

Questioned Document
Sample found in a Brazilian house after Josef Mengele's alleged death.

Authentic Handwriting of Josef Mengele from a résumé written in 1937/1938.

Lebenslauf:

(Ausführlich und eigenhändig mit Tinte geschrieben.)

1 Am 16. III. 1911 wurde ich als Sohn des Fabrikleiters
2 Ing. Karl Mengele und seiner Ehefrau Walburga
3 geb. Hupfauer in Günzburg a/Donau geboren. Nach 4
4 jährigem Besuch der Volksschule in Günzburg, kam ich auf
5 das dortige Gymnasium, wo ich Ostern 1930 das Zeugnis
6 der Reife erhielt. Darauf studierte ich in München u. Bonn
7 Medizin. Im Sommer 1932 legte ich die ärztl. Vorprüfung in Bonn
8 ab und studierte dann weiter in Wien u. München Medizin
9 u. Naturwissenschaften. Im Herbst 1935 promovierte ich an der
10 philosophischen Fakultät 5. Sektion der Universität München zum
11 Dr. phil. und bestand vor dem Prüfungsausschuss in Wien
12 eben im Sommer 1936 meine ärztl. Staatsprüfung.
13 Am 1. September 1937 erhielt ich die Bestallung als Arzt. Im
14 Sommer 1938 promovierte ich an der Med. Fakultät der
15 Universität Frankfurt a/M. zum Dr. med. Nach meinem
16 Studium war ich als Medizinalpraktikant zuerst 4
17 Monate an der Medizinischen Universitätsklinik in Leipzig,
18 von 1.1.1937 ab am Universitätsinstitut für Erbbiologie u.
19 Rassenhygiene in Frankfurt a/M. tätig. Seit 1.9.1937
20 bin ich Assistenzarzt am letztgenannten Institut.
21 Vom 29. IV. 31 bis 31. I. 34 gehörte ich dem „Stahlhelm",
22 dann bis Oktober 1934 der S.A. an, aus der ich wegen
23 eines Nierenleidens ausschied. Im Mai 1937 beantragte
24 ich meine Aufnahme in die N.S.D.A.P., im Mai
25 1938 meine Aufnahme in die SS. Zur Zeit diene
26 ich als Jäger im Gebirgsjägerregiment 137/13. Komp. in
27 Saalfelden i/Tirol.

Josef Mengele.

28 [boxed inset:]
1 gegen den Darwinismus u.
2 widerlegen konnte. Gegen d...
3 die Evolution als einen
4 ... vorgang an die b...
5 ... des Umwelt durch
...

Given Material: Handwritten résumé of Josef Mengele from the years 1937/1938
One questioned document found in a Brazilian House, 1985

Document Examination: Josef Mengele

Given Material:
One page of Josef Mengele's résumé from the years 1937/1938.
One sample of a Questioned Document found in a Brazilian house.

Question:
Are the writings identical?

Interpretation

      The two given handwritings, Josef Mengele's handwritten résumé from the years 1937/1938 and the Questioned Document, found in a Brazilian house just before the discovery of his alleged remains must be compared with each other to establish their identity.
      We see the speedy rhythm, the same connective forms, (supported garlands and softened angles with the smeary corners), the same logical continuity of writing interrupted in letter-groups to leave space for intuitive ideas. The greatest similarity consists in the strong *t*-crossings which appear in both writings in the same short manner and in about the same height of the *t*-stem:

Questioned Document
Evolution as written in the
Questioned Document

Authentic
The t-strokes often fly higher, but
we see the same strength and the same
pastosity in both writings.

One of the essential similarities between the authentic and the Questioned Document writing is the construction of the capital *D*.

Questioned Document
Darwinismus, Dieser

Authentic
Darauf, Dr., Dr., Donau, NSDAP
The D-capital has the extra stroke
at the top.

The simplified construction of the *E*-capital is the same in both writings.

Questioned Document
Evolution

Authentic
Ehefrau, Erbbiologie

Questioned Document
Umwelt

Authentic
Am, zum, meinem, med.

The tendency to let the three stems of the letter *m* in a word fall down successively, as in the Questioned Document's *Umwelt*, is also seen in the résumé in *Am, in, zum, am, meinem.*

Questioned Document
konnte

Authentic
Medizinalpraktikant, Frankfurt,
Oktober, Universitätsklinik

The smeary, blotted construction of *konnte* (Questioned Document) is also visible in the résumé writing of 1937/1938 in the words *Medizinalpraktikant, Frankfurt, Oktober, Universitätsklinik.*

Questioned Document
Umwelt

Authentic
Universitätsklinik, Universitätsinstitut
Universität

The construction of the capital *U* in *Umwelt* (Questioned Document) is the same in both writings with the speedily written capital *U*, in its smeary downstrokes with the blotted corners, filled with ink.

Questioned Document
Umwelt

Authentic
erhielt, Fakultät, Frankfurt, Universität

The strongly extended *t*-stroke in *Umwelt* (Questioned Document) is visible in the résumé-writing of 1937/1938 in *Institut, erhielt, Fakultät, Frankfurt,* and *Universität.*

Questioned Document
Dieser

Authentic
seiner, Hupfauer, vor, für,
September, Sommer, der, war,
der, Nierenleidens, Medizinalpraktikant

The sharp downward-turning terminal *r* (in the Questioned Document) *Dieser* is recognizable in all **1937** résumé *r*'s: *seiner, Hupfauer, vor, für, September, Sommer, der, war, der, Nierenleidens, Medizinalpraktikant.*

Questioned Document

Authentic

Summary

We see in the Questioned Document the same blotted, pastose, smeary letter-formations as in the original résumé. Especially in *Josef Mengele*, the signature, we see in the *f* and the last *e*, the indications of criminality: a smeary stroke-picture. We see the blood, the mud and the impurity early, in the 26 year-old Mengele who just had completed his medical examination. One sees the aggressive *r*'s with their negative downstrokes, kicking downwards as if to hurt everyone below his social class.

The stroke-picture of the Questioned Document is many degrees more smeary, and blotted with ink in the corners of every letter, and shows Mengele's dirty work during these years of killing and experimenting with his helpless victims in Auschwitz. The identity of both writings is established and this shows us once again that the brain pattern is already drawn in early years and does not change.

Courtesy of The Federal Archives, Koblenz, West Germany
Original Hitler writing: Sample from Hitler's *Testament,* written in 1938

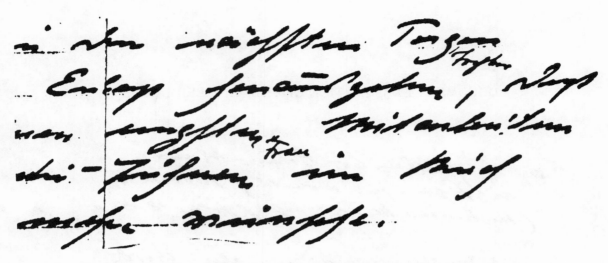

Questioned Document: Sample of alleged Hitler Diaries

Questioned Document E-capital   *Authentic E*-capital

Without going into the detail work of examining the singular letter-formations of the Questioned Document writing, as compared with the authentic Hitler script, we observe at once the more pastose, fat, indistinctive stroke picture of the Questioned Document, compared with the pastose, but more indifferentiated stroke picture of the original. There is more variation, more shading in the authentic writing, and more precision, more legibility in spite of the also slightly pastose stroke picture. The Questioned Document seems to be written by a more primitive writer who has less fantasy in creating new, different letter formations. After he had invented one capital *E*, for instance, in *Erlass* (line 2), he used this form in all his writing without changing, whereas in Hitler's writing we have a different *E*-capital, another movement, enrolled at the base-line and not at the top as in the Questioned Document *E*-capital. The Hitler *E*-capital seems more flexible, whereas the Questioned Document *E* has an even pasty form with a very simple movement without the round, efficient curves of the Hitler writing.

Let us compare the *T*-capital of the Questioned Document, *Tagen* (line 1). Again we see the doughy, undistinguished, muddy form of *Tagen* without a chiselled vowel *a*, a blotted *g*-head and an illegible *en*, almost brush-like, painted instead of drawn.

Authentic: Tochter, Testaments, Testament, Tode, Tempel

The original *T*'s show variations, compared with the primitive fat stroke picture of the Questioned Document writer:

Questioned Document: Taugenichtsen, Truppen

In the Questioned Document we see the wide-spread letters which lack concentration, variations and rank. All letters look the same: brush-like, plump and wasting space. He is not able to draw delicate upstrokes as in the capital *T* of the original writer: *Tode, Tempel.* The sudden change in Hitler's writing from 'wolf in sheepskin' strokes, from refinement to fanatic willpower as in *Testaments,* is more dangerous than the oily pastosity of the Questioned Document writer.

Questioned Document: Hitzköpfe, Himmler, Herrgott

The Questioned Document forger's treasure of letter formations is limited. Although he needed two years to practice the Hitler signature, he seems happy to fabricate just one pattern of capital-H, whereas Hitler's H-capitals vary continuously.

Authentic: Heerwesen, Hoffnung, Haus, Herrn, Herr, Hitler

1908

1920

1925

1929

1937

1938

1943

1944

29. 4. 1945

Authentic signatures

Questioned Document: Hitler's "signature"

Not one of the gathered original Hitler signatures comes close to the exaggerated large forgery, not even the overlarge 1929 authentic Hitler signature. In spite of long years of practice the forger failed to see the always-turned-down-to-the-abyss-*f*-crossing in *Adolf*, and that the downstroke of his *f* is too long. The garlandic successively decreasing downstrokes lack in their exaggerated height the sharpness and fanaticism of the original signatures.

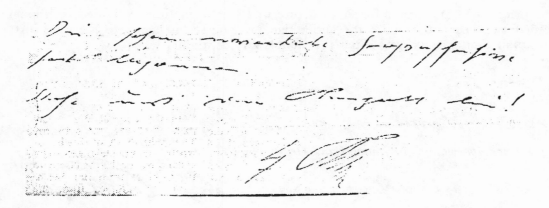

Questioned Document: The forger's conception of a deteriorated Adolf Hitler in the last days before death.

Berlin, den 29. April 1945, 4.00 Uhr.

Authentic: The last signature.

The forger's writing is completely wrong when he tries to dramatize the last days of Hitler, where he constructs a soft and tired downward-falling, weak handwriting, whereas the ataxia of Hitler's progressive muscular weakness and tremor which impaired his voluntary writing movements — shaking palsy — made it impossible to write curves — only rigid strokes.

Questioned Document: Frau

Authentic: Franz

The whole structure of the Questioned Document is wrong in comparison with the authentic Hitler writing. The upper *F*-crossing is divided equally on both sides of the *F*-stem, touching or crossing it to some degree so that the stem penetrates the upper "protective" curve. In the capital *F* of the Questioned Document writing, the stem has a slight to-the-left turn, whereas the Authentic *F*-capitals are drawn straight. The Questioned Document has a wider, more outstretched appearance, whereas the original is written concentrated, with less width. The original vowel *a*'s of the original are blotted with ink, whereas the Questioned Document *a*-vowel is differently constructed with a round loop which leaves an upenness in the *a* which assures the naiveté of the Questioned Document writer. The covered *a*'s in the authentic belie secrecy and cunning.

The proportion of the Questioned Document and the Authentic differ completely in slant, width, size and construction of the letter forms. The middle crossing stroke of the *F*-capital is curved in the original, for instance, and straight in the Questioned Document *F*-capital.

Questioned Document: Leid, Lumpen

Authentic: Lebenszeit, Lammers, Linge, Loyd

The plump Questioned Document's, compared with the more differentiated of the Authentic show errors in the construction of the capital *L*. The base line loop is too wide in the Questioned Document *a*-vowel is differently constructed with a round loop which leaves an openness original capitals *L* in *Lebenszeit, Lammers* and *Linge*. We see again the usual negligence of the forger in his *m* row of *Lumpen* in comparison to the exact *m*-row in the original *Lammers*.

Questioned Document: Grund, Gelegenheit

Authentic: George, Gas, Ganz, Gefängnis

In the Questioned Document writing we see again this clumsy, fat stroke picture in comparison with the more differentiated, legible thin stroke picture of the authentic writer: the precision of his diacritical signs (the little strokes above the *a* in *Gefängnis*), his wide intuition-gaps inside longer words where the letter groups are separated widely from each other, also as in *Gefängnis*. The forger knows only one construction of the capital *G* which, once established, he uses constantly, whereas the authentic *G*'s have a number of differentiations, sometimes simplified, sometimes with elaborated upper curves as in *Gas, Ganz*.

Questioned Document: Wilhelm, Warschau   *Authentic: Weltrevolution, Was*

The construction of the capital *W* is completely wrong; the forger draws round, simplified curves without the know-how of the German Gothic school writing which is often used in Hitler's letter formations. All precision is lost in the forger's try to imitate the original and the outcome is an undistinguished, pasty row of illegible letters. In spite of the speed of the authentic writer, every letter is legible and carefully chiselled.

Questioned Document: Vizekanzler, Verdienste   *Authentic: Vermögen, Verträge*

The pastosity and the thread-like endings in the forger's writing, wide-spread and negligent in form and proportion, are different from the more complicated, accurate formation of the letters in the authentic writing.

Questioned Document: Befehl,   *Authentic: Berliner, Bücher,*
Buchhaltertyp   *Briefschaften*

The forger tends to bring the last downstrokes of his capitals below the base line as in *Befehl, Buchhaltertyp, Vizekanzler* (above).

Questioned Document: Die, Drang

Authentic: Die, Der

Again the forger shows carelessness in his attempt to imitate Hitler's handwriting. The forger prefers the lower regions of materialism whereas the original writer emphasizes the upper regions of ideas.

Questioned Document: Kundgebungen

Authentic: Kaiserismus, Kannenberg

In the word *Kundgebungen* the forger overlooks the variations of Hitler's capitals, as we see in the differently executed *K*-capitals. But the most important trait the forger has not observed is the downward slope in Hitler's handwriting, as in the word *Kannenberg*. The forger is an optimistic personality, carefree and superficial in work and in character, whereas the original writer is a deeply depressive character. We can go on and on with samples which do not bear the slightest similarity to the original writing and wonder only why the world did not recognize right away the *"Hitler Diaries"* as a clumsy forgery.

INSINCERITY IN HANDWRITING

It is important for the graphologist to be aware of signs of insincerity in handwriting. We know that this unpleasant character trait exists and must try to determine when it became dominant. How does insincerity develop in a person? Is it a residue of childhood carried into adulthood? Is it due to a restricted environment, fear of the future? Whatever the reason, it is worthwhile to look for the manifestations in the graphic elements.

We begin with *façade writing*. It is a mask, an artificial over-evaluation of the form. The aesthetic stylization—the façade—is born out of a slow, non-spontaneous mental process. The inessential is exaggerated out of vanity, to conceal feelings of emptiness. Ridiculously inflated forms are an effort to mask identity. The result is that the writing distracts us and we can hardly read the words.

Another form of façade is created when the letter forms are too regular, artificially planned in every detail to match conventional form, resembling the dress of an undercover agent who wears a disguise to blend in with the crowd. In slow and deliberately non-spontaneous movement, insincerity has time to develop.

If the handwriting has rigidity of form and also both concealing arcades and monotonous circular traits, then the nature of the person is insincere and basically egocentric. The girl in the sample on the next page tries to hide both egocentrism and insincerity.

I have felt this need to go out and pass the word of God to my fellow man. And for that reason, I am now taking a ___ on the Bible. I feel ___ and feel that it is

It is erroneous to think that insincerity develops slowly. The insincere writer can attain virtuosity in presenting automatic, almost playfully offered lies; so much so that there is no need to slow down. The artful revelations flow from his quick-working mental fantasy world in graceful packages. Always ready to fabricate an appropriate explanation for any new, unforeseen situation, his spontaneity will not suffer.

In these spiral-shaped initials we find symptoms of secrecy, dishonesty of intention, a whole complex of hidden thoughts. The truth is symbolically rewound like the spring of a wind-up toy. Vanity, delusion, and egocentricity are pictured in these initial upper movements.

The most significant signs of insincerity are revealed in the covered form by the concealed stroke and the concealed curve. The *concealing stroke,* either up or down, retraces itself so the two strokes become one. Psychologically it demonstrates unsatisfied ambition, or shyness and inhibition. It occurs especially in the middle zone, the seat of heart and soul. Instead of continuing the stroke to the right in an expansive gesture, the shy writer clings to the same up or down stroke. He hides himself symbolically behind a tree, not to be discovered, not to be held accountable for his deeds—an ostrich with head in the sand.

Look at the concealed *e* and *r* in the middle zone of *prayers.* In *yours,* the *r* and *s* are

389

concealed. The word *you* has two concealed strokes in the *o* and in the *u* which looks like an *r*. In the word *can*, the *a* and *n* are filled with ink and covered.

If the concealing strokes occur in the upper zone, we speak of intellectual inhibition, a manifestation of intellectual self-deception.

If the concealing strokes occur in the lower zone, as shown by the *g*'s in the sample below, any instinctual desire will remain suppressed. Little effort will be made in that direction. If concealing strokes are drawn with a light pressure (shown), privacy will be the rule in material matters as well. Such writers will be secretive in matters of money and sexuality, for example.

If the lower lengths are drawn with pressure, a stronger *libido* than usual is revealed. The covered lower lengths in the sample below reveal a person generally hiding strong instinctual urges.

In the sample below, the writer creates spiral vowels in the middle zone and in the *d* and *g* heads. This demands more skill and is done by more advanced liars, those who lie efficiently. The writer circles the truth like a cat circles a hot plate of food. He makes detours and excuses with great showmanship.

The covered *a* vowel in *mama* is drawn with such precision that only the darker edges show the double covering up.

The covered forms in the middle zone are typical of deception in the emotional sphere and often reveal compulsive secrecy. Covered garlands reveal shyness.

[handwriting sample: "subconscious"]

The arcade in its arch form is a construction under which the writer can hide fine manners, culture, morality. He shows us whatever he wants us to believe.

[handwriting sample: "feelings between us. I am very sorry for"]

The *covered arcade* symbolizes insincerity by use of an added concealing stroke. It is also called the *supported arcade*. It shows signs of cunning, calculation and cautiousness (the hypocrisy of Molière's Tartuffe).

[handwriting sample: "am much"]

The covered form created by angular connective strokes is the sacré coeur connective form, taught in European convents to strengthen the morals and ethics of teenaged nobility. This writing form is responsible for the disguise and lack of spontaneity of a 'lady.' As in the sample below, she has learned to conceal her emotions. She has learned to dole out the truth in small doses.

[handwriting samples]

Related to *sacré coeur* is the *shark tooth*. It is found in the middle zone and gives the writer a sharpness with words. The writer has the ability or habit of attacking people verbally, either politely or cunningly.

[handwriting sample]

A special kind of covering occurs in puberty. It is used by youngsters to hide and protect awakening emotions.

[handwriting sample]

The *terminal arcade* is so called because the last letter is bent to the left in an arcadic form. It expresses calculation, cautiousness and taciturnity.

[handwriting sample]

If it is drawn with pressure it may signify brutality. Theologically speaking, it is a sin of omission. The writer of such terminal arcade says less than honesty demands.

Another sign of insincerity is the one we find in *the thread* connective form. This kind of writing is eel-like. The strokes slip, evade, and turn aside to avoid strict, decisive connective forms. A writer with this connective form shows psychic insight, diplomacy and adaptability at any price. He has psychic and intellectual versatility. Because he understands people he can deceive them easily. The snake-like connective form may indicate a lying, calculating impostor who bluffs, breaks promises and is unreliable.

Another form of insincerity is the opening of letters towards the base line. The letters are closed at the top and open on the base line, a reversed process (for instance, a garland is usually written with raised arms to receive the grace of heaven. Here, it is shut off on top and open at the bottom.) Very often we see open *b*'s = *bitter*

so that the truth can "fall out." Some separate the vowel *a* instead of *a = Ol*

to construct more visually the closed circle of the a-vowel.

If turned around loops appear in the lower zone, we have the symbol of sublimation of instinctive urges, as in the writing of Oscar Wilde.

If in a connected handwriting the *a*-vowel begins with an arcadic transformation, (like ⌣) and is connected in a rolling fluent movement with the letters to the right, this *a* will look like a horizontally lying *s*. Psychologically speaking, it is a deception. This is the *counterstroke movement,* which can be created four ways: the reversed opening at the bottom, the arcade in its purest form, breaking of a single stroke into two separate parts, and a substitution of the deceiving letter *s*.

A very important sign of insincerity is the correction of wrong spelling, the Freudian *'slips of the pen.'* The writer has something else deep in his subconscious mind and he stumbles over his own lies in writing and speaking. (Writing is loud thinking). The reason for many mistakes and corrections may be nervous disturbances, illness, or lack of education. The corrections of misspelling make the script worse. Early graphologists spoke of *parasitic behavior.* If the correction is done clumsily, causing an exposed ugly blot, it is a sign of neurosis.

As such, this type of writing is symptomatic of exaggerated sensibility, irritability or lack of self-control.

A smaller signature than usual shows us that the writer deliberately plays the modest person. He hides his arrogance behind a consciously constructed mask, portraying false modesty. Other signs of insincerity are the omission of letters, giving us neglected, careless, incomplete words. This we notice especially in the *m* and *n*'s shown below.

Looped garlands are a sign of exaggerated amiability, not necessarily genuine. This holds true with illegible handwriting—the writer hides the true nature behind unrecognizable letters.

Looped arcades are a sign of concealed calculation, courtesy and politeness. In this sample above we have looped garlands, looped arcades and illegibility.

Sharp strokes, especially in the initials, mean cruelty and sadism. Sharpness throughout the writing means intellectual sharpness and hypercritical malice. This writer's priority is self-preservation. He must overcome impulses toward humanism. His feelings are turned into aggressiveness, cruelty, and may even involve sadomasochistic perversion.

If the last stroke of the *m*, as in this word *from*, turns suddenly in another direction, we call it the *counter-stroke*, which shows mistrust, caution, a sudden check of emotions and unforeseen changes in mood.

In a handwriting, pressure is always important. If graceful *lasso movements* are done with light pressure, light-handedly, the writer is one who charms, envelops or enwraps people. If the writing pressure is flickering and pastose (thick) in the stroke picture, we see a seducer. In this case, friendly persuasion is done in the area of sexuality.

393

Table of Insincerity in Handwriting

Sharp handwriting, connected elegantly, means abuse of others' trust and confidence.

Arcadic initial upstrokes with hooks mean cruelty hidden by a benign mask.

Long initial upstrokes with hooks mean tyranny or continual contradiction of others.

Sharp initial strokes mean sadism.

Initial and terminal loops mean rhetorical insincerity.

Calligraphically enriched capitals mean hiding true purpose behind amiability.

Blotty, smeary script shows criminal tendency.

Illegibility means desire not to be known.

Enlarged flickering strokes mean irritated oversensibility of the schizoid type (as an expression of the influence of the vegetative nervous system).

Sudden senseless pressure strokes show parasitic behavior.

Difference in pressure means psychic irritability.

Insecurity in strokes means easily hurt psychologically.

Speed with exaggerated right slant means overrunning, arousing other person's suggestibility.

Diminishing word-endings mean gift of psychic insight and diplomacy.

Widened terminal strokes mean expansion, lack of inhibition and conceit.

Small compressed middle zone with great differences of letter-lengths means high-striving aims by small, restricted inner personality.

Ink-blotted circles in vowels of *a* and *o* show anal-erotic tendencies.

THE FOUR FUNCTIONS
C. G. JUNG'S PSYCHOLOGICAL TYPES

As we discussed earlier, Jung categorized behavior in two large character groups which correspond to two fundamental attitudes which determine the individual's behavior in the world: the *extraverted type* and the *introverted type*. In the extravert, the libido is directed toward the outer world. He is sociable, adventurous and is in need of steady human contact. The introvert is opposed to the extravert. Often timid, extremely sensitive, he lives in his shell and hesitates to contact others. He is often regarded as egotistic because he is more exclusive and his interests are basically subjective.

Jung further created the four functional types, all of which exist in an individual and all of which are used in dealing with the world. These are *SENSATION, THINKING, IN-TUITION, FEELING*. The dominance of one function over the others determines the type. There are no functionally pure types; the four functions are not equally developed in any individual. One function is always more differentiated and "conscious" than the others and it is called the *superior* function. It reacts more spontaneously and reliably than the others, whose powers stay, to a large degree, in the unconscious and are not expressed.

Referring to the diagram, if Thinking, for example, is the superior function, then Feeling (the function opposite) is the inferior support function, hidden in the subconscious.

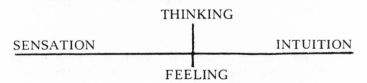

THINKING

SENSATION   INTUITION

FEELING

To the left and right of the Thinking/Feeling axis are Sensation and Intuition, which act as auxiliary functions to the superior function.

Jung considered Thinking and Feeling rational functions because both work through evaluation and judgment, as for instance, true/false, pleasant/unpleasant. A Thinking type reacts to situations and people by using his intellect. And the Feeling type knows exactly what he feels and can describe it. Jung called Sensation and Intuition the irrational functions because they are dependent on perceptions which cannot be evaluated.

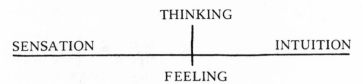

THINKING

SENSATION   INTUITION

FEELING

In the drawing we see *Thinking* as the principal function. The lower opposite function is *Feeling*. The *auxiliary* function is *Intuition* and the fourth function is *Sensation*. Experience shows us that one rational function tends to be accompanied by one irrational function: Thinking may be completed by Intuition which results in the kind of scientific thinking wherein intuitive ideas will be logically analyzed and explored, the outcome being innovation. Conversely, if Feeling is the superior function (rational) and Sensation the auxiliary (irrational), the individual may be an excellent housekeeper, with love for her family, but with no intellectual interests.

The *Thinking* type deals with the world logically and analytically, is punctual, plans well and is principled.

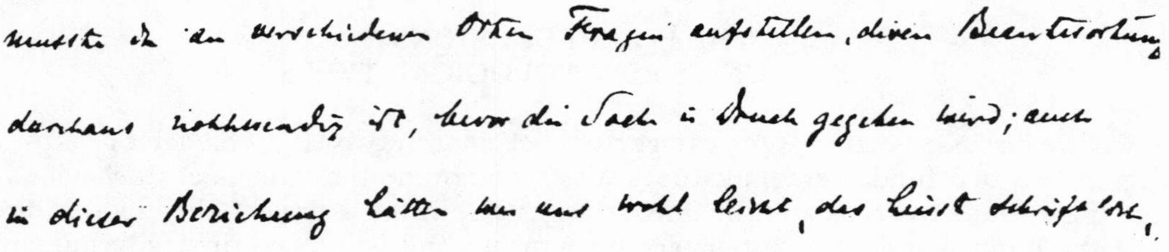

[handwritten German text]

Thinking type: W.K. Roentgen (1845-1923), German physicist

Personal traits for Thinking type	*Graphological indications*
Detached, logical, principled	Small writing, simplified
analytical, conceptual, objective	Clear spacing between lines, words
theoretical, vulnerable to emotions	Emphasis on upper zone
	Original letter forms
	Keen-pointed finals
	Weak lower lengths
	Typographical capitals

Feeling is a rational function. For Jung, the judgments of a feeling type have the same authority as those of a thinking type. They simply have another scale of value. Pascal, great mathematician, physicist and philosopher, said: "The heart has its reason which reason knows nothing of."

The heart has its reason which reason knows nothing of

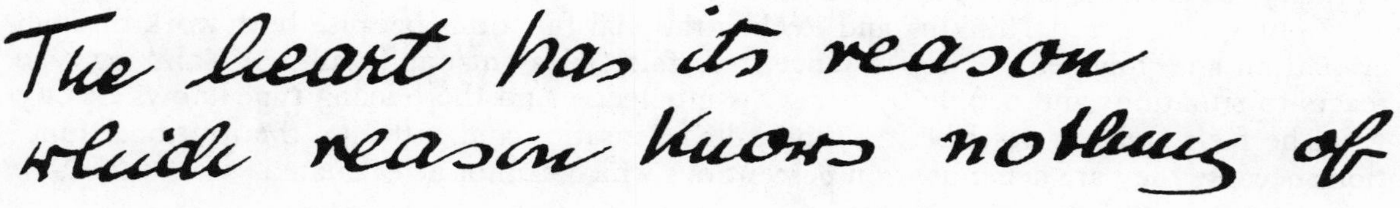

Personal traits for Feeling type	*Graphological indications*
Past-oriented	Unvarying right slant
Emotionally aware	Large open curved finals
Impressive, expressive	Full ovals, large middle zone
Conservative, nurturing	Firm or angular garlands
Loyal, moral, warmhearted	Wide garlands
Responsive, self-pitying	Wavy base line
Vindictive	Pastose, velvety stroke
Moody, romantic	Caressing pressure, arcades, looped garlands

396

The *Sensation* type belongs to the irrational functions because one cannot judge (rational) but only receive sensations and record them. You smell, for instance, the perfume and enjoy it, but one cannot judge how much or why.

[handwriting sample: "Congress ... about me"]

Personal traits for Sensation type

High sensory awareness
Competence, matter of fact
Takes charge in a crisis
Magnetic, bossy, mobile
Likes variety, easily bored
Lives in the present
"Doubting Thomas"

Graphological indications

Normal or large size
Firm pressure
Colorful or pasty writing
Right slant, compact
Dense writing, stylized
Abrupt finals
Pressure in the lower zone
Line and word spacing
Prolonged extensions
Closed ovals, regularity

Intuition is an irrational function. It conceives a "given" by way of the unconscious, and true intuitive types often do not know whence their intuition comes. Jung, in *The Real Problems of the Psyche*, said: "I have often been asked, I could almost say, reproachfully, why I had fixed the number of functions at four, neither more nor less. The number four was first of all suggested by my experiences, but logical reasoning will show in its own right that the total of four functions permits a certain totality of conception."

[handwriting sample]

Intuition type, John F. Kennedy

397

The Four Functions

Personal Traits for Intuition type	*Graphological indications*
Future-oriented	Sharp, light pressure
Inspirations, visions, imagination	Original forms, full ovals
Speculations, guesses	Simplified and all connective forms
Optimistic prophecies	Speedy writing
Things go on endlessly	Right trend
Impractical	Uneven, irregular, illegible
Charismatic, arrogant	Threads, extended upper lengths
Does not like to be pinned down	Curved lower loops open to the left
Dislikes closure and resolution of problems	

Every person has all four functions, but none are as developed as the superior function. The ideal would be if we could be in full possession of the totality of functions. We should therefore constantly try to develop our less differentiated functions.

LIST OF PARTICULAR WRITING ELEMENTS

Description

1) Distorted and incomplete letters

2) Occasionally over-exaggerated size of middle zone letters (*a, o, e*)

3) Quick descent in size of some words

4) Great variations between very large and very small middle zone letters

5) Circular movements flowing together into a blotted point

6) Double flourishings at the lower loops

7) Missing letter-parts

8) Correction within a word and patching up

9) Very meager and tightened *a* and *o* vowels of the middle zone

10) Supported and concealed strokes

11) Fullness in side-parts

12) Fullness in the *d*-heads

13) Some accentuated fullness

Interpretation

1) Occasional break-down in body and spirit, memory lapses, often deceitful and insincere

2) Self-inflation and exaggeration, extravagance

3) Fast fading of momentary vivacious impulses

4) Disturbances of self-esteem, often connected with irritability

5) Insincerity due to vanity, impenetrability; complexes

6) Suppressed desire for tenderness (feminine traits of a male)

7) Poor concentration; nervous irritability; negligence

8) Nervous self-control; if illegible, guilt complexes

9) Repressed anxiety

10) Suppressed softness (inhibition)

11) Phrases, lies, vanity, exaggerations of minor matters

12) Egotistical, delusions of grandeur; phrase-monger

13) Pretending to have more emotions than exist. Passing turmoil in puberty or other transition-phases

List of Particular Writing Elements

Description   *Interpretation*

14) Some emphasized meager parts in a full handwriting

14) Showing more seriousness than exists; in transitional phases a sign of temporary unevenness

15) Lower and upper zone fuller than middle zone letters

15) Worldly interests are more important than personal interests

16) Middle zone fuller than upper and lower zone

16) Personal interests more important than worldly interests

17) Increased pressure in the lower part of middle zone letters

17) Willpower, ambition, drive and intellect are repressing natural emotions

18) Displaced pressure (pressure on side-parts)

18) Psychic energy is channeled into other interests, displaced *libido*

19) Pointed pressure spots

19) Critical sharpness; sudden weakening of strength; undermined self-confidence

20) Dot-like pressure

20) At the initial stroke, possessiveness (for instance, at the capital *M*); in the middle of the text, due to stopping of the pen: inhibition, inclination to complex formations

21) Pressure in the middle zone

21) Emphasis on the personal sphere

22) Change of regularity and irregularity in the script

22) Imbalance between willpower and emotions; people who never learn from their mistakes

23) Disturbances of regularity by fluctuations in width

23) Unbalanced relations to environment; unbalanced social behavior alternating between approach and remoteness

24) Disturbances of regularity by fluctuations in slant

24) Contradictory interests; immaturity; need for variety in social contacts

25) Smeary, smudged, darkened angles

25) Repressed sexual urges for ethical reasons

26) Supported angles

26) Cunning, pseudo-sincerity

27) Angular forms besides the angular connective forms, upper and lower loops

27) Impatience, irregularity

Description	*Interpretation*
28) Weak thread	28) Easily tired; dull
29) Terminal thread	29) Temperament; indifference to unimportant matters; diplomacy; intuition
30) Supported thread (sacré coeur)	30) Rigid fixation upon formality together with inner insecurity; sanctimonious, self-righteousness
31) Mixture of phonetic symbols	31) Self-taught person
32) Alternating phonetic symbols	32) Instability
33) Concealed and supported strokes due to narrowness	33) Neurotic; disturbances of self-reliance and tendency to cover up
34) Angular arcades	34) Excessive efficiency and willpower
35) Small *d*-head bending leftward	35) Lyrical; poetic
36) Initial letters bending leftward	36) Bound to the past; parental and childhood influences
37) Terminal strokes bent to the left (oral hooks)	37) Embarrassment, longing for the past (oral phase)
38) Terminal strokes bent to the left, weakly executed	38) Cowardice
39) Terminal strokes bent to the left with strong pressure, done with sureness	39) Rude determination
40) Directional curving to the left	40) Guilt complexes; burdens from the past
41) Directional curving to the right	41) Fear of the future
42) Lower lengths twisting to the right, with pressure	42) Opposition: obstinacy; criticism; scorn; bitterness
43) Lower lengths twisting to the right with weakness	43) Depression; disappointment; discouragement
44) Open bowl of the lower length is turned to the left	44) Receptivity to pictures from the collective subconscious embracing Jung's archetypal concept of the world; openness to the culture of the past

Description   *Interpretation*

45) Sharp angular points (instead of loops) turned to the left

45) Not admitted irritability

46) Excessively blown-up, round lower loops, turned to the left

46) Materialistic aims; sexual desires; mother-bound; puberty fantasies

47) Over-blown angular lower loops turned to the left

47) Unsatisifed vanity

48) Upper zone twistings and snail-like coilings

48) Vanity; sophisticated argumentations (especially if i-dots are set to the left and connected: humor and flashes of wit)

49) Snail-like coilings in the middle zone

49) Dishonesty; cleverness; stubbornness; insincerity; self-indulgence; obstinacy; dogmatic person

50) Long upstrokes (spring-board-strokes) with hooks

50) Stubborn; aggressive; contradictory

51) So-called 'pigtails' instead of loops in the lower zone

51) Obscenity; lasciviousness

52) Spiral forms instead of loops in the lower zone

52) Hidden thirst for revenge; pre-occupation with self; resentful

53) Left-bent arcades instead of loops in the lower zone (like claws)

53) Grasping for material security; rejection of emotional ties; desire for independence

54) Bending off to the right in the upper zone

54) Need for emancipation; resentment of family restriction

55) Turning off to the right in the middle zone

55) Search for communication and understanding; unquestioned acceptance of society

56) Bending off to the right in the lower zone

56) Transformation of experiences and wisdom into independent activity (altruism)

57) Extension to the right; in the upper zone extended horizontal stroke without pressure

57) Lively, but not firm, willpower

58) Small extra strokes and threads to the right

58) Nervous and foolish talkativeness; playful embellishment of details; no objectivity

Description	Interpretation
59) In the middle zone vertical and left slant; in the upper lengths, right slant	59) Easily excited, but controlled by the intellect; contradictory inconsistency
60) Upper and lower lengths vertical slant, middle zone	60) Neurotic disturbances excessive need for recognition; obstinacy; seeking approval of society
61) Irregular fluctuations of the slant in the middle zone	61) Neurotic restlessness; indecisiveness; subject to moods
62) Crippled lower lengths	62) Lack of vitality; insecurity; irritability; crippled sex life
63) Pointed sharp, channel-like narrow lower lengths	63) Prudishness; easily offended
64) Pointed narrow lower lengths; pastose, smeared, smudged, blurred	64) Hidden desire for 'sweet things'
65) Lower lengths closed below base line	65) Sexual resignation; subconscious, repressed desire to please
66) Accentuation of lower lengths by manifold loops	66) Suppressed desire for tenderness; wanting to be spoiled
67) Long and large executed lower lengths without crossing the base line. Parallel downstroke and upstroke instead of loops. Often with knots and un-motivated pressure spots	67) Sexual frustration; fear of communication and contact; repressions
68) Cut off lower lengths	68) Severe sexual disturbances; inhibitions; split-personality
69) Loops instead of angular strokes	69) Imagination; illusions; enthusiasm; exaggeration
70) Additional loops to patch up meagerly constructed loops	70) Self-deception with regard to idealistic strivings
71) Bent, cracked, meager, small *d*-heads	71) Sensitivity; easily hurt
72) Bent-down *d*-heads which are drawn downward	72) Obstinacy
73) Bending off to-the-left loops of the *b* or immediately drawn to the right-downward	73) Contradictory opposition to own better judgment, puberty obstinacy due to inferiority complex

Description   *Interpretation*

74) Transforming of upper zone loops and points into arcadic forms

74) Representation-talent; cultivating intellectual and artistic interests without being creative; tendency to imitation and phrases; want to take credit for others achievement

75) Middle zone interference with upper zone: over the base line suspending letters (lettre suspendue)

75) Superficiality; poor accuracy; inconsistency; living in 'higher' regions

76) Interference of the upper length-letter with the lower length-zone, reaching into the lower zone

76) Materialistic conception of the world; physical vanity

77) Middle zone letters reaching into the lower zone, e.g. the last downstroke of *y, r, a*

77) Knowing everything better; intellectual oppression; likes to lecture others

78) To-the-left-twisted upper lengths

78) Striving for independence; insecurity; need for glorification of own image in puberty; passing symptoms

79) To-the-right-twisted upper lengths

79) Disappointment; disillusion in idealistic regions

80) Singular, especially high-rising upper lengths

80) Ambition to achieve great things; speculation-fever; exaggerations

81) Singular, especially deep-descending lower lengths

81) Looking for hold and stabilization without consistency

82) To the right convex, long lengths

82) Discouragement; disillusions; eaily influenced; apathetic

83) Narrowing and diminishing of singular curves

83) Inhibitions; emotional insecurity

84) Neglecting of down strokes

84) Weak determination; no vitality; passive receptivity

85) Small distances between words in conjunction with straight lines

85) No self-reliance, with outward composure and pretended superiority; imitation of life-styles of others; need for guidance

86) Small spaces between words with extra-wide distances of lines

86) Neurotic anxiety symptoms

Description	*Interpretation*
87) Extreme narrowness of letters	87) Inhibitions; immaturity; no self-confidence; need to lean on someone's shoulder
88) Diminishing distances between lines (except at the end of a letter)	88) Lack of estimation of time and space; procrastination; reluctance to start anything new; clinging to the old and accustomed; introversion
89) Changing distances between lines due to unchanging size of letters and differences in lengths (disregarding printed lines and size of paper)	89) Lack of adaptability; disregarding reality; following own interests recklessly
90) Use of lined writing paper	90) Desire to impress people with correctness; pretending order and organization; schematism
91) Need for forming paragraphs	91) Need for order and systematic work
92) Inner structure of the script	92) Analytical thinking; ethical tendency; love of correct behavior; need for clarity. In rare cases, fake generosity
93) Occasional extreme inner structure in poorly organized writing	93) Pedantic in small matters narrow horizon; cannot distinguish between the essential and the unimportant

BIBLIOGRAPHY

Adler, A. *Menschenkenntnis.* Zurich: Rascher, 1954.

Allport, G. W. *Gestalt und Wachstum in der Persönlichkeit.* Meisenheim am Glan: Anton Hain,

Ammann, R. *Die Handschrift der Kuenstler.* Switzerland: Bern, 1953.

Avé-Lallement, U. *Graphologie des Jugendlichen.* München/Basel: Ernst Reinhardt Verlag, 1970.

Baldi, Camillo. *Trattato come da una lettera missiva si conoscano la natura e qualità dello scrittore.* Milano, 1625.

Becker, M. *Beziehungen zwischen Graphologie und Schriftexpertise.* Hamburg, 1949.

—. *Graphologie der Kinderschrift.* Freiburg: Walter Verlag, 1926.

Carus, C. G. *Symbolik der menschlichen Gestalt.* Leipzig, 1931.

Cobbaert, A. *Graphologie.* Genf, Switzerland: Ariston Verlag, 1973.

Crépieux Jamin, J. *L'écriture et le caractère.* Paris: Flammarion Editeur, 1888.

—. *Traité complet et pratique de graphologie.* Paris: Flammarion Editeur, 1885.

—. *Les éléments de l'écriture des canailles.* Paris: Flammarion Editeur, 1923.

Daim, W. *Handschrift und Existenz.* Graz, 1950.

Donig, K. *Betriebsgraphologie.* München: Wolfgang Dummer & Company, 1975.

Freud, S. *The Psychopathology of Every Day Life.* New York: W. M. Norton, 1914.

—. *New Introductory Lectures on Psycho-Analysis.* New York: W. M. Norton, 1933.

—. *An Outline of Psychoanalysis.* New York: W. M. Norton, 1949.

—. *Five Lectures on Psycho-Analysis.* New York: W. M. Norton, 1977.

—. *Inhibitions, Symptoms and Anxiety.* New York: W. M. Norton, 1977.

—. *Three Contributions to the Theory of Sex.* New York: E. P. Dutton, 1962.

—. *General Psychological Theory.* New York: MacMillan, 1963.

—. *Beyond the Pleasure Principle.* New York: W. M. Norton, 1961.

—. *Bildende Kunst und Literatur.* Frankfurt: Fischer Verlag, 1969.

—. *Beitraege zur Psychologie des Liebeslebens und anderen Schriften.* Frankfurt am Main: Fischer Taschenbuch Verlag, 1981.

Fromm, E. *The Anatomy of Human Destructiveness.* Holt, Rinehart and Winston, 1973.

—. *Man for Himself.* New York: Fawcett Premier, 1947.

Gille, J. C. *Psychologie de l'écriture.* Paris: Dervy Livres, 1969.

—. *Types de Jung et Tempéraments Psychobiologiques.* Paris:Maloine, 1978.

Green, J. N. *You and Your Private Eye.* St. Paul, Minnesota: Llewellyn Publications, 1975.

Grünewald, G. *Graphologische Studien.* Zurich: Rascher Verlag, 1954.

Hartford, Huntington. *You are what you write.* New York: MacMillan, 1973.

Heiss, R. *Die Deutung der Handschrift.* Hamburg: Claassen Verlag, 1966.

Henze, A. *Die Chirogrammatomantie.* Leipzig, 1863.

Hocquart, E. *L'art de juger de l'esprit et du caractère des hommes sur leur écriture.* Paris, 1812.

Hofstätter, Peter R. *Psychologie.* Frankfurt: Fischer Taschenbuch Verlag, 1960.

Jacobi, Hans. *Analysis of Handwriting.* London: George Allen & Unwin Ltd., 1939.

—. *Selfknowledge through Handwriting.* London: George Allen & Unwin Ltd., 1941.

—. *Handwriting and Sexuality.* Berlin: Marcus & E. Webers, 1932.

Jung, C. G. *Psychologische Typen.* Zurich: Rascher Verlag, 1921.

—. *Über die Psychologie des Unbewussten.* Zurich: Rascher Verlag, 1943.

—. *Welt der Psyche.* Zurich: Rascher Verlag, 1954.

—. *Symbolik des Geistes.* Zurich: Rascher Verlag, 1948.

—. *Wirklichkeit der Seele.* Zurich: Rascher Verlag, 1934.

—. *Gestaltungen des Unbewussten.* Zurich: Rascher Verlag, 1950.

Klages, L. *Grundlagen der Characterkunde.* Leipzig: Johann Ambrosius Barth, 1928.

—. *Handschrift und Charakter.* Bonn: H. Bouvier, 1968.

Bibliography

—. *Grundlegung der Wissenschaft vom Ausdruck.* Bonn: H. Bouvier, 1964.

—. *Graphologisches Lesebuch.* München: Johann Ambrosius Barth, 1954.

Knobloch, H. *Die Lebensgestalt der Handschrift.* Saarbrücken, 1950.

—. *Graphologie.* Düsseldorf: Econ Verlag, 1971.

Kretschmer, E. *Körperbau und Character.* Berlin: A. Springer Verlag, 1967.

Kroeber-Keneth, L. *Buch der Graphologie.* Düsseldorf: Econ Verlag, 1968.

Langenbruch, W. *Praktische Menschenkenntnis auf Grund der Handschrift.* Berlin, 1929.

Lersch, Philipp *Gesicht und Seele.* München: Johann Ambrosius Barth, 1949.

—. *Aufbau der Person.* München: Johann Ambrosius Barth, 1962.

—. *Der Mensch in der Gegenwart.* München: Johann Ambrosius Barth, 1964.

Lombroso, C. *Handbuch der Graphologie.* Leipzig, 1896.

Lüke, A. *Die menschliche Vielfalt in der Handschrift.* Dortmund: Koffler Druck, 1982.

—. *Du bist, wie Du schreibst.* Dortmund: Koffler Druck, 1983.

Malone, M. *Psychetypes.* New York: E. P. Dutton, 1977.

Marcuse, I. *Disturbed Personality through Handwriting.* New York: Arco Publishing, 1969.

—. *Guide to Personality through your Handwriting.* New York: Arco Publishing, 1965.

Maser, W. *Hitler's Letters and Notes.* New York: Harper & Row, 1974.

Mendel, A. O. *Personality in Handwriting.* New York: Stephen Daye Press, 1975.

Meyer, L. *Lehrbuch der Graphologie.* Stuttgart, Germany, 1895.

Michon, J. H. *Système de Graphologie.* München: Kindler Verlag, 1964.

—. *La Méthode Pratique de Graphologie.* Paris, 1978.

Müller/Enskat. *Graphologische Diagnostik.* Bern: Hans Huber, 1971.

Olyanova, N. *The Psychology of Handwriting.* Hollywood, California: Wilshire Book Company, 1977.

Pfanne, H. *Lehrbuch der Graphologie.* Berlin,1961.

—. *Handschriftenverstellung.* Bonn: Bouvier Verlag, 1971.

Pokorny, R. *Psychologie der Handscrift.* München: Ernst Reinhard Verlag, 1967.

—. *Moderne Handschriftendeutung.* Berlin: Walter de Gruyter, 1963.

—. *Uber das Wesen des Ausdrucks.* München: Ernst Reinhardt Verlag, 1974.

Pophal, R. *Die Handschrift als Gehirnschrift.* Rudolstadt: Greifen Verlag, 1949.

—. *Zur Psychologie der Spannungserscheinungen in der Handschrift.* Rudolstadt: Greifen Verlag, 1939.

—. *Grundlegung der bewegungs-physiologischen Graphologie.* Leipzig, 1939.

—. *Das Strichbild.* Stuttgart: Georg Thieme, 1950.

—. *Graphologie in Vorlesungen.* Stuttgart: Gustav Fischer Verlag, 1963.

—. *Die Schrift und das Schreiben.* Volume I. Stuttgart: Gustav Fischer Verlag, 1965.

—. *Eidetische Graphologie.* Volume II. Stuttgart: Gustav Fischer Verlag, 1966.

—. *Kinetische Graphologie.* Volume III. Stuttgart: Gustav Fischer Verlag, 1968.

Preyer, W. *Zur Psychologie des Schreibens.* Hamburg, 1895.

Pulver, M. *Symbolik der Handschrift.* Zürich: Orell Füssli Verlag, 1955.

—. *Trieb und Verbrechen.* Zürich: Orell Füssli Verlag, 1934.

—. *Intelligenz im Schriftausdruck.* Zürich: Füssli Verlag, 1949.

Reis, Hugo. *Deine Handschrift — dein Charakter.* Bad Homburg: Siemens-Verlags-Gesellschaft, 1954.

Remplein, H. *Psychologie der Persoenlichkeit.* München: Ernst Reinhardt Verlag, 1975.

Revers, W. J. *Deutungswege der Graphologie.* Salzburg, 1966.

Roman, K. *Handwriting, a Key to Personality.* New York: The Noonday Press, 1952.

—. *Encyclopedia of the Written Word.* New York: Frederick Ungar, 1968.

Sainte Colombe, P. *Graphotherapeutics.* Hollywood: Laureda Book Publisher, 1966.

Saudek, R. *Experimentelle Graphologie.* Berlin, 1929.

—. *The Psychology of Handwriting.* London: George Allen & Unwin L.T.D., 1954.

Sonnemann, U. *Handwriting Analysis.* New York, 1950.

Teillard, Ania. *L'Ame et L'Ecriture.* Paris, 1948.

—. *Handschriften Deutung.* München: Franke Verlag, 1952.

Teillard-Mendelsohn, Ania and George Mendelsohn. *Der Mensch in der Handschrift.* Leipzig, 1930.

409

Bibliography

Teltscher, H. O. *Handwriting, the Key to Successful Living.* New York: G. P. Putnam & Sons, 1942.

Victor, F. *Die Handschrift eine Projektion der Persoenlichkeit.* Zürich: Rascher Verlag, 1955.

—. *Beethoven als Mensch.* Frankfurt: Graphologische Schriftenreihe, 1961.

Vels, A. L. *Diccionario De Grafologia.* Barcelona: Ediciones Cedel, 1983.

Wagner, L. *Graphologische Forschungen.* Wien: Wilhelm Braumüller Universitäts Verlags-Buchhandlung, 1973.

Wieser, R. *Der Verbrecher und seine Handschrift.* München: Ernst Reinhardt Verlag, 1952.

—. *Persönlichkeit und Handschrift.* München: Ernst Reinhardt Verlag, 1956.

—. *Mensch und Leistung in der Handschrift.* München: Ernst Reinhardt Verlag, 1960.

—. *Rhythmus und Polarität in der Handschrift.* München: Ernst Reinhardt Verlag, 1973.

Wittlich, B. *Graphologische Praxis.* Berlin: Walter De Gruyter, 1961.

—. *Konfliktzeichen in der Handschrift.* München: Ernst Reinhardt Verlag, 1971.

Wolff, W. *Diagrams of Unconscious.* New York: Grune and Stratton, 1948.

INDEX

Absolute size, 289
Abzug, Bella, 87
Acquired form, 157
Acrophobia, 25
Action speed, 104-105
Address, 329-330
Adenauer, Konrad, 323
Adler, Alfred, 130
Adolescence, 140, 167
    See also: Puberty
Aesthetic type, 132
Age, 343-344
Agraphia, 127
Airbridge, 63
Akinesia, 123
Alcoholism, 72, 111, 226, 227
Alexander III, Pope, 184
Alexia, 127
Altruism, 197, 291, 306, 402
Ambidexterity, 350, 351
Ambivalence, 221, 223
American Indian, 351
Amorphous stroke, 5, 157, 226
Andersen, Hans Christian, 268
Angle, 31-33
Anima/Animus, 347, 348
Antennae strokes, 92
Arcade, 38-45
Arcade, covered, 391
Aristotle, 4, 9
Arp, Hans, 73
Arrangement picture, 25, 257-259
Arrêt du Penseur, 63
Art of Graphological Seeing, 7-8
Ataxia, 111, 112, 140, 223
Atchison, David, 188
Augstein, Rudolf, 299
Augustus, Emperor, 2
Autogenic training, 7
Auxiliary function, 395, 396

Back-lash stroke, 198
Baldi, Camillo, 2, 3, 100, 159

Balzac, Honoré de, 84
Baseline, 232, 274
Beethoven, Ludwig van, 47, 48, 121, 283
Behavior, sexual, 304-308
Belafonte, Harry, 17
Ben-Gurion, David, 250
Bergman, Ingrid, 229
Berkowitz, David, 157, 361-365
Berle, Milton, 176
Berlin, Isaiah, 64
Bernhardt, Sarah, 216
Betz Vladimir, Alexandrovich, 125
Biotypes, Pophal's, 115-133
Bismarck, Otto Fürst von, 68, 164
Blotting, 74, 88, 394, 399, 400
Blotted vowels, 74, 219, 394
Body language, 257
Bonaparte, Napoleon, 47-48, 63, 103, 105, 106,
    214, 215, 228, 246-247
Borge, Victor, 18
Boustrophedon, 1
Brain, 5, 115-118, 121-129
Brain Hemispheres, 121, 349, 352, 353
Brainstem, 127-128; Béjart, M., 128
Brain-writing, 5
Bryngelson, Bryng, 351
Buber, Martin, 109
Buffet, Bernard, 215
Burton, Richard, 50
Byron, George Gordon, 243

Capsula interna, 123
Carnegie, Andrew, 93
Carter, James, 316
Caruso, Enrico, 176
Casals, Pablo, 93
Centrifugal movement, 257, 267
Centripetal movement, 253, 257, 264
Cerebrum, 127
Chagall, Marc, 127
Charles, Prince of Wales, 253
Charcot, Jean Martin, 8
Chardin, Pierre Teilhard de, 264

Chevalier, Maurice, 250
Child-like writing, 55, 193
Chinese writing, 12, 278, 340
Chopin, Frédéric, 249
Chorea, 123
Christianity, 12
Claustrophobia, 25
Claw stroke, 41, 98, 194, 306
Cliburn, Van, 17
Cocteau, Jean, 333
Collins, Joan, 302
Columbus, Christopher, 93
Compact pressure, 67
Compulsive writing, 169, 223, 253-254
Concave lines, 314
Concave margin, 324
Concealed stroke, 389-390
    See also: Covered stroke
Connectedness, 59-61
Connective forms, 30
Conscious mind, 4
Convex lines, 314
Convex margin, 324
Correction, 392
Cortex writing, 126, 129-133
Cortico-Spinal Tract, 125
Counter-stroke, 197, 392, 393
Cousteau, J. Jacques, 168
Covered Stroke, 391
    See also: Concealed stroke
Crépieux-Jamin, J., 4, 5, 159
Curie, Marie, 83
Cursive writing, 1-2
Curve, Double, 46
Custer, General George A., 21

Dali, Salvador, 62, 334
Däniken, Erich von, 187
Darwin, Charles, 106, 135, 326
Dead Sea Scrolls, 1
Decreased word endings, 193
Delicate writer, 90
Depth in handwriting, 76-83, 233
Development of human brain, 115-117
Dickens, Charles, 248, 249
Dickinson, Emily, 66
Dietrich, Marlene, 52
Difference in lengths, 284-291
Directional pressure, 217
Disciplined writing, 30, 56
Disconnectedness, 62-66

Displaced pressure, 67, 400
Disraeli, Benjamin, 61
Distance between lines, 311, 312
Distance between words, 309-310
Direction of lines, 313-317
Disturbed rhythm of movement, 150
Doolittle, Hilda, 13
Double curve, 46
Downstroke, 233
Drilled handwriting, 169
Drug addiction, 111, 227
Dürer, Albrecht, 82, 351
Dyslexia, 350

Early Hebrew, 1
Economical type, 132
Edison, Thomas A., 95, 157-158
Ego, 4, 167, 189, 190, 260, 264, 267, 288
    309, 331
Ego Island, 309
Egyptian syllabary, 1
Einstein, Albert, 191, 237, 264, 346
Eisenhower, Dwight, D., 264
Elasticity of vibrations, 115
Elements of particular writing, 399-405
Elevated letter, See: Lettre suspendue
Emerson, Ralph Waldo, 60
Encirclement, 249
Engels, Friedrich, 132
Enrichment, 176-178
Enskat, Alice, 5
Erasmus, von Rotterdam, 126, 130
Ethical type, 131
Evans, Linda, 45
Evenness, 210-211
Extra-pyramidal tract, 124
Extraversion, 4, 251-254, 395

Façade writing, 388
Faulkner, William, 24
Feeling type, 5, 395-398
Fischer, Hans, 75
Flamed stroke, 71, 105
Fluctuating slant, 283
Foch, Marshal Ferdinand, 56
Fontaine, Joan, 58
Forgery, 177-178
Form niveau, 4, 47, 159-163
Form picture, 23-24, 157-158
Formrhythm, 215-224
Four functions (Jung), 395-398

Franklin, Benjamin, 350
Freud, Sigmund, 4, 8, 311-312
Fromm, Erich, 104
Frost, Robert, 28
Fullness, 183-185
Function-types (Jung), 5, 395-398
Furtwängler, Wilhelm, 276

Galland, Adolf, 44
Gandhi, Indira, 244
Gandhi, Mahatma, 69, 288
Garbo, Greta, 250
Garfield, John, 252
Garland, 34-37, 47
Garland, supported, 36
Gaulle, Charles de, 344
Gaynor, Janet, 252
Gender, 347-348
Gestalt, 20, 99, 199, 247
Getty, J. Paul, 229,
Goebbels, Joseph, 142, 254
Goethe, Johannes Wolfgang von, 8, 97, 274
Goya, Francisco de, 10
Grant, Gordon, 80
Granulated stroke, 5, 227
Grauman, Sid, 72
Greek alphabet, 1,
Greek theater, 164
Greeley, Horace, 120
Green, Jane N., 5
Grock, 55

Hamilton, Charles, 338
Handelsman, Bud, 151-154
Handedness, 349-354
Harlan, Veit, 346
Hartford, Huntington, 5
Havilland, Olivia de, 58
Hebrew alphabet, 1
Hedin, Sven, 237-238
Heiss, Robert, 5, 206
Hepburn, Katherine, 195
Herodotus, 12
Herzl, Theodor, 291
Hesse, Herrmann, 53
Heydrich, Reinhard, 14, 90, 142, 249
Hildegarde, 204
Himmler, Heinrich, 14, 142
Hinckley, John, 70, 356-360
History of Graphology, 1-6
Hitler, Adolf, 43, 195, 229, 242, 248, 258, 317

"Hitler-Diaries," 381-387
Hocquart, 100
Homogeneous stroke, 5, 157, 225, 230
Homosexuality, 98, 304, 306
Hooked left-handedness, 353, 354
Houston, Jean, 10, 11, 135-136
Houston, General Sam, 13
Hughes, Howard, 309
Hysteria, 252

Id, 4, 299
i-dots, 199-205
Illegibility, 36, 135, 213, 237, 241, 242
Infantile writing, 30, 55
Initial accentuation, 189-191, 192
Insincerity in handwriting, 178, 388-394
Introversion, 4, 13, 177, 190, 251-254, 395
Intuition type, 5, 8, 397, 398
Inverted lefthand
    See: Hooked left-handedness
Irregularity, 172-175, 323

Jackson, Jesse, 204, 335
Jefferson, Thomas, 40, 264, 318
Johnson, Lyndon B., 194
Jugo, Jenny, 67
Jung, Carl Gustav, 4, 5, 85, 251, 311, 347, 395-398
Jung's function types, 5, 395-398
Juxtaposed handwriting, 278

Kafka, Franz, 189
Kanfer Test, 5
Kant, Immanuel, 167
Karloff, Boris, 89
Kearny, Philip, 94
Keitel, Wilhelm, 195
Kennedy, Edward M., 234
Kennedy, Jacqueline Onassis, 28, 285
Kennedy, John F., 188, 242, 397
Kinematography, 5
King George, 350
King Signature, 237
Kirchner, E. L., 43
Kissinger, Henry, 47, 195
Klages, Ludwig, 4, 7, 68, 159, 161, 172, 184
Klee, Paul, 352
Koch, Edward, 192
Kokoschka, Oscar, 141
Krauss, Werner, 55

Lammers, Hans, 194

Large size writing, 260-263
Lasker-Schüler, Else, 310
Lasso movement, 393
Latin writing, 1, 2, 260
Lavater, 162
Left-handedness, 349-354
Lehár, Franz, 17
Lengths, Accentuation, 292-303
Leonardo da Vinci, 352
Lersch, Philipp, 347
Lettre Suspendue, 197, 404
Lewis, Jerre, 354
Liberace, 190
Libido, 221, 230, 390, 400
Liddy, G. Gordon, 106
Ligature, 181
Lines, Distances between, 311, 312
Lombroso, Cesare, 351
London, Jack, 136
Looped arcade, 42
Looseness, 141
Lower length accentuation, 299-304
Ludwig II, 220

MacKay, Colin, 7
Maillol, Aristide, 85, 146-147
Manet, Edouard, 107
Mann, Thomas, 314
Mansfield, Jayne, 16
Manson, Charles, 70
Margins, 318-328
Marie Antoinette, 86
Marinetti, Emilio, 147-148
Marx, Karl, 213
Masochism, 304
Masters, Robert, 183
Mata Hari, 71, 72
Matisse, Henri, 131, 132
Meagerness, 186-188
Meander-arcadic writing, 39
Mechanical structure, 331
Meir, Golda, 74
Mengele, Josef, 376-380
Menzel, Adolf von, 47, 48, 120, 121
Medulla oblongata, 124
Mentally disturbed writing, 72, 219, 220, 221
Mesmer, Franz Anton, 236
Meyer, Conrad Ferdinand, 219
Michelangelo, Buonarroti, 351
Michon, Jean H., 3, 63, 68, 157

Miller, Anne, 261
Miro, Joan, 85
Mondale, Walter, 36
Monet, Claude, 331
Monroe, Marilyn, 145, 285
Montcalm, General Louis Joseph de, 187
Montenegro, Conchita, 40
Montez, Maria, 94
Mood, 313
Moore, Henry, 37
Morgan, Michèle, 215
Morgan, J. P., 93, 343
Moser-Pröll, Annemarie, 19
Motorcenters of the brain, 118, 127, 129
Movement, Picture of, 20-22, 26, 27
Movement, Rhythm of, 144-154
Mozart, Wolfgang, 18, 86, 95, 220
Müller, Enskat A., 5
Musical symbols, 15, 17, 220
Mussolini, Benito, 228

Narrowness, 270-273
Nationality, 340-342
Negligence, 179, 181
Negri, Pola, 32
Newton, Isaac, 96
Nietzsche, Friedrich, 159, 220, 221
Nixon, Richard M., 49, 248
Nucleus caudate, 121, 122
Nucleus lentiform, 121, 122
Nucleus ruber, 118

O. Henry, 196, 241
Okakura, 162
Olivier, Sir Laurence, 132, 250, 296
Oppenheimer, Robert, 62, 191
Oral hook, 197
Osborn, Albert S., 101
Oswald, Lee Harvey, 363

Paganini, Nicolo, 86
Pallidum, 5, 118-124, 129, 134-135
Palmer method, 23, 53, 54, 162, 339
Parapsychology, 5
Parasite behavior, 392
Parkinson's disease, 112, 118, 124
Particular writing elements, 399-405
Pascal, Blaise, 100, 106
Pasteur, Louis, 240
Pastose writing, 84-88, 228-229

Pathological cases, 161, 219, 220-221
Paulus, Friedrich V., 33
Pen speed, 101, 103, 105
Persona writing, 4, 164-165
Pfanne, Heinrich, 5
Phallus symbol, 16, 219, 300
Phoenician alphabet, 1
Picasso, Pablo, 47, 88, 160, 173, 212, 345, 352
Pissarro, Camille, 29, 337
Planck, Max, 129
Plato, 12, 129, 351
Plutarch, 12
Political type, 133
Pons, Lilly, 234
Pope, Alexander III, 184
Pope, John Paul II, 131
Pope, Pius XII, 167
Pophal Rudolf, 4, 5, 101, 115-140, 134, 157
   225
Pophal-Spranger Types, 130-133
Pophal Tension Degrees, 134-140
Potok, Chaim, 10
Pound, Ezra, 279
Pressure, displaced, 67, 221
Pressure, irregular, 67, 70, 72
Pressure, strong, 67-72
Pressure, weak, 73-75
Preyer, Wilhelm, 4, 100, 167, 324
Prokofieff, Serge, 92
Protection stroke, 243
Psychological types, 5, 395-398
Psychology, 5, 7, 8, 236
Psychology of handwriting, 4, 167
Psychopathic stroke picture, 226-227
Puberty, 39, 140, 175, 254, 295, 307
Pulver, Max, 4, 9, 12
Pyramidal tract, 124-125

Randall, Tony, 172
Reagan, Maureen, 261
Reagan, Nancy, 245
Reagan, Ronald, 245
Regularity, 167-171
Reinhardt, Max, 55
Relationship of the three pictures, 26-29
Relative size, 289
Religious type, 131
Rembrandt, van Rijn, 76, 77
Renoir, Pierre, 148
Rhythm of movement, 144-154
Ribbentrop, Joachim von, 31, 32, 33

Rigidity, 142-143, 223, 254
Rilke, Rainer Maria, 53
Robespierre, Maximilien, 186
Rockefeller, John D., 192
Rockefeller, Nelson, 350
Rodin, Auguste, 74, 353
Roentgen, W. K., 396
Roman, Klara, 5
Rome, 1-2
Roof-tile lines, 314
Roosevelt, Eleanor, 332
Roosevelt, Franklin D., 133, 345
Rousseau, Jean Jacques, 290
Rubens, Peter Paul, 78, 79

Sacré Coeur writing, 40, 164, 178, 391, 401
Sadism, 393-394
Salk, Dr. Jonas, 130, 186
Sand-banks, 331
Sandburg, Carl, 14
Saudek, Robert, 5, 102
Schizoid type, 394
School writing, 30, 53-54, 157, 215
Schultz, J. H., 7
Schweitzer, Albert, 131, 210, 291
Self-representation type, 132
Sensation type, 5, 395-397
Senses, 7
Sexual behavior as seen in lower loops, 300,
   301, 302, 303, 304-308
Shakespeare, William, 366-374
Shark-tooth, 40, 99, 196, 391
Sharpness, 89-91
Shaw, George Bernard, 194
Siegel, Ralph Maria, 21
Sierra Leone, 350-351
Signac, Paul, 137
Signature, 4, 236-250
Signes Fixes, 4, 157
Sills, Beverly, 183
Simplification, 179-182
Special forms of simplification, 181-182
Size, 260-266
Skeleton writing, 64, 181, 188
Slant, 274-283
Slowness, 108-114
Small size writing, 264-266
Société de Graphologie, 3
Socrates, 129
Sontag, Susan, 63
Special forms of formrhythm, 217-224

Speed, 100-107
Spoon-*e*, 97, 177
Spranger Types (Pophal), 130-133
Stalin, Joseph, 133, 289, 297
Stern, Isaac, 17
Strauss, Richard, 45
Stravinsky, Igor, 87
Striatum, 5, 122-123, 137-139
Strindberg, August, 65
Stroke picture, 5, 225-231
Stroke direction, 232-235
Stroke disturbances, 228
Stroke variations, 228-231
Structure, 331-338
St. Vitus Dance, 123
Stylized writing, 30, 57, 58, 166
Substantia Nigra, 124
Sudan, left-handedness in, 350
Superego, 4
Suppé, Franz von, 17
Superior function, 395, 396
Symbolism, 4, 15
Symbolism of handwriting, 4, 9-11, 232
Symbolism of direction, 12-14
Symbolism of letters, 15-19, 219, 220

Taft, William H., 234
Taki, 162
Taylor, Elizabeth, 250
Teillard, Ania, 4-5
Teltscher, Henry O., 5
Temple, Shirley, 245
Tenacity hook, 207
Tension degrees, 5, 134-140, 143
Terminal accentuation, 192-198
Terminal arcade, 391
Tesla, Nikola, 107
Thatcher, Margaret, 243
Theoretical-scientific type, 130
Thinking type, 5, 395-396
Thread, 47-50
Three zones, 9
Tiro, 2
Toscanini, Arturo, 45, 65, 345
Toulouse-Lautrec, Henri de, 144-145
Trajan column, 260
Tranquillus, 2
Transvestite, 304
Trend, Right, 92-94
Trend, Left, 95-99
Truman, Harry S., 194, 318

Trump, Donald, 32
t-Strokes, 206-209

Uncial letter, 260
Unconscious mind, 4, 9
Undefined form, 30, 51-52
Underscoring, 176
Unevenness, 212-214
Ungar, Frederick, 90-91

Ventral horn, 124
Verdi, Guiseppe, 80
Vertical slant, 278-282
Vidor, King, 67
Voluntary movement, 124, 125

Wagner, Lutz, 5
Wagner, Richard, 35, 220
Wagner, Wieland, 35
Walbrook, Anton, 119
Waldow, Ernst, 363
Wallace, George, 67
Walter, Bruno, 270
Washington, George, 245-246
Wassermann, Jacob, 265
Wayne, John, 10
Welles, Orson, 50
Wertheimer, Max, 199
West, Mae, 15
Whitman, Walt, 95, 240
Width, 267-269
Wieser, Roda, 5, 200, 309
Wilbur, Richard, 168
Wilde, Oscar, 64, 85, 160, 297, 306, 392
Wilder, Thorton, 68
Wolff, Werner, 5
Words, distance between, 309-310
Wouk, Herman, 68
Wright, Frank Lloyd, 243

Ying and Yang, 12
Yogananda, Guru Paramahansa, 35
Young, Andrew, 252

Zola, Emile, 179